P9-DDY-826

Lincoln Christian College

The Yale Edition of the Works of St. Thomas More

MODERNIZED SERIES

Published by the St. Thomas More Project, Yale University,
under the auspices of Gerard L. Carroll and Joseph B. Murray,
Trustees of the Michael P. Grace, II, Trust

Hans Holbein, *ca.* 1527. Frick Museum, New York City.

ST. THOMAS MORE: SELECTED LETTERS

edited by

ELIZABETH FRANCES ROGERS

New Haven and London: Yale University Press, 1961

Copyright © 1961 by Yale University.

Set in Baskerville type and

printed in the United States of America by

Vail-Ballou Press, Inc., Binghamton, N.Y.

All rights reserved. The editorial content of this book

may not be reproduced, in whole or in part, in any form

(except by reviewers for the public press),

without written permission from the publishers.

Library of Congress catalog card number: 61-14944

828.2
M83

FOREWORD

WITH THIS VOLUME, we begin our modernized series of the selected works of St. Thomas More, a series that will, we hope, eventually comprise about seven volumes. The modernized series is designed as a complement to the projected Yale Edition of More's complete works, in fourteen volumes. As a general rule, the publication of any text in the scholarly series will precede its appearance in modernized form. The *Selected Letters,* however, is a special case, for Dr. Rogers' standard edition of More's *Correspondence* has been available to scholars since 1947. Her edition, in revised form, with the text of the letters to Erasmus added and with translations of all the Latin letters, will eventually appear as Volumes 12 and 13 of our scholarly series. In the interval, we are most happy to offer a selection of the letters in modern dress.

LOUIS L. MARTZ
Chairman

RICHARD S. SYLVESTER
Executive Editor

18140

Remembering happy years at Wilson College,
I dedicate this book in gratitude to
the memory of a beloved colleague:
ELEANOR FRANCES WARFIELD, 1896–1946

CONTENTS

INTRODUCTION

When Guillaume Budé, the most distinguished Greek scholar of his day, planned to publish his correspondence with learned friends, More wrote that "it would be safer if you would wait a while, at least until I revise my letters. It is not only that I fear there may be passages where the Latin is faulty, but also, in my remarks upon peace and war, upon morality, marriage, the clergy, the people, etc., perhaps what I have written has not always been so cautious and guarded that it would be wise to expose it to captious critics."

Fortunately for us, we need no longer observe More's caution: we are at liberty to read the 127 letters by More that remain, out of the thousands that he must have written. Several of these extant letters are in fact dedications or prefaces for his writings and in the Yale edition of his works will appear in their appropriate places, before the *Epigrammata* or the *Utopia;* but these letters are interesting in themselves as evidence of More's many friendships with other scholars. The letters we read may sometimes be disappointingly few or tantalizing in their brevity, but they nevertheless show the wide circle of his friends, not only in England, but also in the Low Countries and in France. He frequently visited the Continent on diplomatic embassies and met with the councilors of Charles of Castile, Francis I of France, or the Regents Louise of Savoy and her sister-in-law Margaret of Austria-Savoy. There were long delays in diplomacy, perhaps waiting while one side or the other demanded new commissions for the diplomats with whom they dealt. More used such leisure to make learned acquaintances, and to visit scholars whom he had previously met, often through Erasmus.

He seemed indeed, as Erasmus said, "born and made for friendship." The letters to Erasmus show the tiresome errands he kindly performed in securing a horse or assuring the payment on the Continent of the pension based on the rectory of Aldington which Archbishop Warham had granted, or the support he gave in trying to secure a canonry at Tournai when the King had taken the city. On other occasions, there is intelligent and critical praise for Erasmus' or others' scholarly works. Of his own writings, he speaks with sincere modesty or even anxiety.

It is largely through the deep regard of his friends that More's letters have come down to us. Erasmus and Budé, for example, took care to publish More's letters to them; while another friend, Francis Cranevelt, a member of the Great Council of Malines, kept More's letters, along with those from many others, in packets arranged in chronological order. These were inherited by his descendants and in 1914 an heir gave the collection over to two scholars of the University of Louvain to be edited and published. One of them, Professor de Vocht, carried the packet with him as he fled from the sack of Louvain in 1914; by 1928 the letters were printed, among them six from More. Without such care by personal friends, many of these letters would have been lost, as More's papers were confiscated by the King and Thomas Cromwell after his trial and conviction, and More's rough drafts would have been included in the confiscation.

Other groups of letters were preserved with state papers. For some years, More was a royal secretary to Henry VIII, having long periods of residence at Court, following the King as he moved about from one royal house to another, and with specific hours of duty morning and afternoon. Over twenty letters written by him for the King to Wolsey are extant in the British Museum, usually in More's autograph. It was Wolsey himself who had had the genius to see the importance of preserving letters, and his own correspondence is the basis of the early volumes of the State Papers.

Most precious are More's letters to his family. After his death his daughter Margaret Roper was arrested, briefly imprisoned, and asked to give up all of More's papers. Margaret said that she had only personal letters, of no importance to others, and begged to be allowed to keep them. These were later taken to the Continent when members of the More circle went into exile for religion's sake under Edward VI and again

under Elizabeth. Margaret's maid, Dorothy Coly, the wife of
John Harris, More's secretary, lent these papers to Thomas
Stapleton to use in writing a biography of More, and many
were quoted in whole or in part. The originals were lost, possibly worn out by use in the devoted family.

More had secretaries, often young scholars, studying Latin
and Greek and serving also as tutors to the children. They
copied out his letters, preserved the rough draft, and gave
More the neat copy to sign and seal. On one letter, which the
secretary had signed, More added a line saying that he had
been saved even the trouble of adding his signature. Sometimes the original autograph was sent and the secretary's copy
retained. John Harris was so devoted to More that he even
copied his handwriting.

Many letters can now be dated only by external and internal evidence. The date for several others can be determined
by the collection in which they were first printed. Items of
news mentioned may date still others. It is important that the
letters be read in proper order; read in chronological sequence, they take on new meaning. The earliest are newsy
and full of atmosphere, like the one to John Holt (No. 1) or
the first extant long epistle to Erasmus (No. 5). As time went
on and More and his correspondents entered public life, less
could be frankly said, lest the letter fall into wrong hands and
its secrets be divulged. Important messages were given verbally
to the servant or secretary or personal friend who carried
the letter and the recipient was told that he could fully trust
the messenger and the added news that he would give.

Note paper, instead of parchment, was now available and
relatively cheap, a fact which accounts for the wealth of personal records so strikingly new in the sixteenth century. A
letter was usually written on a sheet of rag paper about eight
by eleven inches. The top of the letter was folded down, and
the lower part folded up so that the edges just overlapped.
The sides were folded in, deeply overlapping. A pen-knife
then cut slits through these folds. A wedge of paper was in-
serted and its narrow end caught with sealing wax. The wide
end of the wedge was wrapped around the letter to prevent
its being opened, and that end was sealed with wax. The

writer's die (More sometimes used an antique gem) was pressed into the wax. The folded letter was then a rectangle about three by five and a half inches. Even so, letters were often broken open by unauthorized persons, perhaps destroyed, perhaps re-sealed and sent on.

More's hand is admirably clear and legible. This is true even of the two holograph letters from the Tower, to the King and to Thomas Cromwell, and an autograph copy of each, preserved in the British Museum and the Public Record Office. For the other letters in the sad series from the Tower, we have sixteenth-century manuscript copies and the texts as printed by his nephew William Rastell in "The Workes of Sir Thomas More Knyght . . . wrytten by him in the Englysh tonge," London, 1557.

Of the letters in this volume, forty-four were written in Latin. The translations are from different hands. T. S. K. Scott-Craig has translated No. 19, which previously appeared in Elizabeth M. Nugent's *The Thought and Culture of the English Renaissance: An Anthology of Tudor Prose 1481–1555,* Cambridge, 1956. It is reprinted here with the permission of Mr. Scott-Craig, Miss Nugent, and the Cambridge University Press. Burns, Oates, and Washbourne, Ltd., kindly gave us permission to use the translation of letters in Thomas Stapleton's *Tres Thomae,* Part III, made in 1928 by the late Philip E. Hallett, Rector of St. John's Seminary, Wonersh, and to make some changes if needed. My brother, Robert Samuel Rogers, Professor of Latin at Duke University, translated one (No. 34) to Goclenius, for private printing by the late Arthur Rushmore and by Edna Rushmore.

The rest of the letters have been translated by the Rev. Dr. Marcus A. Haworth, S.J., of the Latin department of St. Louis University. A number of these, notably the Epistle to Martin Dorp (No. 4), have never been translated before, and even Latinists will be grateful to him that they now can read quickly More's clear arguments in favor of Erasmus' early work. The final responsibility for these translations is mine.

For the original texts of both the Latin and English letters the reader is referred to my *The Correspondence of Sir Thomas More* (Princeton, 1947) and to P. S. Allen's *Erasmi*

Epistolae (12 vols. Oxford, 1906–58). I am grateful to the Princeton and Oxford University Presses for permission to reproduce material from these volumes. The numbers in square brackets at the head of each letter indicate its number in the *Correspondence* and, where relevant, in Allen's edition. Angle brackets ⟨ ⟩ enclose places of origin or dates which are conjectural. The text of the English letters is presented here in modern spelling and punctuation and glosses have been supplied for those words or phrases which have either changed their meaning or become obsolete since More's day. Within each letter, all archaic words are glossed on their first occurrence; in some of the longer letters glosses have occasionally been repeated in order to facilitate comprehension of the text. The headnotes and the historical notes endeavor to supply essential information about the correspondents or persons mentioned in the text and to put the letters in their proper context as parts of More's extant correspondence. The reader who desires fuller annotation may consult the editions cited above and the bibliography which follows this introduction.

From the beginning of this work in 1958, I have had constant help and encouragement from the Executive Editor, Richard S. Sylvester, and record my deep thanks to him. I should like also to express my gratitude to the trustees of the St. Thomas More Project, whose generous grant has provided for the editing of all of More's Works, Latin and English, and has made it possible for a devoted group to work together, happily and efficiently, on this task.

Elizabeth F. Rogers

New York, N.Y.
January 1961

BIBLIOGRAPHY

THE FOLLOWING LIST of books is designed both to serve as a guide for further reading and to supplement the short titles used in headnote and footnote references. It is of necessity selective. For further information the reader should consult my edition of More's *Correspondence*, especially pp. 567–74, and Conyers Read, *A Bibliography of British History*, 2d ed., Oxford, 1959.

I. BIOGRAPHIES

A. Sixteenth Century

William Roper, *The Lyfe of Sir Thomas Moore, knighte* (1557), ed. Elsie Vaughan Hitchcock, London, 1935, Early English Text Society.

Nicholas Harpsfield, *The life and death of Sir Thomas Moore, knight, Sometymes Lord high Chancellor of England* (1557), ed. Elsie Vaughan Hitchcock, London, 1932, Early English Text Society.

Thomas Stapleton, as Part III of his *Tres Thomae, The Life and Illustrious Martyrdom of Sir Thomas More, formerly Lord Chancellor of England* (1588), trans. Philip E. Hallett, London, 1928.

Ro. Ba., *The Lyfe of Syr Thomas More, Sometymes Lord Chancellor of England* (1599), ed. Elsie Vaughan Hitchcock, P. E. Hallett, and A. W. Reed, London, 1950, Early English Text Society. (The author is not identified).

B. Modern Biographies

William Holden Hutton, *Sir Thomas More*, London, 1895.

T. E. Bridgett, *Life and Writings of Blessed Thomas More*, London, 1891, 3d ed. 1904.

R. W. Chambers, *Thomas More*, London, 1935 (the best modern treatment).

E. E. Reynolds, *Saint Thomas More*, London, 1953 (modern standard life, written by a Catholic).

C. Biographical Studies

The Fame of Blessed Thomas More, London, 1929.

E. M. Routh, *Sir Thomas More and His Friends*, Oxford, 1934.

R. W. Chambers, *The Place of St. Thomas More in English Literature and History*, London, 1937.

II. COMPLEMENTARY STUDIES

Allen, Don Cameron. See under Fletcher.

Allen, P. S., *Erasmus: Lectures and Wayfaring Sketches*, Oxford, 1934.

Allen, P. S., and H. M. Allen, *Letters of Richard Fox, 1486–1527*, Oxford, 1929.

Baumer, Franklin Le Van, *The Early Tudor Theory of Kingship*, New Haven, 1940.

Benians, Ernest Alfred, *John Fisher: A Lecture*, Cambridge, 1935.

Bradner, Leicester, and Charles Arthur Lynch, *The Latin Epigrams of Thomas More*, Chicago, 1953.

Bush, Douglas, *The Renaissance and English Humanism*, Toronto, 1939.

Chester, Allen G., *Hugh Latimer*, Philadelphia, 1954.

Delaruelle, Louis, *Guillaume Budé, Les Origines, les débuts, les idées maîtresses*, Paris, 1907.

Delaruelle, Louis, *Répertoire analytique et chronologique de la correspondance de Guillaume Budé*, Toulouse and Paris, 1907.

Emden, A. B., Vol. 2 of *A Biographical Register of the University of Oxford to 1500*, 3 vols., Oxford, 1958.

Ferguson, Wallace K., *Erasmi Opuscula,* The Hague, 1933 ("Dialogus, Iulius Exclusus e Coelo," pp. 38–124).

Fisher, John, *The Defence of the Priesthood,* trans. P. E. Hallett, London, 1935.

Fletcher, Harris, "The Earliest(?) Printing of Sir Thomas More's Two Epigrams to John Holt," in Don Cameron Allen ed., *Studies in Honor of T. W. Baldwin* (Urbana, 1958), pp. 53–65.

Fulton, J. F., "Early Medical Humanists, Leonicenus, Linacre, Thomas Elyot," *New England Journal of Medicine,* 205 (1934), 141–46, 158–59.

Gee, John Archer, *The Life and Works of Thomas Lupset,* New Haven, 1928.

Hexter, J. H., *More's Utopia: The Biography of an Idea,* Princeton, 1952.

Hogrefe, Pearl, "Sir Thomas More's Connection with the Roper Family," *PMLA,* 47 (1932), 523–33.

Hudson, Hoyt Hopewell, *The Epigram in the English Renaissance,* Princeton, 1947.

Hughes, Philip, *The Reformation in England,* 3 vols., London, 1952, esp. Vol. 1.

Janelle, Pierre, "Humanisme et unité chrétienne: John Fisher et Thomas More," *Études,* 223 (1935), 442–60.

Knowles, Dom David, *The Religious Orders in England,* 3 vols., Cambridge, 1948.

Letters and Papers Foreign and Domestic of the Reign of Henry VIII, ed. J. S. Brewer, J. Gairdner, and R. Brodie, 21 vols., London, 1862–1910 (referred to as *L.P.*).

Mattingly, Garrett, *Catherine of Aragon,* Boston, 1941.

Mitchell, R. J., "Linacre," *English Historical Review,* 50 (1935), 696–98.

Mortimer, Robert C. (Lord Bishop of Exeter), *Western Canon Law,* Berkeley, University of California Press, 1953.

Nugent, Elizabeth M., *The Thought and Culture of the English Renaissance: An Anthology of Tudor Prose, 1481–1555,* Cambridge University Press, 1956.

Osler, William, *Linacre Memorial Lecture,* Cambridge, 1908.

Pollard, A. F., *Wolsey,* London, 1929.

Reed, A. W., *Young More,* in *Under God and the Law,* Papers read to the Thomas More Society of London (2d ser., London, 1949), pp. 1–27.

Reynolds, E. E., *Saint John Fisher,* London, 1955.

Schenk, W., *Reginald Pole, Cardinal of England,* London, 1950.

Schoeck, R. J., "Sir Thomas More's Schooldays," *Times Literary Supplement,* 18 December 1953.

Spahn, M., *Ioannes Cochlaeus, Ein Lebensbild aus der Zeit der Kirchenspaltung,* Berlin, 1898.

Sturge, Charles, *Cuthbert Tunstal,* London, 1938.

Surtz, Edward, S.J., *The Praise of Pleasure,* Cambridge, Mass., 1957.

Surtz, Edward, S.J., *The Praise of Wisdom,* Chicago, 1957.

Sylvester, Richard S., *The Life and Death of Cardinal Wolsey by George Cavendish,* Early English Text Society, Oxford, 1959.

de Vocht, Henry, *Jerome de Busleiden, Founder of the Louvain Collegium Trilingue, His Life and Writings,* Turnhout, Brepols Press, 1950.

de Vocht, Henry, *Literae Virorum Eruditorum ad Franciscum Craneveldium 1522–1528,* Louvain, Uystpruyst, 1928.

de Vocht, Henry, *Monumenta Humanistica Lovaniensia. Texts and Studies about Louvain Humanists in the First Half of the XVIth Century,* Louvain, Uystpruyst, 1934.

Vulgate, 6 vols., Basel, Froben, 1502 (Vol. 5: the Gospels). Bible text interlined with the Gloss of Anselmus Laudunensis, the Glosses of Walafrid Strabo and others, the Postillae and Moralitates of Nicholas de Lyra, the Additiones of Paulus de

Sancta Maria (Bishop of Burgos, 1354–1435), with Matthias Doring's replies.

Wegg, Jervis, *Richard Pace, a Tudor Diplomatist,* London, 1932.

Weiss, Roberto, *Humanism in England during the Fifteenth Century,* Oxford, 1941.

SHORT TITLES

Allen   P. S. and H. M. Allen, *Erasmi Epistolae,* 12 vols., Oxford, 1906–58.

Correspondence Elizabeth Frances Rogers, *The Correspondence of Sir Thomas More,* Princeton, 1947.

L.P.   *Letters and Papers Foreign and Domestic of the Reign of Henry VIII,* ed. J. S. Brewer, J. Gairdner, and R. Brodie, 21 vols., London, 1862–1910.

LETTERS

1

[2] To John Holt.

John Holt, a distinguished grammarian, B.A. and M.A. Oxford, Fellow of Magdalen College, 1491, Usher of Magdalen College School in 1494, became Master to the boys in the household of Cardinal Morton at Lambeth Palace, 1495, and c. 1497 wrote for them *Lac Puerorum,* the first Latin grammar of note in English. Young Thomas More composed Latin Epigrams to introduce and close the little book. Holt was some years More's senior, but More may have known him early in London, perhaps at Oxford, and again when More returned to London during Holt's years at Lambeth. After the Archbishop's death in 1500, Holt became schoolmaster-prebendary of the Chichester Prebendal School, which the bishop, Edward Story, had re-endowed.

More was admitted to Lincoln's Inn on 12 February 1496. The Law Inns in the fifteenth and sixteenth centuries provided training in the law, not then taught in the universities. He was called to the Bar c. 1501. Practising law, and living in or near the Charterhouse to test himself for the monastic life, More used his scanty leisure to study the classics.

William Grocin (1446?–1519) entered Winchester in 1463 and distinguished himself in Latin. He went on to New College in 1465 and was a Fellow there from 1467 to 1481. For a short time he held a college living, but returned to Oxford in 1483 to be Reader in Divinity at Magdalen College. He studied in Italy from late 1487 or 1488, and returned by June 1491. He probably had learned some Greek in England and in Italy he studied with Chalcondyles and Politian (Allen, 2, 441). He held the living of St. Lawrence Jewry (1496–1517), and later resided in another of his livings, in Maidstone, where he died in 1519.

⟨London
c. November 1501⟩

THOMAS MORE SENDS HIS GREETINGS TO JOHN HOLT.

I have sent you everything you wanted, except the additions I have made to the comedy about Solomon; those I

1

could not send you at the moment, as I did not have them with me. I shall arrange for you to get them next week, along with any other of my materials you wish.

I am glad you have left Smarden, an unhealthy spot, and have moved to Chichester, which is a healthier location, with more sunshine. I suppose you will be glad you made the move; the local bishop, I hear, is very fond of you.

As for myself, thanks be to God, I am feeling quite well; and—something few people can say for themselves—I am living my life just as I desire; so please God, may my desires be good. You ask how I am doing in my studies. Wonderfully, of course; things could not be better. I have shelved my Latin books, to take up the study of Greek; however, while dropping the one, I have not as yet completely caught up with the other. But enough on that point.

Grocin, my instructor, recently made a very successful start on his lectures, at Saint Paul's, on the text of the "Celestial Hierarchies," the famous work of Saint Dionysius the Areopagite. It would be hard to tell which is greater—the acclaim for himself, or the profit for his listeners. His audience includes a group of students, whose numbers, unfortunately, are more impressive than their learning; but it also includes very many of the educated class. Several illiterates too are flocking to the lectures, some drawn by curiosity, some out of a desire to appear a little erudite. But the majority of self-styled intellectuals are not attending, so as not to give the impression of admitting their ignorance on matters of which they are ignorant.

Catherine, the illustrious daughter of the King of Spain and bride of our distinguished Prince, lately made her entry into London, amid a tremendous ovation; never, to my knowledge, has there been such a reception anywhere. The magnificent attire of our nobles aroused cries of admiration. But the Spanish escort—good heavens!—what a sight! If you had seen it, I am afraid you would have burst with laughter; they were so ludicrous. Except for three, or at the most four, of them, they were just too much to look at: hunchbacked, undersized, barefoot Pygmies from Ethiopia. If you had been there, you would have thought they were refugees from hell. Ah,

but the lady! take my word for it, she thrilled the hearts of
everyone; she possesses all those qualities that make for beauty
in a very charming young girl. Everywhere she receives the
highest of praises; but even that is inadequate. I do hope
this highly publicized union will prove a happy omen for
England. Farewell.

2

[3] To John Colet.

John Colet (1466–1519) was educated at Oxford, probably at
Magdalen College, and was M.A. 1483. He spent the years 1493–96
in France and Italy, studying theology and preparing himself for
preaching. He returned to Oxford and gave public lectures on St.
Paul's Epistles, which were attended by masters and doctors as well
as students. Erasmus said he lectured "wholesale not retail," for
Colet discussed all the Epistles and compared them with the Book
of Acts and Roman history, in order to know the man Paul and the
conditions in the churches under his care. He served St. Paul's
Cathedral probably as early as 1503, and was appointed Dean in
1504, though not taking office formally until late June 1505.

Thomas Linacre (1460–1524) was born in Canterbury, and educated there (under William de Selling) and at Oxford, being elected
to a Fellowship at All Souls College in 1484. He accompanied Selling to Italy about 1485–86, on his mission to the Pope, and continued the study of Greek with Politian at the court of Lorenzo de'
Medici in Florence. He was in Rome for a time, and must have
gone to Ferrara to study medicine—as a part of Humanism, by the
reading of Hippocrates and Galen in Greek—with Nicholas Leonicenus (1428–1524). He took his doctorate in medicine at Padua,
1496, delighting the professors with his quickness and intelligence
as well as his learning. He lived for several years in Venice in the
home of Aldus Manutius, in order to assist in the publication of
the Greek Aristotle.

Linacre returned to England in 1499. Leonicenus had asked him
to arrange for publication of several medical works which he had
translated from the Greek, but this was delayed until 1522, when
Galen's work on *Muscles* appeared. Meanwhile Linacre had published his own translations of three of Galen's treatises. In 1509,
Linacre became physician to Henry VIII and tutor to the Princess
Mary. He was ordained to the priesthood and received many preferments from 1509 on. The income gave him leisure for study,
and he made a distinguished reputation as a grammarian, by the
publication of *De emendata structura Latini sermonis,* 1524. In
1518, he was one of the founders, and the first president, of the

Royal College of Physicians in London. There were a few physicians,
who were often ecclesiastics, and a few surgeons, but general practice was by the barber surgeons and apothecaries. For Grocin, see
above, the headnote to Letter 1, and for Lily, Letter 11, note 1.

London

23   October   ⟨1504⟩

THOMAS MORE TO HIS JOHN COLET, GREETING.

As I was walking in the law courts the other day, unbusy
where everybody else was busy, I met your servant. I was delighted to see him, both because he has always been dear to
me, and especially because I thought he would not have come
without you. But when I heard from him not only that you
had not returned, but that you would not return for a long
time, I cannot tell you from what rejoicing I was cast into
what dejection. For what could be more grievous to me than
to be deprived of your most pleasant companionship, whose
prudent advice I enjoyed, by whose most delightful intimacy
I was refreshed, by whose powerful sermons I was stirred, by
whose example and life I was guided, in fine, in whose very
countenance and nod I was accustomed to find pleasure?
And so when encompassed by these defenses I felt myself
strengthened; now that I am deprived of them I seem to
languish and grow feeble. By following your footsteps I had
escaped almost from the very gates of hell, and now, driven
by some force and necessity, I am falling back again into
gruesome darkness. I am like Eurydice, except that she was
lost because Orpheus looked back at her, but I am sinking
because you do not look back at me.

For in the city what is there to move one to live well? but
rather, when a man is straining in his own power to climb
the steep path of virtue, it turns him back by a thousand devices and sucks him back by its thousand enticements. Wherever you betake yourself, on one side nothing but feigned
love and the honeyed poisons of smooth flatterers resound;
on the other, fierce hatreds, quarrels, the din of the forum
murmur against you. Wherever you turn your eyes, what
else will you see but confectioners, fishmongers, butchers,
cooks, poulterers, fishermen, fowlers, who supply the materials

for gluttony and the world and the world's lord, the devil? Nay even houses block out from us I know not how large a measure of the light, and do not permit us to see the heavens. And the round horizon does not limit the air but the lofty roofs. I really cannot blame you if you are not yet tired of the country where you live among simple people, unversed in the deceits of the city; wherever you cast your eyes, the smiling face of the earth greets you, the sweet fresh air invigorates you, the very sight of the heavens charms you. There you see nothing but the generous gifts of nature and the traces of our primeval innocence.

But yet I do not wish you to be so captivated by these delights as to be unwilling to fly back to us as soon as possible. For if the inconveniences of the city so displease you, your country parish of Stepney (of which you should have no less care) will afford you hardly less advantages than where you now dwell, whence you can sometimes turn aside, as to an inn, to the city (where there is so much that needs your service). For in the country, where men are of themselves either almost innocent, or at least not ensnared in great sins, the services of any physician can be useful. But in the city because of the great numbers that congregate there, and because of their long-standing habits of vice, any physician will have come in vain unless he be the most skillful. Certainly there come from time to time into the pulpit at St. Paul's preachers who promise health, but although they seem to have spoken very eloquently, their life is in such sharp contrast to their words that they irritate rather than soothe. For they cannot bring men to believe that though they are themselves obviously in direst need of the physician's help, they are yet fit to be entrusted with the cure of other men's ailments. And thus when men see that their diseases are being prescribed for by physicians who are themselves covered with ulcers, they immediately become indignant and obstinate. But if (as observers of human nature assert), he is the best physician in whom the patient has the greatest confidence, who can doubt that you are the one who can do most for the cure of all in the city? Their readiness to allow you to treat their wounds, their trust, their obedience, you have yourself proved in the past, and now the universal desire and anticipation of you proclaim it all again.

Come then, my dear Colet, for Stepney's sake, which mourns your long absence as children their mother's; for the sake of your native place which should be no less dear to you than are your parents. Finally (though this will be a weak force for your return), let regard for me, who am entirely devoted to you and hang anxiously upon your coming, move you.

Meanwhile, I shall pass my time with Grocin, Linacre, and our dear friend Lily, the first as you know the sole guide of my life (in your absence), the second my master in learning, the third the dearest partner of my endeavors. Farewell, and love me ever as now. London, 23 October.

3

[8] To John Colet.

Colet founded his new school c. 1509, dedicating it to the Child Jesus and erecting buildings in St. Paul's Churchyard. The fortune his father had left him provided a generous endowment for 153 boys to have their education free, and to pay the three masters well. Latin was thoroughly taught and Greek was introduced in an English school for the first time since the revival of letters. This "new learning" caused Colet and his school to be suspected of heresy. Colet wrote to Erasmus that "a bishop, held to be one of the wiser ones, has been blaspheming our school before a large concourse of people, declaring that I have erected a useless thing, even an evil thing, yea more—a temple of idolatry."

<London?
c. March 1512?>

I don't much wonder if *they* are bursting with jealousy of your excellent school. For they see that, just as the Greeks who destroyed barbarian Troy came out of the Trojan horse, so from your school come those who reprove and overthrow *their* ignorance.

4

[15] To Martin Dorp.

Martin van Dorp (1485–1525) was born at Naaldwyk in South Holland, near The Hague. He was educated at the Lily, the first college in the University of Louvain to teach Renaissance studies. He was promoted M.A. in 1504 and was appointed to teach Latin. His method was new, as he based his lectures not on abstracts, but on full literary texts, and as few had yet been printed, he taught those with such thoroughness that it was possible for his students to present the Latin plays which they had read. In 1505 he was chosen to teach philosophy, and lectured on Aristotle in very conservative, scholastic fashion. This he later deeply regretted, as time lost from the study of the Bible or of Cicero. At the same time, probably, he began to study theology, though he said he did it at first only in the hope of being preferred to benefices. Meanwhile he published his earlier writings on the classics. This brought him to the notice of Erasmus as early as 1503; in 1514 he was entrusted with seeing Erasmus' *Opuscula* through the press.

It was therefore a shock when in late September 1514 Dorp wrote Erasmus a long letter to report criticism of *The Praise of Folly* by the theologians at Louvain, at whose instigation, indeed, he wrote. He said that their authority over the common people must be maintained and Erasmus should now write a Praise of Wisdom. Dorp approved Erasmus' editing of St. Jerome's correspondence, but strongly criticized the proposed edition of the Greek New Testament and the correction of the Latin Vulgate by comparison with it, thinking that casting doubt on the authority of the Vulgate would undermine the faith (Allen, 2, Ep. 304).

Copies of this letter were circulated to others before Erasmus received it. Not until March 1515, when he reached Antwerp on his way to England, did he see a copy, lent him by a friend. On his return from England at the end of May, he wrote his defense (ibid., Ep. 337). More immediately called it an Apologia (see below, Letter 5), and it was included in later editions of the *Folly*.

Erasmus wrote in a conciliatory tone, and with much common sense. He said he had criticized the theologians only when their teaching consisted chiefly of idle debates and not when it was based upon adequate study of the biblical languages and of the teaching of the Fathers. He was sure the critics would also condemn the edition of the works of St. Jerome because, in his exegesis of the Scriptures, Jerome cited the Hebrew and Greek texts. Finally, Erasmus defended the printing of the Greek New Testament, which the Fathers had considered the best text, not the Latin Vulgate which had not been approved by any council. After sending the letter to Dorp, Erasmus rewrote it, with somewhat more explanation, for publication. Dorp answered the original, shorter form, not now extant, and More also wrote from that.

Dorp's second letter is much sharper (Allen, 2, Ep. 347). Dorp had received his doctorate before 30 August 1515 and was admitted to the Council of the Faculty of Theology. His letter to Erasmus was dated 27 August, and fully supported the Louvain theologians.

Dorp again denied the need of a knowledge of Greek. He maintained the superiority of the Latin Vulgate over the Greek text,
which, though it was the original, had lost its value, he said, because
the Greeks had become heretics. He named distinguished scholars
of the Western Church who did not know Greek. Finally he told
Erasmus that he wrote what others said of him in his absence, but
averred that he was to these critics a public herald of the name and
renown of Erasmus, even though in some matters he did not agree
with that learned man.

   More wrote the following long letter in defense of Erasmus. He
said later that he had suppressed it, but that does not mean that
he did not send it to Dorp. The copy which was evidently sent sur-
vives in the Bibliothèque Nationale in Paris, and the one sent to
Basel for Erasmus and his friends to see is in the Humanistic Library in Sélestat. From that, it would seem, it was printed in More's
Lucubrationes at Basel in 1563.

Bruges

21 October ⟨1515⟩

THOMAS MORE SENDS HIS GREETINGS TO MARTIN DORP.

   If I were as free to visit you as I strongly desire to do, my
dear Dorp, I could then discuss with you personally and more
appropriately these matters which I now put down, quite in-
appropriately, in writing. Then too for the time being I would
be enjoying your actual company—the sweetest pleasure I
could have enjoyed; for Erasmus has implanted in my heart
an extraordinary longing to see you, to get acquainted with
you and to love you; he is very fond of both of us and, I hope,
dear to both of us alike. His greatest pleasure is to praise ab-
sent friends to friends present. Since he is greatly loved by so
many men and that too in different parts of the world, because of his learning and most charming character, he tries
earnestly to bind all men together with that same affection
which all have for him alone. And so he constantly mentions
each one of his friends individually to them all, and, to in-
sinuate them into the friendship of all the others, he constantly talks about those qualities each one has that deserve
affection. Now while he constantly deals in this manner with
all his friends, with no one, my dear Dorp, does he do so
more often, more effusively, and more readily than with you.
He has sung your praises in England for so long a time that

every scholar there knows and respects the name of Dorp as much as do the scholars of Louvain, who most respect him (as they should). When we were alone, he described you in such accurate terms that long ago I conceived a very beautiful picture of you, one that conformed exactly to the picture I received from the reading of your splendid writings, after I came here.

So, as soon as I got word from our Invincible King that I was to serve in the embassy [1] to this country, rest assured, my dear Dorp, the possibility of my being offered a chance to meet with you somehow was not, in my opinion, the least reward for my lengthy journey. But the transaction of the business entrusted to me has deprived me of this opportunity, which I had hoped was offered to me, and has detained me at Bruges, for a previous agreement had been made with the noble representatives of our Illustrious Prince Charles to discuss our business here. Consequently, now, though my mission may be successful for many other reasons, I am very unhappy, because my luck has completely abandoned me just where I had hoped I was particularly lucky.

But—to get down to the point which has compelled me to write at the present moment—while I have been staying here, I have chanced upon some persons who, to my way of thinking, are not unacquainted with the world of letters. In conversation with them, I have introduced Erasmus' name, and yours too. Erasmus they knew from his writings and reputation; you too they knew, but also for other reasons. They told me a story that was not only unpleasant, but quite unbelievable. They said that you are acting in a rather un- friendly manner toward Erasmus, and that this attitude is obvious from your letters to him.[2] They promised to bring me those letters the next day, as they were aware I was not easily inclined to accept their word. They came back the next day, bringing me three letters; one was addressed by you to Erasmus. This letter, as I gather from his answer, he had not

1. More served in this embassy from early May to the end of October.
2. The Latinist should read Dorp's letter to Erasmus (Allen, 2, Ep. 304), Erasmus' reply (ibid., Ep. 337), and Dorp's second letter (ibid., Ep. 347), all with notes. Erasmus wrote a reply but suppressed it, and it is not now extant.

received; but he had read through a copy of it, just as I have
done, given him by somebody. In this letter you make some
charges against the *Folly,* and you suggest that he write a
"Praise of Wisdom"; and as for his plan to emend the text of
the New Testament with the aid of Greek manuscripts, you
give such little approval of it and encourage him to restrict it
within such narrow limits that you practically oppose the
entire plan. The second was a letter of his in which he apol-
ogized to you briefly, because he was travel-weary and still
very much occupied with the same trip, but promising to
write at greater length after reaching Basel. And then there
was a third letter containing your answer to this letter of
Erasmus.

I read through this letter in their presence. There was nothing in it to convince me of any hostile intent on your part
toward Erasmus; nor could there be anything to convince me
of that. There was, however, some evidence that you were
confused beyond my expectations. But as I desired rather to
uproot this view from their minds than corroborate it, I
claimed I read nothing in the letter which might not proceed
from a friendly heart. "But," one of the group remarked,
"I am not criticizing what he wrote, rather the fact that he
did write; for that reason, in my view, he by no means acted
as a friend." For if the *Folly* gives so much offense to any
person—and I have never heard of that happening, not even
at Louvain, although I have often been there since the *Folly*
has been published, and for long periods of time—except
from one or the other person, and they were soured old men
in their second childhood, the object of derision even of
children in that place—with this exception the work has met
with universal approval, here at Bruges and at Louvain,
so much so that many people even memorize several passages
of the work.

But as I started to say—if the *Folly* gives so much offense
to any person that it seemed necessary to challenge Erasmus
to write a retraction, still since Dorp was summoned to the
side of Erasmus not so very long ago, and, on his own evidence, all by himself, what was the purpose of writing a
letter? If he thought he ought to deliver some admonition,

why did he not give it when present personally with Erasmus? Why did he not give his orders face to face (to quote from Terence) as to what was to be done instead of departing and shouting them out in the middle of the street, while Erasmus was so far away that he was the only one not to know for some time and finally heard only from others a matter which he should have been the first or even the only one to hear? "Consider," he said, "the sincerity of his action in this matter. First, he makes a pretense of defending before the public a man against whom no one brings any charges; then the reasons for his defense are read openly by everybody, though I have my doubts whether anybody, except the one who ought to, listens to his objections." After he finished, different remarks were passed by the others, not necessary to retail here. My rejoinders and my manner of dismissing them were such that they readily grasped the idea that I would not listen to any untoward remarks about you and that I was almost as well disposed toward you as toward Erasmus, and I could not possibly be better disposed toward him. For as to the fact that you preferred to discuss the matter with him by letter rather than by word of mouth, no matter what your intention was in so doing, I am convinced, in keeping with my opinion of you, that you definitely did not act out of ill will; and he too entertains no doubts in the matter, knowing full well your attitude toward him.

As for your second letter, now widely read with unhappy consequences, I am inclined to believe it was no deliberate action of yours but merely an accident that it reached the public. I am forced to this point of view especially because in this letter there are some things which I am fully convinced you would have changed had you wished to publish it, as they are not quite the sort of thing to be written either to him or by you. You would not have written such harsh words to so important a friend, or in such an off-hand fashion to a man as learned as he; as a matter of fact, I am positive, you would have written in a more kindly vein, in keeping with your temperate character, and with greater care, in keeping with your extraordinary learning. Furthermore, as for the jests and jeers with which your whole letter abounds immoderately,

I have no doubt you would have employed them much more sparingly, or at least, my dear Dorp, more cleverly. I do not make much of the fact that you attack the *Folly,* that you inveigh against the Poets, that you deride all the Grammarians, that you do not approve of the Annotations on Holy Scripture, that you are of the opinion a thorough knowledge of Greek literature is not pertinent—all of these points I do not make much of, since they are views each man is free to hold without offending anybody; and they have been discussed by you up to now in such a fashion that I do not have any doubt that several answers, which ought to be given to your objections, will occur to anyone reading them. Besides, by no means do I think you have said too much against any one of these points; and in certain instances even I miss many points with which I should like to have seen your letter better equipped as it advanced against Erasmus, so that he could have a finer opportunity to fortify his camp with more powerful siege works to oppose you.

But I am definitely very much disturbed because, in your work, you give the impression of attacking Erasmus in a manner not at all becoming to you or him. You treat him sometimes as if you despise him, sometimes as if you looked down upon him in derision, sometimes not as one giving him an admonition, but scolding him like a stern reprover or a harsh censor; and lastly, by twisting the meaning of his words, as if you were stirring up all the theologians and even the universities against him. I do not want this letter of mine to be interpreted as being in opposition to you, for I thoroughly believe that you have done none of these things out of any ill will toward him. While I should need a defender myself, I shall take up the defense of one who, I know, is definitely considered in the eyes of all, and in reality is, too outstanding a man to have to be reduced to their level. Out of love for you and my interest in your reputation, I have wanted to warn you of those matters which men, not fully understanding your temperate character and utter sincerity, are using as an opportunity to think that you are extremely greedy for your own reputation and making sneak attacks on the reputation of another. I wish, Dorp—just as in Virgil, Aeneas, enveloped in a mist, mingled with the Carthaginians and viewed the portrayal of the tapestries of himself and his exploits— so I wish you could view, without being seen, the facial expression of those reading this last letter of yours. I am quite sure you would consider me much more worthy of gratitude for frankly advising you to make corrections than you would consider those people who, when by themselves, criticize the very things they fawningly praise in your presence; for by making corrections you can get everybody to think—as I am doing myself—that the letter was not sent by you, but escaped from you.

However, I am certainly surprised if any person should take it into his head to be so flattering as to extol such matters even in your presence; and, as I began to say, I wish you could watch through a window and see the facial expression, the tone of voice, the emotion with which those matters are read. In the letter to Erasmus more than once you ride roughshod over our theologians, over Erasmus, and over your grammarians, as if, while occupying a throne high up among the ranks of the theologians, you were shoving him down among the poor grammarians. You take your place among the theologians, and rightly so, and not just a place, but the first place. Still he should not be shoved from the throne of the theologians down to the benches of the grammarians. Though I do not think Erasmus will scorn the title of grammarian, which you laugh at with more frequency than wit. As a matter of fact, he deserves that title most of all perhaps. But he is so modest, he does not admit it, since he realizes that the name "grammarian" is synonymous with learned; the function of the grammarian penetrates all types of letters —that is, all the arts. Consequently, a person who has made a thorough study of dialectics can be called a dialectician, of arithmetic, an arithmetician; likewise in the other arts. But it is my definite opinion that only the man who has investigated all the branches of knowledge has the right to be called learned. Otherwise you could attach the name of grammarian even to little children who have learned the alphabet. But you mean by grammarian only those men who, as you put it, with whip in hand instead of a scepter play the king in the

cave of flogging and, though more stupid than Self-love and
Folly, think they understand all branches of learning, just
because they know feeble words and the structure of clauses. I
would admit, my dear Dorp, that such men are far from being
learned. Yet, I really believe that they are much closer to
learning than are those theologians who do not know the
structure of clauses and feeble words. I can think of several,
and you, I suppose, of even more, who belong to that class,
although we both keep it a deep secret. Erasmus definitely
does not belong to that group of grammarians who have
learned only feeble words, nor to that group of theologians
who know absolutely nothing but a confused labyrinth of
petty problems. He does belong to the group of grammarians
such as Varro and Aristarchus, and to the group of theologians
such as yourself, my dear Dorp, and that is to the very best.
He is not ignorant of those petty problems; yet, just as you in
a thorough way have done, he has acquired what is much
more useful, a competent knowledge of good literature, primarily sacred, but also of other kinds.

But, to go on with your letter. It contains another remark
of almost the same stripe: "If ever you see the Decretals,
Erasmus," as if, of course, he could in no way see the Decretal
letters [3] which you imply you have seen. Then, there is that
remark which you fling into his face: "the water was disturbed
by a heron" and likewise "everything is thrown into confusion
by the ignorant whenever they step upon the wrestling floor
of argumentation." And then again: "Erasmus, you are unable
to tell the difference between a dialectician and a sophist, if
you do not understand either art." And a little later: "Unless it be that in your eyes sophists are all those men who get
the better of you in an argument, that is, all dialecticians."

3. From the late fourth century popes solved problems of local
churches in decretal letters, which had the force of law along with the
canons (decisions) of church councils. This law was codified in a textbook by
Gratian of Bologna, c. 1140. Later decretals were published by Pope
Gregory IX, 1234, as five books of "Extravagants," *extra vagantes*, wander-
ing outside Gratian. Boniface VIII, 1298, issued the "Sext," which itself
was divided into five books, and in 1314 Clement V published the Clem-
entine Constitutions. Two later collections were made. All were printed
in 1503 by Jean Chapuis, as the Corpus Juris Canonici. This Erasmus
would of course have seen.

Do you really think, Dorp, that everything is thrown into
confusion by Erasmus when he is engaged in an argument,
and that he does not understand the nature of dialectics, or
just exactly what a sophist is, and that he alone does not
understand what practically all schoolboys know? I do believe that even you will admit that rhetoric is a very special
gift of his, and if you grant that, I do not see how you can so
completely strip him of dialectics. Not the lowliest of philosophers were correct when they maintained that dialectics
and rhetoric were no more distinct than are the fist and the
palm of the hand, because what dialectics holds together more
tightly, rhetoric unfolds more freely, and just as the former
strikes with the point of the blade, so the latter by its sheer
force completely prostrates and destroys. But suppose dialectics
has nothing in common with rhetoric. Just because he does
not argue in the schools, because he does not engage in discussions before groups of schoolboys, and because, as you will
do later yourself, he lets those petty problems stand, you
think he has never learned them; rather, you believe he is the
inferior of all dialecticians in argumentation.

Now notice how completely I disagree with you. Take a
man who has some learning and a moderate supply of talent—
I mean one with far less talent than a man like Erasmus. Such
a man I do not think will take second place in an argument
to every dialectician, provided both parties are acquainted
with the subject under discussion; native talent will supply
the deficiency in formal training. The very precepts of dialectics are merely the product of man's native intelligence; that
is to say, they are methods of reasoning which reason has observed as useful for investigating things. I do not think a
single person would doubt that he could handle even those
petty problems, if he should so wish, not in those quarrelsome
debates where shouting prevails over reason and which men
leave spitting on one another—for his self-control and sense
of shame shrink from such manners; but he will handle
them, in writing or in a serious and earnest discussion, in
such wise as to be not only not inferior to everyone else,
but even the equal or superior of the best. Erasmus, whose
ability and learning are the object of universal admiration,

is far from being inferior in argumentation to absolutely all dialecticians—that is to say, including even schoolboys. But I shall put all that aside; it is too small a matter when the subject under discussion is an evaluation of literature. Quite indiscreetly you introduced the names of Jerome the Hussite and Cresconius the grammarian, both obviously heretics; this is certainly disgusting, since you seem to refer to them for the sake of making a comparison. Your handling of the subject is sometimes so bitter, as if your only purpose were to arouse against him, first, the theologians of Louvain, secondly, everybody in the whole world, and finally all the schools; and to attain that purpose you misinterpret some of his words, completely garbling the text.

To begin with the last point—Erasmus remarked that not all theologians condemn the Folly, but only those who regret the renascence of good literature are causing this commotion, and that those who had condemned the Folly, would not give their approval to the edition of Jerome, which you had said in writing was approved by the theologians. Seizing upon his remark as material for a clever joke, you then make this comment: "A strange distinction, for you to publish what few will approve"; as if there were left only a few to approve, if from the very large number of distinguished theologians, we except one or two soured old men who deserve any title rather than that which they profess. And yet, Dorp, you pursue at greater length the same merry jest. "Well, now," you say, "the theologians will not approve of it" (that was obviously what he said!); "please tell me then, who will approve of it? Lawyers? Doctors? or philosophers? so at least they could apply the sickle to another's harvest? But you are getting it ready for grammarians. Then let the grammarians sit upon the throne, the critics of all branches of learning, and let them produce a new theology for us, one destined to be born at long last together with a ridiculous little mouse. But there is fear that their students will not want to submit to their scepters. For their scepters are whips, with which they play the king in the cave of flogging, and though more stupid than Self-love and Folly, they think they understand all branches of learning, just because they know feeble words and the structure of clauses. Therefore there is no need of academies; the school of Zwolle or of Deventer will be enough. It is definitely the opinion of the great Jerome the Hussite, that universities are as valuable for the Church of God as is the devil. And it does not disturb the grammarians one bit that this opinion was condemned in the Council of Constance, in which it was decreed that all men are ignorant, even one who has some knowledge of Greek." I may be somewhat unfair to you, Dorp, if I keep mentioning your jest; it is strange what sweet pleasure you have received from it for some time. But if you have had enough joking, listen to me now, Dorp.

It is obvious to everyone who reads your words that you descended to the level of mentioning universities without any reason at all, and that this entire passage was declaimed by you in copious language, and very eloquently, to be sure, but it has nothing to do with the point in question; nor is there any need to answer it. I do not think there is any doubt about the attitude of Erasmus toward the universities; he studied and taught in them, not only those branches you called grammar, but many others much more valuable for all Christians, as also those petty problems, which you will later make little of, though at present you make much of them. Everybody knows how long he was held in high esteem at Paris, and at Padua, and at Bologna, not to mention Rome, which, in my view, is the most distinguished of all the universities. He is as highly regarded now at Oxford and Cambridge as he should be; he spent some time in both places, with great success for the students, and not less honor for himself. He is being invited to both places. Both are trying to number him among their theologians, because that is his distinction elsewhere. But what your esteem is of our universities, I do not know; you are so generous in your tribute to Louvain and Paris, as to seem to leave nothing at all, especially of dialectics, for the rest of the world. You claim, if it were not for the fact that the theologians of Louvain and Paris are dialecticians, dialectics would be a stranger all over the world, and would have been such for many centuries.

I was in both universities seven years ago; true, not for very long, but during that time I made an effort to know the sub-

ject matter and method of teaching in both places. I admire
both. But, after having found out all I could by personal
presence or by inquiry when not there, I have up to now no
reason for wanting my children, whose best interests are close
to my heart, to receive their education, even in dialectics, at
either university rather than at Oxford or Cambridge.[4] Still
I shall not deny—for I would not consciously deprive any
man of the honor due him—that our people are very much
indebted to James Lefèvre of Paris.[5] Those of our nation
possessed of finer talent and sounder judgment follow him
as the restorer of true dialectics and true philosophy, especially
Aristotle's; and consequently through his instrumentality
Paris seems to be returning thanks to us for a gift [6] received
long ago, since he is the means of reviving among us the
branches of learning which they received from us at the start.
This fact is so generally accepted that Gaguin,[7] who neither
disparages the honor of the French nor broadcasts our honor,
has recorded it in his history. I should even like to see all the
scholars of Louvain, and of Paris too, adopt Lefèvre's commentaries on Aristotle's dialectics. If I am not mistaken, both
parties would find that subject less troublesome and a little
clearer.

And yet I wonder why, at the mention of dialectics, you
linked together the scholars of Louvain and Paris. They are so
at odds with one another, they do not even agree on the name;
the one group takes for itself the title of Realists, the other, of
Nominalists. However, if both groups adopt Aristotle, and
teach him, if the only subject of their constant arguments is
his meaning, then when the scholars of Paris and Louvain

4. When More so planned for the education of his children, the eldest,
Margaret, was just ten.

5. James Lefèvre (c. 1455–1536) of Étaples in Picardy, was M.A. Paris,
and also studied in Italy. By 1504 he had become secretary to William
Briçonnet, Bishop then of Lodève and later of Meaux. His studies were
chiefly biblical, but for these his knowledge of Hebrew and Greek was
inadequate. He edited St. Paul's Epistles from the Vulgate in 1512, and
with them a paraphrase and commentary of his own.

6. Probably an allusion to Alcuin.

7. Robert Gaguin (1433–1501) was born in Artois, a Fleming by birth
but French by nationality. He went to a school of the Trinitarian or
Maturin order, which he later joined, and studied at Paris. He was an
ambassador to Germany, Italy, and England. He is best known for his
De Origine et Gestis Francorum Compendium, 1495.

give different, and not just different but even opposite, interpretations of him, how can one tell which side to follow? Now
if such quarrels belong to dialectics—though not at all to
Aristotle—then it is not Aristotelian logic, as you say, but
some other brand which one or both parties are professing.
But if such controversial matters do not belong to dialectics
—and certainly they do not belong to it, if they do not belong
to him, provided he gave a complete treatment of dialetics—
it would be a tremendous absurdity to dispute fiercely for so
many years, with the purpose of learning dialectics, over
matters which do not at all pertain to the subject.

Really, Dorp, I am almost led to believe that a large section
of opinions which are the subject of lengthy and bitter fighting, as if for hearth and home, has little to do with logic, or
does not contribute very much to its mastery. In the study of
grammar, for instance, it is enough to learn the rules which
can help one to speak Latin and to understand what others
have written in Latin, but not with worried mind to pursue
numberless rules of grammar and to grow gray amid letters
and syllables. So also, in the study of dialectics, I should think
it enough, once a person has been taught the nature of words,
the force of propositions, and after that the rules for syllogisms,
to make immediate application of dialectics, as an instrument,
to the other branches of learning. Aristotle undoubtedly had
this very idea in mind; his entire treatment of dialectics consists of those ten supreme categories, either of things or names,
plus a treatise on propositions, and finally the rules for syllogisms, those which lead to a necessary conclusion, those
which persuade with probability, and those which involve
clever fallacies. To this Porphyry [8] added, as an approach or
introduction, the five universal predicables, whether you
prefer to call them things or words. Moreover, neither of
them proposed the sort of problems by which minds, still
untrained and in need of more suitable formation, are held
back rather than advanced. Porphyry even explicitly avoided
them. But now they have introduced a jumble of senseless
monstrosities, which were kept distinctly separate by the ancients, but are now given birth for the complete destruction

8. Porphyry (A.D. 223 – c. 304) the Greek scholar who wrote an introduction and commentary on the *Categories* of Aristotle.

of the liberal arts; and with regard to the absolutely pure traditions of the ancients, they have polluted everything by in-
jecting their own filth. In the case of grammar—to bypass
Alexander [9] and others of like kind, who, though teaching
grammar imperfectly, still did teach it in some way—one
Albert,[10] professing to expound grammar, gave us some sort of
logic, or metaphysics, or, really, neither of the two, but substituted for grammar sheer nightmares and wild imaginations.
Yet this nonsensical nonsense was welcomed into public
academies, even given excessive approval by a considerable
number of men, so that practically the only person thought
to carry any weight in the field of grammar is one who has
attained the title of Albertist.

A conviction that is first handed on by stupid teachers and
then strengthened in the course of years is extremely capable
of perverting the judgment of even sound minds. I am not
therefore surprised that, in a similar way, a type of nonsense,
worse than that of the sophists, has gradually displaced dialectics. Under the guise of brilliant wit, this nonsense has a
powerful attraction for its supporters. Recently, while I was
speaking in passing about these matters, a certain dialectician,
considered very learned, made this statement—I shall quote
his very words, else I could not reproduce the brilliance of
his eloquence—: "Aristotle had only a rough style; today
schoolboys are so solidly grounded in the *Little Logicals*—
of this I am positive—that if Aristotle should arise from his
grave and argue with them, they would easily 'shut' him up
again, not just with sophistry, but with his very own logic
too." I took leave of the fellow very much against my will;
I was a little too busy, in the circumstances, to have time for
play.

Now this book, the *Little Logicals*,[11] which is so called,

9. Alexander de Villa Dei (fourteenth century) wrote a Grammar, *Doc-
trinale,* in verse, which was used universally until the sixteenth century.
10. Albert of Saxony, student of Prague, M.A. of Paris, first Rector
of Vienna, 1365, wrote a *Tractatus* used as a philosophical textbook.
11. Parua Logicalia was the title for more than one textbook of logic,
notably for that by Peter the Spaniard, Pope John XX, 1277, and another
by Marsilius of Inghen, ex-Rector of Paris and cofounder of the University of Heidelberg, 1386.

I suppose, because it has very little logic in it, is worth while looking at, with its suppositions, as they are called, its ampliations, restrictions, and appellations, and passages in which occur little rules, not only silly, but even false, as, for instance, the rules by which one must distinguish between these and similar enunciations: "A lion than an animal is braver" and "A lion is braver than an animal," as if they did not mean the same thing. Surely, both enunciations are so silly, they have practically no meaning; though, if they do have any meaning, certainly it is the same in both cases. The same difference exists between "Wine I've drunk twice" and "Twice I've drunk wine"—a great difference, that is, according to these logicians, but in reality none at all. Now if a person eats meat that has been roasted and even burned, they would insist he is speaking the truth if he says, "Raw meat I have eaten," but not if he says, "I have eaten raw meat." And if somebody should take a part of my money, leaving me some of it, I would be lying, of course, if I said, "He has robbed me of my money." But, so as not to be lacking words with which to lodge my complaint in court, I may say, "Of money has he robbed me." And in some possible supposed case, as they call it, this enunciation will be true, "The Pope I have whipped," while, supposing the same case, this one will be false, "I have whipped the Pope"—that is to say, if he who is now pope was as a boy beaten by me. Really, those who teach such stuff in their old age deserve a beating every time they teach boys. And then they claim this to be false: "Every man is a father who has a son," unless absolutely all men were now to have sons, since it obviously is equivalent to saying: "Every man is a father and every man has a son."

But at the same time they maintain this proposition is true, "Sortes will be a father, when Sortes will not be a father"; and also, "John will remain a father, when John will not remain a father." Who can hear such a thing without thinking he is being offered a riddle? The words "I am" and "I can" hold complete sway, and since (as they say) they are expansive, they extend their boundaries far beyond the very limits of nature. For they imagine this as true: "Everything that will be, is," although they interpret it cleverly. They say "Everything that will be is" means "everything that is that will be, is," and in this way they avoid maintaining the present existence of the Antichrist, who will one day exist. For although everything which will exist, does exist, and although the Antichrist will exist, still it does not follow that the Antichrist does exist, for the reason that the Antichrist is not a being that will exist. But if theologians sharp in dialectical subtlety had not pondered the more than clever explanation of this proposition, undoubtedly the Antichrist would have invaded the Christian Republic long ago, not without tremendous disaster for all the others. As for themselves, I do not see how any crisis can be a threat to them, since they admit that these propositions are true: "The Antichrist is lovable" and "The Antichrist is affectionate." Surely neither the Antichrist nor the final day of judgment will be able to destroy the physical world any more than this sort of dialectics, which teaches that such propositions as the following are true: "The living was dead," "The future was past"; the result of these propositions undoubtedly is that the resurrection of the dead seems to be not—as they hold—in the process of becoming (*in fieri*), but an accomplished fact (*in facto esse*). And the following propositions are not less remarkable, but attractive also, and plausible, since they are of course true: "The virgin was a whore," and "The whore will be a virgin," and "The whore is possibly a virgin." It is not easy to say which of the two, virgins or whores, are more indebted to such an obliging dialectics; certainly both groups are very much indebted. And so poets treat of trifles, dialecticians, of serious matters. Poets use their imaginations and tell untruths; dialecticians never speak aught but the truth, even when they affirm as true: "A dead man can celebrate Mass." Although I do not have the daring to refuse to believe them when they make that assertion, almost even with an oath (for it is not right to answer so large a group of professors who are so unanswerable), still to this day, as far as I can recall, I have never found a single person able to report that he had served Mass for a dead celebrant.

Is this the sort of dialectics that Aristotle teaches? that Jerome praises? that Augustine approves? that the mad

Orestes—to quote Persius [12]—would swear to be a madman's? Really I am surprised, how sharp-witted men thought that those statements must be understood in a sense in which no one in the whole wide world except themselves understands them. Those words do not belong to a profession, so as to be their private property and to be taken on loan by anyone who wants to use them. Speech is surely a common possession; but they spoil some words which they have gotten from cobblers. They have taken them from the common people; they misuse what is common. But, they object, their so-called rule of logic tells them that such propositions demand that interpretation. Will this damned rule, designed in some corner by men who hardly know how to talk, impose new laws of speech on all the world? Grammar teaches correct speech; it does not devise unusual rules of language, but advises those who are unskilled in speech not to violate the customs of the language which she notices are ordinarily observed. A dialectics that is sound acts no differently. Assuredly, this syllogism: "Every animal runs; every man is an animal," therefore "every man runs" is not a syllogism for the reason that it is properly constructed in accordance with the precepts of dialectics and fashioned as a *barbara* syllogism, but because reason, which made such a rule for that very purpose, tells us that the conclusion follows from the premises. Otherwise, should reason make the rule in any other way, no matter which way, it would swerve from the very nature of things. So also with regard to the proposition "The whore will be a virgin," let those men not say that it must be interpreted "The whore that is, or that will be" because so the rule demands; but let them produce a reason for such a rule from the meaning of the words. For if that interpretation is correct, it must be evident either from the thing itself, which is put into an enunciation, or from the normal meaning of the words.

Very many people, who have spoken Latin for some time, have possessed both talent and learning and have been the equal, in my opinion, of those men in a knowledge of correct

12. Aulus Persius Flaccus (A.D. 34–62), Roman poet and satirist. The passage in Satire 3: ". . . and you say and do things which Orestes, the hero of madmen, would depose to be the words and actions of a madman."

speech. But why is it that not one of them could see that this
proposition is true: "The whore will be a virgin," or could
distinguish between these two propositions: "Money I do not
have," and "I do not have any money." Although no one
would deny that a change in the position of words often
causes a change of meaning. "Drink before eating," does not
mean the same as: "Eat before drinking." But, when there is
such a change in meaning, I maintain that men are unanimous
in their agreement, under the influence of reason. The rules
of dialecticians do not demand so much as persuade, for it
is their duty to follow our custom in the use of language and
to push us along in any direction, with reasons that are true.
Sophists, however, by their deceptive use of words lead us to
a spot where we find ourselves with surprise. It is a dull-witted
form of cleverness and a stupid kind of ingenuity for men to
proclaim they are the winners in an argument and to decide
the victory in favor of themselves, because we do not know in
what sense they have secretly agreed to use our words, contrary to universal acceptance. While such do not even deserve
the name of sophisms, still they are not considered as sophistic
nonsense, but are counted among the most secret treasures of
dialectics. They are not learned by schoolboys as something to
be forgotten, but are welcomed even by elderly men into the
very inner sanctum of theology. Some men use these sophisms
as stuffing for obscure theological problems; from them they
formulate such absurd propositions that no other source
could produce a greater abundance of ridiculous matter. But
I would much prefer that men who are such fools recover their
sanity than that I derive pleasure from the wild ideas of madmen. Yet why do I mention these things to you, Dorp? I have
no doubt such childish prattle irks you as it does me. You
could change, and perhaps you will be able to, with the help
of men like yourself, provided you do not decide to give in to
the silliness of men who would more suitably be following
your judgment.

But to get back to your letter. I want to point out that the
words of Erasmus did not give you a valid reason for stating,
as you do, that he censured the theologians of Louvain for
ignorance; and your statement about all other theologians

is even less true. Erasmus said he would have nothing to do with those theologians, if such there are and there certainly are, who have learned only sophistic nonsense. He did not mean all theologians, because earlier in the same letter he had said there were many who were distinguished. On that statement of his you remark, "I think he is referring to the theologians of Louvain." Why so, Dorp? Would it be so hard to find in any place at all men of that stripe, or rather, of that stuffing? You certainly have a nice opinion of the Louvain theologians if you think that they alone, and all of them, fit such a description, but that is neither the opinion nor the statement of Erasmus. A little further on, you take his words to refer to all the theologians throughout the world, as well as to the Louvain theologians, but Erasmus referred neither to all theologians, nor to the men at Louvain. And then, as if you were unconscious of what he was saying or what you were saying, you do not just stoop to such language, but you break forth like one swept away by the storm of a raging heart: "Do we not see the lowest form of laborers, even the meanest slaves, endowed with brilliant minds? What then is the meaning of these epithets hurled against all theologians: stupid, ignorant, obnoxious, brainless? To insult anyone does not demand any skill. It is neither a gentlemanly thing to do, nor the mark of a good man, if we ponder the stern statement of Our Saviour: 'Whoever says to his brother, "Raca," shall be liable to the Sanhedrin; and whoever says, "Thou fool," shall be liable to the fire of Gehenna.'" On this passage Jerome comments: "If we are to render an account for an idle word, how much more so for an insulting one. The man who says, 'Thou fool,' to a believer in God, is guilty of impiety toward religion."

These words of yours, Dorp, are laden with piety as well as with seriousness, and truly worthy of a stern theologian. If only they were spoken in their proper place! They are too good to have to perish. If they were hurled from a pulpit down upon a crowd, they would never fail to hit somebody; and it would be obvious whom they struck. But now I am sorry that Erasmus is the sole object of your entire declamation; he is the one man who does not at all fit the description

of any part of your declamation. As for your quotation from
the Gospel, "Whoever says to his brother, 'Thou fool,' shall
be liable to the fire of Gehenna," it has nothing to do with
him. Without mentioning any names, he only means to say
that amidst the large number of human beings there are one
or two fools. Otherwise ten hells would not be enough for
him who said, "The number of fools is infinite." As for your
question, "What is the meaning of these epithets hurled
against all theologians?" that is the question I should be asking you, Dorp. For the remarks he directed toward only a few,
you alone have directed toward all. I am extremely surprised
that you have taken it upon yourself to do this. Just as "to
insult anyone," as you put it, "does not demand any skill," so
also it does not demand any skill to spoil, as you are doing,
fine words by misquoting them; for words, rather well written
against those who deserve them, you are attempting to turn
against those who do not deserve them, to give the impression they were badly written. You yourself easily see how easy
it is to do that in any situation.

Surely, if your own words were garbled in this way, any one
of them could be open to calumny in some way, no matter
how carefully they were written—and you have always been
most careful in writing. Take, for example, your recent, carefully written letter on the edition of the *Quodlibetica* [13] of
the distinguished Hadrian Florentinus of Utrecht. Although
you praise the work highly and its author generously, and
I certainly think you are sincere and correct in so doing, still
if some rather malicious interpreter were to come along, he
could make you appear to be extending in one hand bread,
but in the other, a stone; because, first of all, you were induced
to edit this work, for which you had no inclination, only by
the entreaties and even the tears of others, and you seemed to
be willing to devote yourself to a task for which you had no
great esteem, only because of the feelings of others; and,
secondly, you write that you have put aside your own serious
studies, but only for so long a time as it will take you to cor-

13. The *Quaestiones quotlibeticae* of Adrian of Utrecht, later Pope
Adrian VI. These disputations had been held at the University of Louvain
from 1488 on.

rect the *Quodlibetica,* as if that work did not deserve to be counted among serious studies; and yet Master John of Ath,[14] whose judgment is equal to his great learning, did not feel burdened to spend his labors on that work, often, as you say, far into the night; just as midwives are often called out at night, when women are in labor, so, it seemed, this work could not be corrected by day. What of the fact that, while praising the fairness of Hadrian, you seem to be attributing to him a Lesbian fairness, no doubt referring to the Lesbian level,[15] which Aristotle recalls was made of lead and not always level, but adaptable to uneven surfaces? Do not think, Dorp, I am making these remarks because I think you meant anything of the sort or that you were merely joking when holding up for praise a great man and a great work. For the man, I hear, has in many ways attained an extraordinary degree of honor, and the work I regard, certainly in its own way, as perfect.

I am saying all this only to show there is nothing so insignificant that calumny cannot find a place for itself therein, since even your own writings, despite careful, cautious editing, demand reading with a kindly eye. And yet Erasmus does seem to have forestalled the possibility of having anyone seize the opportunity to say that he was referring his remarks to all theologians, as you accuse him of doing, by the very fact that he said: "Every day I learn from actual experience how men who have learned nothing but sophistic nonsense have no brains." [16] He does not say "How all theologians have no brains," nor "Men who have learned sophistic nonsense" but "Men who have learned nothing but that." Therefore, when you write "As for your assumption, Erasmus, that our theologians are busied only with thoughts of sophisms, you completely miss the point," here, my dear Dorp, you completely miss the point, in making the assumption that Erasmus had made such an assumption about all your theologians

14. John Briard, called Atensis, because he was born at Beloeil in the district of Ath. His *Quaestiones quotlibeticae,* disputed at Louvain 1508–10, were included in the second edition of Adrian's *Quaestiones,* 1518.

15. The Lesbian rule was a mason's rule made of lead which could be bent to fit the curves of a molding (Aristotle, *Eth. Nic.* 5.10.7). So it means a principle of judgment that is pliant and accommodating.

16. More quotes from Dorp's letter to Erasmus (Allen, 2, Ep. 347).

which he made about only one or two, nor does he say anything that must include all your theologians. Therefore not
even the remark which you immediately added is pertinent:
"Tell me, what will keep men, however unacquainted with
poetry, from reading the Gospels, the Epistles of Paul, and
the entire Bible?" Nothing, of course, Dorp, as long as they
do not keep themselves from it, as some men do, who by de-
voting their entire lives to petty questions, never condescend
to search the Scriptures, as if it were not at all pertinent. And
he does think some people are like that, but not all, so that
you may realize your further remark is without justification:
"I shall produce many men from this place who, setting aside
the books and with the help of memory alone, will dispute
with anybody on the text of Scripture. Watch out, do not
think that theologians are enjoying the sleep of an Endymion,
while you are keeping a watchful eye on literature, or that
they are lacking in talent who are not poets or rhetoricians."
Nobody denies, Dorp, that there are men who can set aside
books and dispute on the text of Scripture. As a matter of
fact, one could find in any place more than enough men who
have not just set aside the books, but have never looked into
them, and yet are ready to dispute very stubbornly about any
text of Scripture with any person well versed in Scripture,
with the help not of memory but of Folly. Still I shall not deny
that there are men where you are and in every other place
who know by heart many passages from Scripture. Some of
these men have put forth the effort not just to commit passages
to memory, which even uneducated monks and friars do, but
much rather in order to understand them; these men have
acquired such a facility with the language that they are capable of making a thorough study of the elaborate works of
Jerome, Augustine, Ambrose, and others of the same kind.
These are the men I think who are most deserving of having
their names placed on the list of theologians, even if they
have never written a line, and even, by heavens, if they have
not spent a full century on those trivial quibbles, not to mention if they have neglected them altogether. You too, if you
are willing to admit the facts, will not deny that among so-

called theologians there are on the other hand some who so
set aside the books of Scripture that, once they have been
set aside, they never take them up again, and who devote
themselves so completely to this disputatious theology that
they not only fail to take up poetry or rhetoric but practically
consider as unimportant the most holy Fathers, and also the
most ancient interpreters of the Scriptures, and certainly disregard the commentaries of those men on the sacred writings
as also the study of those writings; that is an established fact.
Finally, they disdain all the things that are the finest, the most
pious, the most Christian, and most worthy of true theologians,
all those things which they call "positive"; they consider none
of those things worthy of any exertion on their part, these
men born for petty quibbles, matters that are obviously so
much more important. And yet, even of those quibbles, they
pursue most of all such as pertain least of all to piety or moral
training.

Therefore, I respect and look up to the former class of
theologians; but I definitely do not regard the latter very
highly. Still, my purpose is not to defend poetry and rhetoric
against them, since I am almost as far removed from poetry
and rhetoric as they are. However, they are almost as far removed from such studies as they are even from theology. From
that they are so far removed that they are not farther away
from anything else, except from the common feelings of hu-
manity. This is true especially because they have added to
an extraordinary ignorance of all subjects a perverted opinion
on all sorts of knowledge, by means of which they so flatter
themselves as to judge themselves alone capable of giving a
ready interpretation, according to their own whims, of any
piece of literature, even of Scripture, of anything they have
heard on any occasion, although they have never seen the passage, have never looked into the work, and do not know in
what context the passage occurs. As a matter of fact, they do
not know whether the passage quoted really occurs in such a
work or not.

Although I have come upon many men of this type, it surely
will not be any bother to recall at least one instance by way

of example, so that one can see what the rest are like. I once had dinner with an Italian merchant [17] who was as learned as he was rich, and he was extremely rich. There was with us at table a religious who was a theologian; an outstanding controversialist, he had recently come from the Continent to engage in controversy in London over some problems which he had been pondering over and had brought with him. His intention was to find out in this arena of controversy what were the capabilities of the English, and also to broadcast his reputation, which was already made at home, among our people. Even though it would take a long time, I certainly would not mind telling the conclusions (so-called) that he reached, and how beautifully the controversy went for the fellow, if the affair were as pertinent as it was jolly. However, at table, no matter what statement was made by anybody, no matter how carefully and cautiously modified, or thought out, it had barely left the lips of the speaker when he would promptly tear it apart with a syllogism; even though the subject of the conversation had nothing to do with theology or philosophy, and was completely foreign to his whole profession. However, at the start of the dinner he had made sure that nothing could be foreign to his profession by claiming he would argue either side of any question. Gradually the merchant came around to problems more concerned with theology. He threw out for discussion the matter of usury, tithes, the permission granted to friars to hear confessions in parishes other than their own. It was a matter of indifference to the theologian which side to defend. But as soon as anyone took a position on either side, he proceeded to attack it. On the other hand, whatever anyone denied, he promptly defended. Then, as a joke, the merchant brought up the topic of mistresses; he maintained it was less sinful to have one woman at home than to be running around town after many. Again the theologian marched forth with a fierce attack. It was not so much that he wanted to appear a mistress hater as to avoid agreeing with anybody on any topic, or perhaps because variety was the spice of life for the fellow. But he maintained it was the well known conclusion of a brilliant

17. Perhaps Antonio Bonvisi. See below, Letters 15 and 65.

teacher, the author of an outstanding book entitled "A Direc-
tory for Men Who Keep Mistresses," [18] that a man who had
one mistress at home was a greater sinner than one who had
ten whores abroad. There was, first of all, the bad example
being given; secondly, there was a more frequent occasion for
sin with a kept woman. The merchant's reply was indeed
learned and shrewd but too long to quote now and, as far as
you are concerned, unnecessary. And when he got wind that
the theologian was not as well versed in the Scriptures as in
petty quibbles, he started to banter the fellow and for some
time to give arguments based on authority. He made up on the
spur of the moment some brief quotations to support his
view. And after freely fabricating these quotations, none of
which had ever been heard of, he cited the references: one
was from some Epistle of Saint Paul, one from an Epistle of
Saint Peter, and another from the text of the Gospels. He was
very careful not to omit even the chapter numbers in his
references; and if a work had sixteen chapters, he deliberately
quoted from the twentieth. Meantime, what was our fine
theologian doing? In handling previous arguments he was
definitely clever, like a porcupine wrapped up in its spines.
But these faked quotations he had difficulty in evading, as he
dodged from side to side; but he did manage to evade them.
Cleverness plus practice in debating is that effective. He did
not know anything about the text of Scripture; nor did he
doubt that those were true quotations, and he considered it
a serious sin not to bow to and yield to the authority of Scripture, but a terrible disgrace to be dislodged and defeated;
though hemmed in by very subtle arguments, do notice how
cleverly this Proteus finally worked his way out of the traps.
As soon as some nonexisting opinion, presumedly from Holy
Scripture, was quoted against him, he would say: "That is a
fine quotation, my dear sir, but this is the way I understand
that text." Then he would give an explanation by distinguish-
ing. In the one sense, he would admit, it upheld his opponent;
the other sense was his means of escape. And if the merchant
would annoy him by insisting that was not the correct mean-

18. *Directorium aut potius Castigatorium Concubinariorum,* published
by Badius Ascensius, 1513.

ing of the passage which the theologian had given, the fellow
would swear a sacred oath, making it credible to all, that such
was the interpretation of that passage given by Nicholas of
Lyra.[19] At that single dinner, my dear Dorp, there were more
than twenty potable quotations and a like number of potable
explanations during the potations; and from the cups, like the
earth-born brethren from the dragon's teeth, they sprang up
and died.

What then do you have to say, Dorp? Do you think that
such men, devoid of a knowledge of Sacred Letters, no matter
how much occupied they are with theological quibbles, deserve the distinction of being called theologians? I do not
think you do. And yet, to tell the truth, these words of yours
make me doubt your attitude: "Do not convince yourself,
Erasmus, that the man who understands in a literal sense the
whole of the Bible is a perfect theologian, nor the man who,
like another Origen, can derive moral interpretations. There
is much more to be learned, that is more difficult to understand and also more practical for the flock for whom Christ
died. Otherwise how shall we know, in the administration of
the sacraments, what is the proper form of the sacrament;
when should a penitent receive absolution, when is he to be
refused it, what are the rules regarding restitution and retainment, and numberless other such problems? Unless I am
badly mistaken, you would learn by heart a good part of the
Bible with much less effort, before you would learn to solve
just one problem. Very many such problems occur every day,
in which one has to stick to just four words and over a long
stretch of time. Unless, whatever relates to the sacraments,
and without them the salvation of man is imperiled, as the
Holy Catholic Church of God maintains—unless you would
refer to that as the ditties of theologians." Really, my dear
Dorp, if these were not your own words, I could never be
brought to believe that such was your opinion. That petty
casuistry of the moderns—and that is what we are talking

19. Nicholas de Lyra (c. 1265–1349) compared the Vulgate O.T. with
the Hebrew text, used Jewish commentaries, and was very independent
in his attitude toward traditional interpretations. He had remarkable
historical and critical sense.

about—is not merely more difficult to comprehend but also more practical for the flock for whom Christ died than a very careful knowledge of all the sacred writings! What an elephant you are making out of a gnat! First of all, you consider that subject so difficult that it would require less effort on the part of Erasmus to learn by heart a good portion of the Bible than to learn how to solve just one problem of the sort that they find by the dozens every day, where there really is no problem at all. And there one has to stick, hours on end, to the clinging, not to say filthy, mud of four words, while you could have been strolling leisurely, almost from beginning to end, through the very lovely, wholesome meadow of the entire Bible. Up to now, therefore, Erasmus has been in danger of not having learned such casuistry. Now, as I understand it, it is more to be feared that it is so far beyond his power of comprehension that he cannot even grasp it. What his capabilities are, I am going to bypass. But this I do know: I have met men, though woodenheads and with brains like a blunt pestle, who, however, not only made progress within a short time in this type of casuistry, but even galloped on white horses ahead of their more talented and equally industrious fellow students in the field of debate. A brazen and unblushing stupidity charges on recklessly, while a sense of shame about playing the fool reins in a noble character and a critical sense that is generally sound.

But you, Dorp, have certainly good reason to rejoice and to refer your boon not to your own powers, but to God, the Giver of all good things. His extraordinary kindness toward you is the source of this rare good fortune that all things seem so easy to you in the Sacred Writings. In the book sealed with the seven seals you would not find everything apparent, unless the Lamb had unsealed the book for you; it is He Who opens and no one seals, Who seals and no one opens. But this very book, Dorp, which seems so easy to you, certainly seemed very difficult to Jerome; Augustine thought it was unfathomable. Not a single one of the ancients had the boldness to say he understood it. They think that the comprehension of this work had been heavily blockaded by some mysterious providence of God, or for the very purpose of challenging inquisi-

tive minds and arousing dormant talents, whose powers had
been buried and needed to be called forth by hard work.
Otherwise, in the presence of treasures lying right in front
of them in the open, they would be lulled to sleep because
they had no need to worry. For the present I shall bypass any
discussion about how this work is not one of ordinary learning, and not one that suits any sort of intelligence, and about
the fact that the very talents which sometimes shrink at first
sight from moral topics are still attracted suitably to moral
topics and so happily that they seem not to have been drawn
away from anything else, but born for this very purpose. Some
men are at present making such an attempt; but the results
are so poor that up to now they have rather succeeded in dis-
locating the subject than drawing it to their own position,
for their work shows neither judgment in content nor charm
in style, with the obvious result that all that moral interpretation, as it is called, grows frigid from lack of attractiveness
and life. But, as I said, I shall bypass a discussion of these
points.

I definitely think that the literal interpretation carries with
it so much difficulty that I do not see how anyone at all can
grasp it. With regard to the words "The Lord said to my
Lord, Sit at my right hand," I do not think their literal sense
is clear to anyone except to him who understands them as
being foretold by the Prophet concerning Christ Himself.
With the exception of the Prophets, no one of the Jews, although they devoted all their efforts to these books, understood this interpretation, until Christ explained to them this
meaning of the passage. Christ did interpret the Scriptures to
His Apostles and disciples; and, as far as I know, he never
argued with them over such quibbles; still, I would not make
bold to say that He gave them an interpretation of the entire
Scriptures while among them, or that He revealed it to them
through the Holy Spirit after His ascension. The Prophets
made many predictions about Christ which eluded the understanding of everyone else, until they were all made clear by
His life, passion, and resurrection; so, too, I think the powers
of mortal man are unequal to the task of finding out whether
there are still concealed prophecies about the Last Judgment

or other matters beyond our comprehension, not as yet known to any man, or mysteries not to be discovered until their fulfillment has revealed them at the time and moment foreseen only by the unfathomable providence of God. But, Dorp, supposing that Scripture is easy, and those petty questions are hard; still there is no reason in the world why a knowledge of the latter is a more valuable training. True, it is harder to dance and pirouette, as some dancing girls and acrobats do, than it is to walk; and it is easier to chew on bread than on pieces of pottery; still, I do not think any person would want to exchange those proper and ordinary natural actions for such extraordinary but useless ones. Which is more difficult, I do not think important. But your view that such casuistry is even more valuable for the flock for whom Christ died than a knowledge of the Sacred Letters is for me completely intolerable. If you would maintain that a knowledge of casuistry was necessary, I would not object; if you put it on the same level with the elaborate works of the Ancients, I would not accept it. But when you not only compare but even prefer those kitchen maids to the Bible, the venerable queen of all letters—pardon me for saying so, Dorp—I simply cannot keep myself from throwing them all out with that saying from Terence: "Get the hell out of here, you wenches, you and your pompousness; do you think we don't know what you are or what you're doing?"

I cannot express enough surprise at reading the words in which you extol them with such magnificence; as if, like the heavens resting on the shoulders of Atlas, as the poets say, the universal Church leans upon such subtle problems— namely, a reed, and would otherwise, of course, be in danger of collapsing completely, falling into ruin! "Otherwise," you say, "how shall we know the manner of administering the sacraments, their proper form, when should a penitent receive absolution, when is he to be refused, what are the rules regarding restitution and retainment?" Do you really think, Dorp, that those points which you assert are found nowhere else except in the writings of modern casuists were completely unknown to all the ancient Fathers, whose learning was equal to their holiness? Were Jerome, Ambrose, and

Augustine blind to the matter and form of the Sacraments? Was the entire Church for more than a thousand years (there were more than a thousand years from the Passion of Christ to the days of Peter Lombard,[20] from whose *Sentences,* as from a Trojan horse, that whole army of problems, rushed forth)—for so many years then, or rather, so many centuries, was the universal Church of Christ without the Sacraments or lacking in those problems? Was it unknown for all those years when a sinner was to be received back, when he was to be rejected? and were they ignorant of the rules for restitution? As for what could be retained, I would be willing to admit that the Early Fathers did not argue with such wit as these men. Like Zachaeus, who, afraid to make too little restitution of ill-gotten gains, promised to make a fourfold return, so those ancient Fathers encouraged men to make more restitution than was demanded. I admit, they were not, in this matter, as interested in definitions and distinctions as these men are. Still I would rather emulate their lack of interest, to quote Terence, than the unintelligible solicitude of these men, who hold earnest discussions, and are concerned not so much with what restitution must be made as what can be retained, not so much with how far sin should be avoided as how close one can come to sin without sinning. Therefore, one who gives advice to an unjust possessor, of course, like an honest steward of somebody else's money, is more careful that he, in making restitution, fall short by even a mile rather than be a finger's breadth in excess.

My dear Dorp, I would certainly maintain, and, I think, without any opposition from you, that whatever is necessary for salvation—that is, the things without which we cannot be saved—those have been handed down to us in abundance, first of all by Sacred Scripture itself, then by their ancient interpreters, furthermore, by the common practice handed down from the Early Fathers, and finally by the sacred decrees of the Church. If these sharp-witted men have made any addition to this tradition by their delving, although I grant much of it is convenient and practical, still I think none of

20. Peter Lombard (c. 1100–64) bishop of Paris 1159–60, wrote a famous medieval textbook of theology.

it is essential for life. But perhaps you will object that not
everything in the writings of the Ancients is as easily found
or as ready at hand as in the works of the moderns, who have
classified all related and similar points under headings, each
thing according to its own division. In this, Dorp, perhaps
I agree with you; I admit there is some advantage in having
in literary matters, as in household equipment, the various
articles so arranged that you can reach out for anything you
want without making a mistake. That is, as I said, an advantage, but some have so misused this great advantage to
disadvantage that it almost seems better not to have this advantage. I do not think there was any more fundamental
reason why all the earliest interpreters of the Sacred Writings
were so long held in neglect than that incompetent men with
bad judgment persuaded themselves and then others that
there was no honey anywhere except what had been stored
up in the jars of those summaries. The result is that, satisfied
with those alone, they are not at all interested in all the
other things. I once happened upon a person of this frame
of mind in the shop of a bookseller; he was an elderly fellow,
with one foot in the grave and, soon after, both feet; he had
held the distinguished title of doctor for more than thirty
years. I happened to mention in his presence that Augustine [21]
once thought that all demons were corporeal substances. He
promptly frowned and checked my rashness with a wrinkled
brow. "That's not my opinion, Father," I said, "nor do I defend Augustine for saying it. He was human and could make
a mistake. I trust him in most things, as much as I do anybody; but I don't trust any one man in all things." By now
the fellow was beginning to burn up, especially because, in
his opinion, I was trying to insult an outstanding Father.
"Do you think," he asked, "that I haven't read Augustine?
Why, I read him before you were born." He would have
knocked me away with his savage words, if I had not conveniently prepared a refutation. There was in the shop a copy
of Augustine's work on *The Divination of Demons*. I picked
it up and turned to the passage and pointed it out to him.

21. Augustine, *De Diuinatione Daemonum,* capp. III–IV (Migne, *40,*
584–86).

He read it once, then again, and finally, on the third reading, with my assistance, he began to understand it; and eventually he was full of surprise. "I am surely surprised," he remarked, "at what Augustine says here in this book, because it certainly doesn't say that in the *Master of Sentences,*[22] which is more of a teacher's book than this." Men of that sort, who do not read any of the Fathers, nothing of the Scriptures, except in *Sentences* and commentaries on them, strike me as being like a person who, disregarding all the Latin authors, looks up Alexander for the rules of grammar and attempts to learn the rest of Latin from Perottus' *Cornucopia* [23] and Calepino,[24] because he is convinced that in these works he will find all the words of the Latin language; certainly he will find very many, and those, carefully chosen.

In the works of more recent theologians, quotations from earlier ones are introduced as an authority; so too in the case of literature, the ancient poets and orators are cited, some even whose works are no longer extant. But such quotations, my dear Dorp, will never make a Latin scholar, nor a theologian, if that is all there are, no matter if the man is equipped with ten thousand thorny problems. I just wonder how such persons can be of any value to the Church, for instance, in debating with heretics, for they usually try to put themselves on the market under such a title. Heretics are either learned or unlearned. If unlearned, as they are for the most part, they will neither understand the subtleties possessed by this theologian all by himself, nor the unusual words which this theologian is used to all by himself. Such a debate is destined to have as much effect as one in which a person, using perfect French (for a Frenchman, that is the only lovely language!), tries to win over to the Faith a Turk, familiar only with his native tongue. But if the heretics be learned, and especially in that type of casuistry (for heretics are practically never anything else)—when will they ever be

22. Peter Lombard's textbook of theology was entitled *Libri Quattuor Sententiarum,* Four Books of Sentences (more correctly, Opinions), so he was called Master of the Sentences.

23. Perottus, *Cornucopiae, seu Commentarii Linguae Latinae,* 1489.

24. Ambrogio Calepino (1435–1511), an Augustinian monk, had published a polyglot dictionary in 1502.

refuted? When will there be an end to the debate? Those quibbles with which they are attacked furnish inexhaustible material to them for counterattacks, so that they are very much like two men fighting naked among piles of stones: each has plenty of weapons, neither has any defense. Of course, some of the principal authors read in the schools are as sharp-witted as they are thought to be; I might omit the fact that they have concocted about God some problems so ridiculous, you would think they were joking, and some statements so blasphemous, you would think they were jeering. Certainly, they are so zealous in forming objections to the Faith, but so slipshod in their solutions, that they seem to be double-dealers, jokingly defending the Faith while seriously attacking it. When will heretics ever surrender, if matched with the type of theologian I have mentioned above, since they are clever in playing the same game? Not very soon, I think, if their respect for one packet of rods were no greater than their dread for several stacks of syllogisms.

But at least he will be suited for preaching to the people. Heavens! That is what they mean by the saying "A bull on a wrestling mat." For he has learned nothing but quibbles, which sound strange to the ears of the people and are not at all suitable. And so of course he has to memorize one of the sermons from *The Disciple,* or *Come with Me,* or *Sleep Soundly;* [25] such sermons are silly in themselves, but when a sillier person untrained in that office handles them, and bellows forth that whole string of words from somebody else's gullet, the entire sermon is necessarily a chilly business. Therefore I do not see at all what value those quibbles are for a man whom they alone are master of, except that they render him ineffectual for anything else. When one of these subtleties, in which he has gone through a thousand practice sessions, is put before him, rather than some subject for solid discussion, then he is perfectly at home; he lifts up his chest like a rooster who struts in his own dung-pit. But if he strays a little too far from that chickenyard, at once strange sights all around shroud him with darkness and dizziness.

25. Books of outline sermons for parish priests.

No longer does dialectics, however strong, however keen, come to his assistance, as he stumbles about in his blindness. For, when she understands things, she gives expression to many different ideas and types of arguments; but when she fails to understand things, she necessarily becomes useless and speechless. Moreover, as he has soaked himself thoroughly in those quibbles, and in nothing else, over the course of many years, when in old age he withdraws, for any reason at all, from the fellowship of the schoolmen, where such things are constantly aired, then within two years all those subtleties, much too numerous indeed, disappear into thin air, like mist and smoke, for they have no solid weight to hold them down; and now those words of Aristotle, usually quoted with reference to the mind of an infant, are verified in his case; for his mind at length becomes a blank page, devoid of any picture. By a strange reversal of things, it happens that one who formerly placed every type of wisdom in argumentative verbosity has now in old age become a speechless infant, laughed at by everybody. He might attempt to cloak his stupidity with a haughty silence to take the place of wisdom, but thereby he makes himself all the more ridiculous; for one who but recently was more vociferous than Stentor now with just the exact opposite vice becomes more reticent than a fish; and while others are conversing, he sits there like a head without a tongue, like a mute mask or a Hermes pillar.

Finally, so you may know briefly my views on this whole subject—I am not criticizing all theologians, and I do not condemn all the problems advanced by the moderns; but those which are not at all relevant, which contribute nothing to learning and are a great hindrance to piety—those problems, in my opinion, should be censured, and furthermore, completely rejected. There are however other kinds of problems which treat of human affairs seriously, and of divine affairs reverently. Such problems, if they show by their modest behavior they are more interested in searching for the truth than in gaining a victory by clever debate, provided they do not lay complete claim on anybody, nor hold anyone too long within their grasp, nor measure themselves by their own feet, nor compare—not to mention prefer—themselves to what is better—problems that are developed in that fashion I am very willing to embrace, but only insofar as I consider them of some value in training the intellect. But I would deny that they are the prop and support of the salvation of the universal Church. I have no criticism for theologians who have acquainted themselves with these problems, but rather praise for those who have joined to a deeper knowledge of Sacred Scripture and a better understanding of the early, most holy, and learned Fathers an acceptable acquaintance with them. But, to be honest, I do not approve of those theologians who grow gray over problems of every kind, and even pine away in death over them, who, hindered by intellectual impotence or goaded on by the childish applause of schoolmen, neglect the works of all the ancients and even disregard the Gospels, which they profess to teach; they have learned absolutely nothing but little quibbles, some of which are devoid of any content, some devoid of any value for men who themselves are devoid of all other things; and when they are old men, they are hopeless, because, without a knowledge of the writings of the Ancients, they cannot discuss the Scriptures intelligently, and because of their ignorance of Latin they are unequal to the task of getting to know those writings.

To return to the study of grammar and to learn along with schoolboys and even from schoolboys is not only a great embarrassment for them, but it is even too late to do so. The last thing in the world I would do, my dear Dorp, would be to praise such characters. Rather, just as the Romans had the custom of forcing incompetent officials to resign their office, so I believe these men, theologians by title rather than actual fact, should be forced to swear to their incompetence for this office which they fill so unworthily. Still it is no surprise that there are some like this among the large number of theologians. For what group can be so carefully fenced in as to prevent an unworthy person from sneaking in by flattery, or bribery, or through influence, or other means of deception; and once that fellow has reached the heights, he helps up to the same position as many similar characters as possible. The result is, there is no group without a large number of unworthy members. Just as in the Roman Senate there were men

whose dignity was equaled by no kings,[26] so also there were
some so mean and dishonorable that they met a wretched
end by being crushed to death at the public games. However,
the baseness of these men was no obstacle to the splendor of
the former, nor did the name of Senator save their meanness
from disdain; so, too, unworthy theologians are not saved
from abuse by their name; and the contempt shown to them
does not detract from the esteem given to individuals who are
theologians in the real sense, nor does it diminish the respect
and dignity of the whole class; and I certainly am as anxious
as any person alive today to have that position of respect and
dignity preserved and augmented. And as for Erasmus, it
would be foolish to make the same claim with regard to him,
for it is common knowledge that any false idea conceived
or expressed in opposition to the sacred ranks of the theologians is the object of his very special and personal interest.
And so, my dear Dorp, you have my views on the matter; and
I do not doubt they are yours too (if you are the person I
think you are). If you approve of them, consider them as being
the views of Erasmus too; if not, consider them as being only
mine, and mine no longer than you will want them to be.
For there is nothing so firmly fixed in my mind that I am not
ready to change it at the order of one who, I know, will never
issue an order unreasonably. But enough of this.

Inasmuch as I have treated this part of your letter somewhat
extensively, though deservedly so, I shall be briefer with regard to the rest; but both sections are receiving due consideration. The points I have been discussing up to now, Erasmus
has never seen; but those I am now going to make, he has
written about and also promises to do so with greater attention. In some of these points even Saint Jerome not only takes
sides with Erasmus by setting a precedent that is like a judgment given beforehand, but has also settled the entire issue
by delivering a verdict, like a decision that is published, in
favor of Erasmus. Every single objection you make to a change
in Scripture based on the reliable text of the Greek manu-

26. Cineas, envoy of King Pyrrhus, reported back to him that the
Roman Senate was an assembly of kings.

scripts was once made against Saint Jerome and thoroughly
refuted by him; unless you consider this a new point—namely,
that all the translations which once had been numerous were
discarded "for fear that the faithful have doubts because of
the variety of texts." This one version, approved by the holy
Fathers, emended by Jerome, and transmitted all the way
down to us, has been recommended by the Church, not in any
one Council, but by the uninterrupted practice of having recourse to it whenever a difficulty concerning the faith came
up in a Council. Nor could it have happened by chance that
this alone came down to us when all other versions perished,
except for the deliberate efforts made on the part of our
predecessors.

First of all, my dear Dorp, I do not think anyone doubts
that this very edition had been accepted by the Church and
given approbation by being continually cited, before the days
of Jerome; otherwise he would not have emended this text
rather than any other; and I think that is the only reason
why this is the sole text that has come down to us. Why then
did Jerome dare to make any change?—and that was done
with the approval of other excellent and very holy men, and
also with the encouragement of Augustine. But Jerome, on
his own admission, changed the Latin text whenever it disagreed in meaning with the Greek text. He thought this a
more valuable procedure than what you are trying to persuade
Erasmus to do—namely, only to add a note to those passages
which the translator might have put in more appropriate and
clearer language, but to let the meaning stay as it is, whenever there is lack of agreement, and not to point out to the
Latins an obvious correction. What Saint Jerome did not consider worth too much attention, you consider the object of
special attention. What he judged most important, you steer
away from most of all. But then you reply by admitting that
Jerome was correct in doing what was obviously necessary at
a time when this text, which has since become the commonly
accepted one, was not sufficiently corrected; but now that the
errors have been removed, a second emendation would be
superfluous. Certainly, if the need were as great today as it

was at that time, there is no reason why he does less a service who today performs the same task as did Jerome at that time. First of all, I do not think there is a single individual—and to be somewhat bold, not even Jerome himself—who has had the brashness to claim he was so sure of himself that nothing could possibly escape him in making a translation. This is so true that a point will sometimes be noticed by men of average ability who happen along in the wake of superior men, and even in a task in which those superior men are properly engaged.

"Well, is there ever an end to translating then?" you ask. Very easily, if someone happens to make such a perfect translation or corrects someone else's imperfect translation so well that, as long as this version remains intact, future generations will find nothing which, in their opinion, needs to be changed. But, you object, there is still danger that the different versions will cause doubts in the minds of the faithful as to which version they should accept as the more correct one; for, you believe, the reason why all other versions were purposely discarded and this one preserved was to avoid causing doubts for the faithful. In this matter, I so completely disagree with you that what you attribute to the anxiety of our predecessors I attach to the lack of interest of those times; for this very same reason not only those versions but many other things too have perished. Otherwise, even if they had retained just one version for use in the churches, what need was there to discard the others, when there was no danger that they would cause doubts for the faithful? But just as now, from the different narratives given by the Evangelists, the sequence of events takes on a clearer light, so in those days, from a comparison of the various translators, a scholarly reader would be given the opportunity of inferring the true meaning from the other versions, whenever the meaning of an ambiguous word escaped him, or when he was tricked by a passage with a double meaning, or deceived by an idiomatic expression. Augustine was aware that that was very valuable; Origen [27]

27. Origen (c. 185 – c. 254) put the Hebrew text of the O.T. side by side with various Greek versions and tried to find the basis for a more reliable text of the Septuagint.

learned it by experience; and James Faber showed it by his edition of the Psalter [28] with five different texts. I have mentioned this to point out that Saint Jerome should not be criticized even if his work had remained intact up to the present day; and if anyone should find that something had been overlooked by him, then he should gather it in, like ears of grain left behind by a reaper.

But does not everyone think there is no less need now than formerly for an emendation of the Latin manuscripts from the Greek ones when the text has become so corrupt that not even traces of Jerome's emendation are in evidence? This fact is so well known that even you who most of all deny it still do admit it. For although you contend that the task of emendation is particularly futile, because, you maintain, the corrections made by Jerome have been preserved intact thanks to the careful vigilance of the Fathers, yet in almost the very next line you added: "Answer this question, Erasmus; to which text does the Church give its approval, the Greek one, which it does not use? or the Latin one, which alone it cites whenever a definition is to be made from Sacred Scripture, even disregarding Jerome's text in the case of a variant reading; and this is not just an occasional incident." Now, my dear Dorp, you just answer my question; if, as you say, and you are correct, Jerome not occasionally reads differently from the Vulgate, how can your previous statement be true, that the same text remains emended, just as he had emended it? I do not think anyone would believe that he had proposed a reading contrary to his own emendation. Therefore there is as much need for an emendation now as there was in the past. Whether it will be permitted to the same extent, is still open to question. However, this fact, I think, is neither to be questioned nor doubted—that emended texts are as valuable to the Church today as they were in the past.

But, you say, the Church has now given its approval to this text. As I said above, the same Church had given its approbation in the same way to the same text before the emenda-

28. Lefèvre d'Étaples gave the Psalter in five versions—St. Jerome's first revision, his second revision, his translation from the Hebrew, the pre-Jerome text, and Lefèvre's own revision, with critical and exegetical commentary.

tion of Jerome. However, it will be no bother to re-examine
those words of yours, which you consider irrefutable, for fear
you may think I am secretly bypassing anything. It seems to
me this is your argument: Augustine did not think credence
had to be given to the Gospels except under the compelling
authority of the Church. But the Church has given its approbation to the veracity of the Gospels in this translation.
Therefore, wherever the Greek manuscripts have readings
that differ from the Latin, those passages cannot contain the
true Gospel. This is a brief summation of your argument,
as I see it; and it strikes me as not being difficult to solve.
For, first of all, the Church believes that the Gospels are
contained in the Latin manuscripts, while still admitting that
they are a translation from the Greek. The Church gives
credence therefore to the translation, but still more so to the
original. It gives credence to the veracity of the Gospels in
the Greek, and also in the Latin, but only insofar as it puts
trust in the translator; and, I believe, it never puts so much
trust in the translator as not to realize that he could have
erred out of human frailty. But, you object, in the councils
it is the Latin, not the Greek text, that is cited. Remarkable,
is it not, for Latins to cite from a Latin text! As if they did so
for the explicit purpose of depriving the Greek originals of
credence. Did not the Apostles, in quoting the Prophets, use
the Septuagint version [29] when writing to the Greeks, without
any implication as to the veracity of the Hebrew text? And so
Jerome did not think that therefore a precedent had been
set, whereby the Greek version was to be considered more
genuine than the Hebrew text on the authority of the Apostles.
I certainly am convinced, and in this I think I am correct,
that whatever has come down to us from the Apostles has
never been translated more accurately than were the original
words of the Apostles. Consequently, whenever a passage occurs in the Latin texts that seems to be contrary to faith or
morals, Scriptural commentators examine the meaning of this
doubtful passage in the light of other passages; or they place
such doubtful passages side by side with the Gospel of the

29. Translation of the Hebrew Bible into Greek at Alexandria,
c. 250 – c. 50 B.C.

one faith, which has been implanted in the hearts of the faithful throughout the universal Church, and which, before being written down by anyone, had been preached to the Apostles by Christ, and by the Apostles to the whole world; and so they examine such passages according to the unbending rule of truth. If they cannot reconcile the passage with that rule, the commentators do not hesitate to admit they do not understand the passage, or that the passage is corrupt. The remedy for such a defect, they believe, must be solicited from different translations, as from physicians (a dangerous procedure, to your way of thinking), or it must be sought from the language which was the source from which the Scriptures flowed into the Latin tongue.

You admit, my dear Dorp, that those men were right who, in times past, emended the Latin text from the Greek, although it was the Latin text which had been accepted and approved by the Church; but still you deny it would be right to do that today, for the reason that probably the texts of the Greeks have been deliberately corrupted by themselves, as they broke away from the Church of Rome long ago; or at least that they became defective at a later date through lack of interest; and that it is incredible that the texts of the Greeks have endured up to the present in an incorrupt state, although the faith of the Greeks has long since been corrupted, while the texts of the Latins, despite their constant regard for the faith, have gradually deteriorated. Such reasoning, Dorp, did not deter Jerome from translating the Old Testament from the Hebrew. However, if this reasoning has any validity in the present case, it should have had much more in that situation; for, as everyone knows, the Jews were avowedly more bitter enemies to all Christians, whom they opposed as a group, than the Greeks were to the Latins, with whom they shared the common name of Christians, despite a lack of agreement in some matters. Surely, to be truthful, it strikes me as not being exactly credible that a nation would ever have planned to enter into a conspiracy to tamper with texts—not to mention that it would have been impossible to do so. What assurance could there have been that not a single person would oppose the idea? or that the plan would be kept secret? and if it were discovered (as it was bound to be, since every day there were refugees from the Jews over to Christ, and from the Greeks to the Latins), would they not anticipate the fact that, while their efforts would be of no avail, they would, in addition, cause prejudice to their own sect, if, on their own admission, they would be supporting a cause which they knew they could defend only by corrupting the texts. But let Jerome take care of the Jews. The Greeks are certainly freed from such a suspicion of deception by the fact that their texts agree with ours in those matters over which we have engaged in controversy with them. There was never any question about the text, but only about the meaning of the text. However, it is obvious, if they had wanted to make any change, they would have changed those texts first, and only those texts, which support us, but oppose them. And if they had falsified those texts, there would have been no reason for thinking they would do the same with other texts. Now, can you imagine any reason why they would have wanted to falsify other texts, although they left those texts intact which were the only ones they would have wanted to falsify? But, you also object, it is credible that the books became defective at least through lack of interest, especially if ours suffered that fate; for it is likely that we have devoted greater care to the books of faith, just as we have to the faith itself. On this point I could cite as witness Augustine, as well as Jerome; both are of the opinion that the Greek manuscripts are in a better state of emendation than the Latin ones. But I would rather base my argument on reason than on authority.

I certainly insist that no person is so indifferent toward any book as to hire someone to copy it who would not care one bit whether his reproduction was defective or perfect; for he could spare himself the effort and the expense by not having the transcription made at all. Therefore, I am convinced that the Greeks too were interested in having exact copies made of their books; no one would doubt this who ever made a careful examination of their books. Furthermore, I maintain that because of the breathing, punctuation, and accent marks, the Greeks were less liable to err in transcribing; and I am not deterred from making this statement just because you used the same argument to prove the exact opposite, in saying that error is more likely to occur where one has to attend to many details. But I maintain the contrary; error is less likely to occur where it is likely to occur, to use a riddle as the dialecticians do. That is my view, and it is based on my experience; for when we are rushing along, without any worry, over a level stretch of ground, where no one expects any mishap, we often do fall; but in climbing down a steep descent, we test our way, making certain of each step, and gradually reach safety. The same thing happens in transcribing manuscripts; in following a scrambled model, the more attentive the scribe is, the more accurate will be his copy; while the very unconcern causes lapses in copying a manuscript that is neat. It is also obvious that our manuscripts are defective and theirs are reliable from the fact that we notice in our manuscripts the very same errors which Jerome long ago thought needed emendation. In these manuscripts one can still see the very same words which, we know, Jerome emended. And so shall we be forbidden today to delete a second time from these manuscripts the mistakes which he once did away with? And while it is right to reform all religious orders, since defects keep recurring, shall we consider it a crime to purge a second time texts which have once been purged, since errors have sprouted up again?

Upon posing the question "Why do the Latin texts remain defective?" you give your own answer: "Because of the carelessness and incompetence on the part of the printers." Then you add the comment: "Just observe which group of printers is more unusual—competent printers of Greek texts or of Latin texts; then you will find out which manuscripts must be regarded as being more carefully corrected." I do not understand what you mean by this remark, Dorp. I do not think you suspect Erasmus is employing printed editions for his Scriptural Commentaries; for there is no lack of handwritten manuscripts; nor could he, even if he wished to, use printed books for this task, since, to my knowledge, the New Testament, over which he is laboring, has not as yet been printed in Greek type. If you meant to say that, just as printers make

more mistakes in setting up Greek type than Latin type, so
too did the ancient scribes of both languages; then let us disregard printers who set up Latin type so that it looks more
like Greek than Latin, or those who set up Greek type so
that it looks more like Arabic than Greek. Let us compare
the work of printers qualified to set up type in both languages;
Aldus Manutius [30] Romanus was an outstanding example, so
is John Frobenius of Basel. I dare to assert, and this information I have gained from personal experience, that such men
print Greek texts with greater accuracy and reliability than
even Latin texts. This fact and many other likewise relevant
facts you will grasp more clearly from your own reading than
from hearing it, if eventually you will concentrate on a
thorough study of Greek; this I desire very much; yet my attempts to convince you are destined for failure; not even
Erasmus succeeded in doing that; for you are putting up a
strong resistance to him, or rather, to yourself, for fear of
being forced to benefit from a knowledge of Greek literature.

Therefore, since you feel so antagonistic toward that type
of learning, I am not going to encourage you to take it up;
but because of my affection for you, I am not going to stop
wanting it for you; and I shall never lose hope that some day,
in the not too distant future, you will stop your arguments
on this subject—your endless triumphs in them make it difficult for you to want to retreat—and that you will convince
yourself of this point of view, for, as I see it, no one else can
do that for you; and that either after you use more mature
judgment and forget all about those generals under whom
you are now serving and all those whose good will you at
present prefer to the coterie of high learning, or, even better,
after you convince those very men it would be more ad-
vantageous to both you and their stratagems for you to fell
the Greeks with their very own weapons and to dispute with
them with greater prestige than at present, for now you are
discussing a subject about which you know nothing. Yet, while
you give the impression that you do not consider the effort
spent on the study of Greek as being worth while, you definitely do not convince me you are writing what you really
feel. For it is unlikely for a man of your good sense not to

30. Aldus Manutius had died 6 February 1515.

appreciate the values of that language, or for one with such an enthusiasm for all the liberal arts not to feel a passion for it, especially since, at the very moment you argue for its omission, you practically propose the strongest motives for urging you to pursue it. According to your own perfectly correct and wise observation, a language outranks and is superior to other languages most of all because of this endowment, that it happens to possess in its literature, as in a chest, a richer treasure of the liberal arts. Everybody knows that it is because of this one reason you have given that Greek is the language to be most highly cherished by all men, and, for a very distinct reason, by Christians, because through Greek all the other branches of learning have come down to us, and also, very fortunately, almost the entire New Testament—unless you think that this language, because of daily publication of translations, like constant childbearing, has finally become sterile and exhausted.

First of all, in your work written in elegant style—whether its purpose be to censure Laurentius [31] or to praise Aristotle, you do both with an equal amount of spirit—you make mention of some commentators on Aristotle, such as Alexander, Themistius,[32] Ammonius, Simplicius, Philoponus, and Olympiodorus.[33] With the one exception of Themistius, how little there is of the works of these men that is not still read only in the original language!—of course the problems of Alexander have made their way into the Latin language. Whatever else is available in a Latin translation—and I am aware of the existence of fragments of Alexander and Simplicius—all of it, and too little at that in Latin, is almost more incom-

31. Lorenzo Valla c. 1450 wrote *Annotations on the New Testament*, in which, after study of several Latin and Greek manuscripts, he came to the conclusion that the Vulgate translation contained a number of errors.

32. Themistius (317–?387) taught at Constantinople. His paraphrases of several of Aristotle's works are valuable. His works were first published at Venice in 1534, so More knew them in manuscript. For Alexander, see above, note 9.

33. Ammonius Hermiae (fifth century A.D.) wrote commentaries on the logical treatises of Aristotle. Simplicius of Cilicia wrote commentaries on Aristotle. John Philoponus, a Greek philosopher in Alexandria in the late fifth and early sixth century, probably wrote the life of Aristotle attributed to Ammonius. Olympiodorus the younger wrote a life of Plato, and also tried to reconcile Plato and Aristotle.

prehensible for Latin readers than is the original Greek. I
am not going to say anything now about the poets or orators,
nor am I going to mention other philosophers or even other
commentators on Aristotle. However, just one of them, John
the Grammarian, possesses such subtleness of mind and depth
of knowledge, in particular of Aristotle, that if you could
converse with him in his own tongue, I am positive this one
grammarian, all by himself, would reconcile you with all
grammarians, toward whom you do not appear right now to
be well-disposed. Moreover, notwithstanding the fact that the
vast majority of ancient writers on Christian learning wrote
in Greek, very few in proportion to their large numbers have
been translated; and some of those versions are much more
like subversions. Now I come to Aristotle, whom I love above
many, but still along with many. In your work referred to
above you seem not only to cherish him above many, but
also instead of many, even instead of all. Now he could never
be completely known to you without a knowledge of Greek.

I might omit the fact that there is no translation of Aristotle so suitable as to have the same powerful effect on one's
spirit as does the original; also, the fact that some of his
works are as yet available only in Greek, and I am not sure
if the Latins have the titles of those works. Certainly, of the
works they do have at present, some they have in such a way
as really not to have them. It is known that his *Meteorologica*
has shared the same fate; and that is regrettable, since I doubt
whether any other of his numerous works deserves more to
be known, or whether nature herself is more marvelous in
any of her phases than that which, though so close to us and
completely embracing us, is still more unknown and uncertain
than the position of the stars and the movements of the con-
stellations, which are so remote from us. However, I have
hopes that this work will soon be presented to Latin readers
by my fellow countryman Thomas Linacre,[34] the physician of
our illustrious King, as he has already finished two of the
books. He undoubtedly would have completed and published

34. Linacre translated several treatises of Aristotle, but his work was
not published because of his extreme fastidiousness, with which Erasmus
reproached him.

the entire work by now, if Galen, by reason of his high rank
and authority in medical matters, had not prevailed upon
Linacre to set aside even Aristotle for the moment and first
attend to a Latin version of his own work. Aristotle then
will make his appearance somewhat later, but he will appear,
with equal grace and, in addition, with a retinue. For Linacre
is going to publish in the same volume a translation he is
making of the commentaries of Alexander Aphrodisiensis,[35]
for which he is destined to win the undying favor of all
Latins. It will be no little advantage for them that he will
combine a remarkable commentator with an outstanding work
of a remarkable philosopher; and his labors will have this
result, that at long last the Latins can understand what, to
my surmise, no one, ignorant of Greek, has up to now understood. Some time ago I was listening to Linacre read and explain to me the Greek text of this very work of Aristotle,
and occasionally, for the sake of experiment, I would take a
glance at a popular translation of it; as a result of reading
it, I was suddenly reminded of a comment once made by the
same philosopher about Aristotle's *Physics*. Linacre said it had
been edited in such fashion as not to have been really edited
at all; so too this work seemed to have been translated in
such fashion as not to have been translated at all, and so
much so that what I thoroughly understood from the Greek
was unintelligible to me in translation. Nor can we hope for
any assistance from the Latin commentators; even Albert,[36]
surnamed the Great, to emulate Alexander the Great, while
professing to be the "Circumlocutor" of Aristotle, would
more correctly be considered, in that work, the "Contralocu-
tor." Although his duty is to put the meaning of Aristotle
in other words, he introduces a meaning that is diametrically
opposed to it. Cajetan,[36a] also a writer of commentaries, de-

35. Linacre did not publish the commentary of Alexander Aphrodisiensis on the *Meteorologica* of Aristotle. It was first printed at Venice in
1527, and again in 1548.

36. Albertus Magnus (c. 1206–80) desired to make Aristotle's philosophy
"intelligible to the Latins," and to use its forms in the exposition of
church doctrine.

36a. Gaetano Tiene, who wrote commentaries on Aristotle's *Meteorology*,
published in Venice, 1491 and 1496.

scribes to us into how many handfuls of water a handful of
earth liquifies, and into how many handfuls of air a handful
of water dissolves—and what are his limits in such a process?
While he is measuring out these immeasurable measures, he
does not arrive one bit at the meaning of Aristotle. It would
be an endless task, my dear Dorp, to explain how much is
lacking to one who lacks a knowledge of Greek. Still I am
aware that many men, above all you yourself, without a
knowledge of Greek, have advanced toward the citadel of
learning to a point which many, even learned in Greek, cannot reach with all their sweating and puffing. But I should
dare to make this one assertion: if you would add a knowledge
of Greek to the rest of your learning, you would then surpass even your present accomplishments as much as you now
surpass others, though they are skilled in Greek. But enough
about literature.

Now about *The Folly;* since Erasmus, who once dedicated
the work to my patronage, has taken up a second defense of
it, I need not make many explanations to you; a task, of itself easy, has been rendered easier by a sharing of the labor.
And so I have no doubt he will make such remarks—in fact,
he has already done so in his brief letter—as should suffice for
everybody. Still, what I have to say, no matter what little
effect it may have upon others, upon you, I think, it can have
quite an effect. First, I wonder what you mean by the words:
"Now, suddenly, the ill-starred Folly like Davus throws everything into confusion." How can you say, "suddenly"? As if
The Folly has just now for the first time suddenly appeared,
which for more than seven years has basked in the most
brilliant light, meanwhile undergoing seven revised editions,
and has been welcomed into everybody's pocket. And why is
it "ill-starred"? Is not its birth under a lucky star abundantly
proved by the simple fact that numberless copies of it would
never have been sent broadcast had it not found so many
who took great delight in it? And these were the best educated
men, not the scum of the people—for I would not be surprised
at the popularity of a product that delights the illiterate, who
swarm everywhere. The fact that it delights only the learned
is also an indication that only the learned understand it,

which is perhaps the reason why the two or three theologians who were disturbed by *The Folly* lost their tempers; at the persuasion of others, they think it says more than it really does; otherwise perhaps they would not become angry, if they understood what it actually says.

You are of the opinion, my dear Dorp, that no theologians should have been ridiculed; and yet, you admit, in a rather serious tone, that they are just as *The Folly* describes in a jesting tone, for you say, "Biting wit, mingled with much truth, rankles in the memory." What you say is certainly true. For those "theologists" would not have suffered this wit with such rankle if it had not been as true as it was biting. Since they are exactly what even you admit they are, do you approve of them? I do not think so. Then, do you censure them? In your own mind, I am sure you do; you would do so in the open if you had not determined to oppose no one, and if you had not resolved to conduct yourself in such a way that absolutely all men might praise you, no matter of what kind they may be, learned, unlearned, good or bad. You admit you like it, if they pet you even with a puppy's tail as a sign of their friendship. Your way of acting, my dear Dorp, is more cautious; but still one who attacks evil men openly and plainly, as does Gerard of Nymegen, does not do any worse. Much less so is the case with one who, like Erasmus, puts on the mask of Folly, and jests with greater prudence and restraint, although you cannot stand his jests and wit, and want him to recant. Yet, according to your own words, you found nothing you would want changed in the *Satires* of Gerard of Nymegen,[37] although those *Satires,* even when most benign, are more pungent than *The Folly* in its most pungent though truthful passages. Such does the nature of the poetry demand; unless it is biting, it is not satire. And so it is worthwhile to hear how satirically he inveighs against the monks everywhere, and the friars, as he draws pictures of their haughtiness, debauchery, stupidity, their drinking

37. Gerard Geldenhauer of Nymegen (c. 1482–1542) had composed eight *Satyrae* which were published 13 June 1515. About 1525 Geldenhauer went over to the Reformers, married in 1527, and in 1532 became professor of history at Marburg (Allen, 2, 379).

bouts, their gluttony, lustiness, and hypocrisy. His language is as elegant as it is biting, and also just as true. Although many do not deserve such insulting attacks, there are some to whom individual remarks apply; there are also some to whom all the remarks apply. I am not surprised then that you found nothing in the *Satires* you would want changed, just as I certainly did not. But I am surprised at this, why you do not allow *Folly* to make theologians the butt of her jests with impunity, while you permit the *Satires* to chastise the religious in such a stinging way, and among the religious, also theologians. But no more about Gerard's *Satires*.

If a person would examine your letters, my dear Dorp, could he find nothing wherein you have reprimanded any class of men with some stinging remark? Do you think that those words had absolutely no bite to them, with which, in your well known letter to Abbot Dom Meynardus,[38] you splatter the bishops? While you praise him, you moan over the others in this fashion: "Alas for me, alas for those poor wretches who do not act as religious; but thronged by a herd of nags, they remind us of the triumphal parades of Caesar. It were better for them to crawl along the ground, than to spur their steeds on to hell; unless they are afraid they would arrive there too late on foot." My dear Dorp, this very biting wit seems so charming to you that you obviously made special mention of horses, for fear of letting a *bon mot* go by unused. Otherwise, I think you see it is not so terrible a crime for abbots to ride horses, and use animals for the purpose for which they were made. I have also heard that other bishops do not always ride horses, and that your friend does sometimes. So that your little joke almost bounces back upon him, while you are anxious to deflect it away from him toward the others. Every man is charmed by his point of view, just

38. Printed as the dedication of Dorp's *Oratio,* 1513. Meinard Man (d. 1526), trained in the University of Louvain, was ordained and served as a parish curate, and then entered the Benedictine Abbey at Egmond, and in 1509 was elected Abbot. He reformed his monastery, largely by his personal example, improved its intellectual life, and made it an influence in neighboring monasteries and in the diocese of Haarlem. Dorp was his protégé (de Vocht, *Monumenta Humanistica Lovaniensia,* pp. 64–72).

as each person thinks his own wind smells sweet. While we frown upon the jokes of others and cannot stand their bitterness, we hug our own jokes, which are not more jolly, but more stinging. You will say that these were not jokes aimed at religious bishops, but rather lamentations, especially since you commence with the inauspicious outcry, "Alas." No matter what form a joke is given, I think it is intended to make everyone who hears it laugh. What difference does it make whether your sting is made jestingly or seriously? All the difference in the world! Almost everybody can smile at a pleasant joke directed at himself. But no one can take a gibe. Otherwise, if you think lamentations are all right, but not jokes, it would be easy for Folly as a joke to prefix an interjection of woe to her entire work, and, changing her form, go back again and with the same language lament the theologians she laughed at before. One could not easily tell whether he ought to lament them or laugh at them. But maybe it should be all right to make any remark at all about bishops, even second-rate ones, but not one word against theologians, no matter what they are like.

That is almost the point of your words in your most recent letter to Erasmus. You say, "You are surprised that your Folly, a source of delight to many men, both theologians and bishops, has caused such a disturbance. But I am surprised at you, Erasmus, for putting more value, in this matter, on the opinion of bishops than that of theologians. You are acquainted with the life, the morals, the learning, or rather the illiteracy, of the bishops of our day. True, there are some worthy of their high rank; but their number is remarkably small." In these words, Dorp, while you resent having the theologians spattered with a very mild joke, you very ceremoniously drown the bishops with downright insults, as you not only fail to find any learning in them, while carping at their illiteracy, but you also slanderously condemn their life and morals. But, according to you, it is most imperative that the theologians maintain an unblemished reputation with the people; as if it made no difference what the people think about the bishops, but you know very well what position they hold in the Church, how far superior it is to that of

your theologians, and you most clearly realize that they are
the successors to the Apostles. And do not think you exercised
a prudent foresight in admitting that some bishops are worthy
of their high rank, since not even you would believe that
Folly ascribes the defects of unworthy theologians to the
worthy ones. She even convinces you that, as far as she is
concerned, there are many worthy theologians. But as far as
you are concerned, the number of good bishops is not only
small, but "remarkably small." But let us grant you that
there is nothing wrong in making fun of bishops with clever
remarks or in attacking them with abuse, provided one does
not assault the all-holy ranks of the theologians. What do
you have to say about the following? In your very witty
prologue to Plautus' play about Pyrgopolinices [39] you almost
tear those theologians apart with your teeth. Of course, you
do not do so by name, but the picture you draw is so clear,
you could not have described them more accurately by nam-
ing them. The mention of Plautus reminds me of the remarks
you gathered from the words of Saint Augustine and which,
in various parts of your letter, you dump upon the poets, and
explicitly upon Terence. Although this subject demands a
more lengthy discussion than I can give in this letter, I do
put this question to you. Do you think, by those words,
Augustine meant that Christians should not read Terence?
If he is not opposed to a thorough study of Terence, that
passage is no argument against the reading of poets. But if
you think Augustine intended to deter Christians from a
study of poetry, then I have another question for you. Do
you yourself think Terence should still be taught? If so, what
is the point of quoting someone carefully who, in your opinion, should not be followed? If not, then obviously you have
been convinced by Augustine. But I certainly wonder; how
did it happen that only now for the first time you have been
convinced by one whom you undoubtedly read long ago?
Yet you did not stop reading Plautus; not only that, you
did not stop teaching him, and presenting and staging his
plays in public; and Plautus is not more free from indecencies

39. "Tower-town-taker," the hero in Plautus' *Miles Gloriosus*.

than Terence; in fact, he is more indecent. Then too, you
enriched *The Braggart Warrior* of Plautus with a very clever
prologue. You wrote not only a prologue for *The Pot of
Gold*,[40] but also a conclusion, which the comedy had lacked.
Whether regarded from the viewpoint of elegance of style,
or of wit, which is truly Plautine, this conclusion of yours
does not seem inferior to any section of the whole comedy.
The following verses will be a proof of that fact, in which,
as I have noted, you draw a very neat picture of those uncultured theologians you are now defending; you jeer at them
as wittily, you attack them as fiercely as anyone else has ever
done. No verses could be more witty or more elegant than
these that I now quote:

First of all, the uncultured and those uninitiated
Into learning that is not plebeian, such men
He tells to go to the devil,
Since those sour-tempered growlers still
Go on doing what they've always been doing:
Bellowing their roaring bombast, and
Belching forth their venomous bile,
Abusing, snarling at, chewing on everybody with fangs
They love to sink into flesh, and like hounds,
Barking at everyone they meet.
Such humans (if they really are humans),
Since they're ignorant yokels, Plautus has
Emphatically ordered me to bounce.
Any who happen to be present, unless they keep their mouths
       shut,
And don't cause any rows, he has warned there'll be whips
With which they'll be given a hell of a reception.

That, my dear Dorp, is how you thought one need not avoid
the poets, and how well you portrayed those uncultured theologians in their true colors! You might deny you were a
theologian at that time, as those lines were written seven
years ago; but hardly six months have passed since you col-
lected and published those writings; you were certainly a

40. Dorp wrote a prologue to Plautus' *Aulularia*.

theologian then, for that was four years after your brilliant
sermon on the Assumption of the Virgin Mother of God. So
what difference does it make whether you wrote those lines
as a theologian or before you became a theologian, but you
gave them your approval by publishing them when you were
a theologian? Really, it makes a vast difference. Usually we
are swept along by an impetuous drive to write. But when we
go over something again that we have set aside for a time, we
act with decision. And so, my dear Dorp, while you judge
that no change should be made in those pointed satires of
Gerard, in which he describes the foulest vices of monks;
while you pity religious bishops so as to laugh at them, and
with a biting laugh too, and while you bitterly censure the
ignorance, life, and morals of the rest of the bishops, with
the exception of remarkably few; and while the very theologians, whose folly it is a crime, in your opinion, for Folly
to poke fun at, you describe as sour-tempered, uninitiated into
learning that is not plebeian, bellowing their roaring bombast,
belching forth venomous bile, abusing, snarling, chewing on
everybody with fangs they love to sink into flesh, barking
like hounds at everyone they meet, ignorant, yokels, and
finally barely human who, according to you, ought to be
told to go to the devil—while you are doing all this, my dear
Dorp, why did you not think of that well weighed advice
you now offer with much friendliness and prudence to Erasmus? Where then was that famous saying of Sallust, "It is
extreme insanity to gain, by one's exertions, nothing but
public hatred"? Where then was that famous saying of Cor-
nelius Tacitus, "Biting wit, mingled with much truth, rankles
in the memory"? Whereto then did that famous saying of
Epictetus vanish: "Do not think that everybody likes to hear
what you like to say"? Assuredly, my dearest Dorp, it is a
natural instinct ever to demand moderation from others, but
to grant liberties to ourselves. I know the type of men who
would not tolerate Reuchlin [41] with any fairness—Good

41. John Reuchlin (1455–1522) was second only to his younger contemporary Erasmus in the revival of learning. He studied Greek with
Rudolf Agricola in Paris and continued it with Contoblacas at Basel,
taking his B.A. there 1475, M.A. 1477. He then returned to Paris and
studied with George Hermonymus. He chose the profession of the law

heavens, what a man!—extremely learned, prudent, and honest, while his rivals, utterly ignorant, stupid, and worthless liars, attacked him with such monstrous injustice that, had he revenged himself with his fists, it would have seemed proper to pardon him. As I say, I know the type of men who would not tolerate him, and yet they were very high in their admiration for him, because with his pen he gave free expression—true as it was free—to his feelings against them. I also know that the very men who did not tolerate this sort of thing, soon after became much more violently angry over a matter of much less importance and one that did not bear so close a relation to themselves. It is undoubtedly so much easier to control other people's feelings than one's own. Therefore, you say, was it not right for me to approve of the satires of Gerard, or to speak out, jestingly or seriously, against uncultured theologians (include abbots and bishops too), provided it was true, and no names were mentioned? As a matter

---

and state service rather than that of teaching, and thus studied law at Orléans and Poitiers, taking his Licentiate in Roman law at Poitiers. His state service was as secretary to the Count of Württemberg, and with him he made his first journey to Italy in 1482, knowing the Medici court and its library, rich in Greek manuscripts, and seeing Pope Sixtus IV in Rome. A second visit in 1490 allowed him to study Greek with Demetrius Chalcondylas.

Around 1482 Reuchlin began the study of Hebrew, continuing it in 1492 at Linz with Loans of Mantua and in 1498 in Italy with Obadiah Sforno of Cesena. From then on, he did more for Hebrew learning than he had for Greek. In 1506 he published *Rudimenta Hebraica,* part dictionary, part grammar, and later wrote on the Hebrew orthography and accents. He knew that he had done well—"I have raised a monument more enduring than bronze." He published the seven penitential Psalms in Hebrew with a Latin translation and compared passages in Hebrew critically with the Vulgate translation.

In 1509 he became involved in the controversy with John Pfefferkorn, a converted Jew who proposed the destruction of all Hebrew books except the Old Testament, in order to hasten the conversion of the Jews. Reuchlin thought the books contained too much of value for scholarship to be destroyed for their anti-Christian view. He had to defend himself against the obscurantists, and when summoned to appear before the court of the Inquisition at Mainz, he appealed to Rome. The case was settled in his favor in 1514, but by 1520 he had lost in the ecclesiastical struggle, because of anxiety over the progress of the Reformation. Nevertheless the Humanists accepted him as their leader, and he was a personality of European renown (Hans Rupprich, *Festgabe seiner Vaterstadt,* Pforzheim, 1955, pp. 10–34).

of fact, my dear Dorp, I think it was so right for you to act as you did, that I do not think you have ever acted better in your life, as long as you have that sense of fairness by which you do not make a matter of a defect in another person what you consider praiseworthy in yourself.

All of this then, my dear Dorp, is my view on Folly. It is without reason that you warn me, since there is no warning that has to be given; and if there were any, you are giving it to me too late, after so many years. Your suggestion at the conclusion of your former letter—namely, that Erasmus would be reconciled with those theologians who were disturbed by the Folly, if he were to write a praise of Wisdom in answer to the praise of Folly—that suggestion really brought a slight smile to my lips. They are indeed wise men, if they think that by this *Praise of Folly* Folly has been so lauded as to want wisdom lauded in the same manner! If that is what they think, why are they angry? They too have been copiously lauded by Folly that has been so lauded. Besides, I do not see how Erasmus could appease the ill-will of such men towards himself; rather he would only aggravate it, whether he wants to or not, because he would be forced to expel them from the coterie of Wisdom, just as now he has been forced to admit them into the company of the most gifted priests of the secret rites of Folly.

While I have been writing this, a letter has reached me from my Prince, recalling me.[42] Though I desire to continue, I am forced at last to stop and, even though unwilling, to put an end to this letter; it is so lengthy, perhaps it might have been shorter, an "*Orestes* written also on the back of the pages, and still not finished." [43] Because of some vague longing to talk with you, it still wanted to go on and on.

Although I have now left nothing untouched, certainly, as far as I know, I have omitted nothing deliberately. I do not think that anyone will expect me to defend *The Folly*

---

42. More was evidently recalled at the same time as Tunstal. (Cf. *L.P.*, 2, 1047). He did not return to England immediately; on 25 October Pace wrote to Wolsey, "I met with Mr. More in the highe waye . . ." (ibid., p. 1067).

43. Juvenal, *Satires* 1.6.

from even a suspicion of blasphemy or lack of piety, as if, because of that book, Christ's Religion has been in bad repute. You have so represented these men in your former letter as to show plainly that you were giving someone else's view, contrary to your own personal opinion; and in your later letter, though much of it was not your own true thoughts, everything you wrote was adorned splendidly and fully, especially in those passages where there was an opportunity for the brilliant style that is typical of your genius and learning; and yet you purposely omitted any mention of this slanderous charge of lack of piety, as if that charge itself were impious and sacrilegious, and not only flagrant, but also idle and absurd. Therefore, I did not have to say anything about that subject; I think I have spoken about everything else. And so there is nothing left of the subjects I wanted to discuss. If I had not been interrupted by the letter from my Prince, I would probably have written more fully about the same matters.

I am not displeased by having to fold up this letter, as I am afraid that, because of its length, it could be bothersome to you. Yet I am not happy to be deprived of the opportunity to revise this letter, and give shape to this crude and ugly offspring of mine by frequently retouching it. I had definitely decided to do that, so it would reach you, most learned Dorp, in a more finished state; for I want myself and all I am to meet your approval. Please, pardon the lack of finish, due to the fact that I cannot even reread it because of my hasty departure, but also to the fact that I had no library here while writing, in fact, almost no books at all. However, your kindness first of all, gives me hope that this letter, no matter what it is like, will not even as it is cause you displeasure; and, secondly, the pains I have taken in writing it, for I trust that I have carefully avoided saying anything that could justifiably offend your ears, unless it be, since I am human, that self-love has deceived me. If that should happen, upon being reminded of my fault, I shall admit it frankly, and not defend it. Just as I am not unwilling to admonish those I love, if it is of any importance to them, so too I am certainly very happy to be admonished by my friends. I am aware also of

this fact, that some of the reproaches you made against Erasmus were not the result of your own irritation, but rather you
were repeating what you had gotten from others. I say this,
so you may in turn realize that many of the answers I have
made in this letter are directed through you against them,
rather than against you. For I not only love you as being a
most affectionate person, and regard you as most learned,
but I also respect you as an excellent man.

Goodbye, my dearest Dorp, and be truly convinced that no
one, even in your native Holland, is more interested in you
than is More among the British, sundered from all the world;
and you are no less dear to him than you are to Erasmus. For
you cannot be any dearer, not even to me. Again, goodbye.
Bruges, October 21.

5

[16, Allen, 2, 388] To Erasmus.

Erasmus' first extant letter to More is dated 28 October 1499,
and the letter printed here is the first from More to Erasmus which
has survived. How many have been lost to us!

Erasmus (27 October 1466 – 12 July 1536) was educated in schools
at Gouda, Utrecht, Deventer, and 's-Hertogenbosch. His parents
had died by 1484 and his guardians had been unwise in the care of
his small inheritance, so the monastic life seemed good provision for
the very studious Erasmus and about 1487 he became an Augustinian canon at Steyn, near Gouda. He was not suited to the religious
life and as a secretary accompanied the Bishop of Cambrai to Paris.
He remained to study, resided in the College of Montaigu and
earned a living by tutoring Lord Mountjoy and other young Eng-
lishmen.

Invited by Mountjoy, he visited England from May 1499 to
January 1500, and his acquaintance with Archbishop Warham,
John Colet and Thomas More and many others began. He came to
England again 1505–06 and 1509–14, teaching at Cambridge from
1511 to January 1514 and working on a new translation of the
Greek New Testament into Latin, and also on St. Jerome, Seneca,
Plutarch, and Cato.

As More wrote this letter, Erasmus was in Basel, seeing books
through Froben's press. He wrote a friend that "Jerome is proceeding finely" (Allen, 2, Ep. 385) and composed a dedication to Pope
Leo X (ibid., Ep. 384) of the first published edition of the Greek
New Testament.

〈London
c. 17 February 1516〉

THOMAS MORE TO HIS ERASMUS, GREETINGS.

Since your departure,[1] my dearest Erasmus, I have received altogether three letters from you. If I claimed to have answered all of them I do not suppose you would believe me, no matter how solemnly I lied; especially since you know me very well as being a lazy correspondent and not so scrupulously truthful as to shrink from a little white lie as if it were parricide. Our friend Pace[2] is on an embassy in your locality, although not exactly in the same place as you; he is separated from me without being with you. He can converse with me by letter, but not with you face to face. May he come home soon with his business happily concluded, so that at least one half of me can be with me. For I do not know when to expect you,[3] since you intend to move on into Italy, where, I fear, you will meet people who will not let you get away. For the present, I shall be missing one half of me, while he is gone; and the other half, while you are gone. I hope that some excellent fortune, worthy of the man, soon happens to Pace.

1. In May 1515.
2. Richard Pace (c. 1483–1536) was of good family, high principles, more than usual intelligence. As he was poor, he turned to the church for his career, and though pious had little of the priest in him. He owed his education to Langton, Bishop of Winchester, who sent him to Oxford and then to the University of Padua. Langton died in 1501, but left Pace £10 a year for seven years, and Pace continued his studies at Bologna. His acquaintance with Erasmus began in Italy in 1508. He was ordained priest in 1510. From 1509 to 1514, he was secretary to Cardinal Bainbridge, Langton's nephew in Rome. After the death of Bainbridge he returned to England and served as secretary to Wolsey, and then to the King, and finally as chief secretary to the King.
He was employed by the King in many diplomatic missions. At this time he spent two years in negotiations with the Swiss, returning to England in December 1517. He supported Henry's cause, in vain, in the imperial election of 1519, and Wolsey's in the papal elections of January 1522 and September 1523. During the latter years he was on embassy to the Republic of Venice.
Pace was paid by the King with the grant of rich church preferments, including St. Dunstan's, Stepney, the Deanery of St. Paul's on the death of Colet, and other deaneries. His life ended sadly in nine years of mental illness and finally complete loss of reason.
3. Erasmus, however, did return in July–August 1516.

I am very much aware that it is the intention of the King and the wish of the Cardinal and the endeavor of all good men to honor and promote him.

As for yourself, I would be entertaining even higher hopes if I were not so constantly disappointed; and yet, why can I not have high hopes for you even now? I have not lost hope for the future, just because my previous hopes have not been realized; rather, I am more confident than ever. No man has the same luck indefinitely, and yours cannot continue to be bad, for you are the idol and the admiration of the Pope, of kings, of bishops, of almost all men throughout Christendom. It would be a waste of words to mention the attitude toward you among our own bishops, particularly the Archbishop of Canterbury, and the special favor you enjoy with our King. Your previous failures to receive a benefice corresponding to your worth and to the deep love shown you by eminent men, have been caused partly by your disregard of the way which others use to solicit support, partly by some accident of fortune, as, for instance, in the recent case of the Tournay canonry, which Lord Mountjoy [4] had reserved for you. Right now, you do not seem averse to it, for, as you say in your letter, you have sent on to him all the documents necessary for its bestowal upon you. However, if you recall, when I was with you at Bruges,[5] I discussed this topic with you; and after listing the advantages and disadvantages of the benefice, you seemed to be uninterested in it; nor did you conceal your attitude from Sampson, who represents the Bishop of York at Tournai.[6] You were forced into that view not only because of

4. William Blount, Lord Mountjoy (d. 1534) was Erasmus' pupil in Paris c. 1496, and invited him to England to visit in 1498. He was lieutenant of Hammes, Picardy, and of the marches of Calais 1509–11. He became chamberlain to Queen Catherine 1511. From 1514 to 1517 he was lieutenant of Tournai. He was present at the Field of the Cloth of Gold, and took part in the war with France 1523. He told the Queen of the contemplated divorce, and warned the Pope that if it were refused, the King would renounce papal supremacy.

5. More was a member of an embassy to Prince Charles of Castile, May–October 1515, which had made a treaty renewing the commercial privileges gained in 1495 and 1506.

6. Thomas Wolsey was bishop of Lincoln at the beginning of 1514, received the bishopric of Tournai on the capture of the city, and on the death of Cardinal Bainbridge received the archbishopric of York 5 August 1514. Richard Sampson (d. 1554) was now at Tournai to further Wolsey's interests, as the French bishop refused to surrender the diocese.

your fear that it would not be a permanent position without the further consent of the other bishop,[7] whose authorization you did not expect for this one action of a man whose every act he endeavors to countermand; but also because of the obligation of making a payment of ten English pounds immediately upon receiving the canonry and an additional two hundred nobles or more to redeem the house. Such is the local custom, and if you fail to comply with it, you will barely realize six nobles a year, and not even that much, as I understand, unless you take up permanent residence there. As a result of these considerations, you gave Sampson and me the impression that you would not accept the canonry.

Shortly after your departure, I went to Tournai. There I found out from Lord Mountjoy and also from Sampson that the Archbishop of York had informed the two of them by letter that the benefice was to be given to another party, to whom apparently he had promised it, without knowing it had been intended for you. Upon hearing this and without disclosing my impression that the benefice did not suit your taste, I urged them to send a return letter saying that it had already been conferred upon you and that the situation was such that no alteration was possible unless some better provision were first made for you. In response, the Archbishop of York said that this post would not at all be suitable for you, as it was not lucrative for one in residence and was totally unproductive for an absentee, and he guaranteed them that he would make you a better offer. So, in my presence and with no dissent on my part, they decided to confer the benefice upon the Archbishop's choice. What happened after that, I do not know. But this I do know: if you are deprived of that benefice, a more profitable one is due to you from the Cardinal, and I hope he makes payment soon. He does often speak of you in very friendly terms.

It was unnecessary for me to ask the Archbishop for your pension. He had thought of it himself, before receiving my letter, and had handled the matter with Maruffo,[8] who, as you know, is regularly employed by him as a broker for such

7. The very young French bishop, Louis Guillard.
8. The banker who dealt with Erasmus's pension from the Archbishop.

transactions, and at stated times they balance their accounts. The Archbishop was at Otford [9] at the time, and, upon receiving my letter, he wrote again to the fellow urging him to send on to you twenty English pounds with dispatch and promising to make good the payment to Maruffo as soon as he was assured by a receipt from you that the money had been delivered. I had a conference with Maruffo. He said that he would ask you by letter to send back promptly to him a receipt, stating that you had received the money; he would take this receipt to the Archbishop, claim the money, and only then arrange to have it sent on to you. When I learned of that plan, I was afraid there was some danger, if the money were not paid out to him right then, that the delay would also affect you. "This subterfuge is not necessary," I told him; "either send the money immediately, charging it to the account of the Archbishop, or, if it irks you to pay out money without first receiving the equivalent, I shall arrange immediately for you to have the money on hand." "No," he said, "there is nothing to worry about. I shall see to it that Erasmus has the money at once; in fact, it is here right now. For Erasmus has a money draft from me entitling him to draw, at will, to the amount of one thousand ducats. Whatever amount he draws from this account, must be paid back to me, according to our agreement, out of this pension of his." That is what he says. But I hardly believe that he has given you a draft entitling you to draw from his account, without the money first being put down on his counter. Consequently, if the arrangements are not as he says, inform me quickly.

The Archbishop of Canterbury has finally been relieved of the office of chancellor,[10] a burden, which, as you know, he had tried extremely hard to shake off for several years; at long last he has attained his heart's desire, a life of privacy, and is having wonderful leisure amid his books and his memories of duties well done. He has been replaced, at the appointment of the King, by the Cardinal of York,[11] who as an administrator is far exceeding everyone's expectations, which were very

9. In Kent, where the archbishops of Canterbury had a manor house.
10. Warham resigned 22 December 1515.
11. Wolsey took the oath of office 24 December.

high in virtue of his other qualities; it is no easy thing to be
the successor of an extraordinary person, and yet to give complete satisfaction.

Our embassy, which like everything else I do is a matter of
interest to you, was quite successful, though it dragged on
much longer than I had hoped or wanted. When I left home,
I expected to be gone at the most two months; but the embassy
lasted more than six. However, those long months were
crowned by rather gratifying results. So, when I say that my
mission was accomplished and also that further complications
were arising which, apparently, would lead to greater delay
(as regularly happens with administrators), I wrote to the
Cardinal and received permission to return, thanks to the
assistance of my friends, especially Pace, who had not as yet
gone. But on my return trip I unexpectedly met him at
Gravelines; he was in such a hurry that he hardly had time to
stop and exchange greetings. Tunstal came back recently, but
was here barely ten days, without spending a single one of
them pleasantly as he wanted, for his entire stay was squandered on a bothersome, disgusting review of all the details
entrusted to him on his mission, and then, without warning,
he has been promptly shoved back again on another embassy.[12]
It is very much against his will, I am sure, but he cannot
refuse.

The office of ambassador has never held a great attraction
for me. It does not suit us laymen as it does you clergy, for
you either have no wives and children at home, or you find
them wherever you travel. Whenever we are away for a short
while, our hearts quickly go back to our wives [13] and children.
Then too, when a priest goes on an embassy, he can take
along with him wherever he wishes, his entire household and,
for the time being, can support them at the expense of the
king, while at home he would have to support them at his own
expense. But when I am on leave, I must support two house-
holds, one at home, the other abroad. A rather generous
allowance was granted to me by the King for the benefit of

12. Tunstal was "to arrange the treaty lately concluded between England and the Prince of Castile" (*L.P.*, 2, 1574).

13. His second wife, Alice Middleton.

my retinue, but no consideration was made for those whom
I had to leave at home; and although I am, as you know, a
kindly husband and an indulgent father and a gentle master,
still I have never had the least success in persuading the members of my family to do without food, for my sake, until I
came home. Finally, it is easy for sovereigns, without any
cost to themselves, to reimburse clergymen for their work and
expenditures by means of ecclesiastical preferments; but no
such generous and handy provisions are made for us, though
the King, it is true, marked me out, on my return, for an
annual pension,[14] which, because of the distinction or the
revenue involved, is not to be scorned. However, I have not as
yet accepted it, and I do not think I ever shall; for its acceptance would mean that I either would have to leave my present
post in London, which I do prefer even to a higher one, or,
what is not at all to my liking, I would have to retain it and
thereby occasion resentment among the townsfolk. If any
dispute over privileges arises between them and the King,
as sometimes happens, they would be skeptical about my
sincerity and loyalty to them and consider me under obligation
to the King as his pensioner.

However, certain aspects of that embassy gave me great
pleasure; first of all, the extended and constant association
with Tunstal,[15] who is second to none in literary attainments
and strictness in life and morals, and yet is a genial companion; secondly, the friendship which I formed with Busleiden,[16] who is extremely wealthy and very generous, and

14. More received a pension in 1518, retroactive from Michaelmas 1517
and charged to the little customs of London (*L.P.*, 2, 875, and No. 4247).
He then resigned as under-sheriff of London.

15. For Tunstal, see below, Introduction to Letter 10. On 17 November 1515 he had become Archdeacon of Chester, which was a rich
preferment, and 12 May 1516 he received the high position of Master
of the Rolls and Vice-Chancellor.

16. Jerome de Busleiden (c. 1470–1517) was educated at the Universities of Louvain, Orléans, and Padua. He knew well the Italian Renaissance, studying Latin and Greek, art and archaeology, coins and medals.
He also studied law, and was promoted Doctor Utriusque Juris, 1503,
at Padua. On his return from Italy he became a member of the Great
Council of Mechlin, the high court of justice for the Netherlands. He
followed an ecclesiastical career, was provost of Aire, and held a large
number of other preferments. He was nonresident, as he had to be present
always in the Great Council.

therefore a magnificent and gracious host. He gave me a tour of his home, which is very artistically decorated and fitted with exquisite appointments; he also showed me his large collection of antiquities, in which, as you know, I am very interested. Finally, he displayed to me his remarkable well stocked library and a mind even more so than any library, so that he completely filled me with amazement. I understand that he will very soon be sent on an embassy to our King. However, the most pleasant experience of my entire trip was my personal relationship with your host, Peter Gilles [17] of Antwerp; his learning, his wit, his modesty, his genuine friendliness are such that, bless my soul, I would be happy to pay a good part of my wealth to purchase the companionship of that one man. He sent me your *Apology* and also your commentary on the Psalm *Beatus Vir,* which you dedicated to Beatus Rhenanus,[18] a man truly blessed with this wonderful, lasting memorial of a friend. Dorp has had his letter printed and included as a preface to your *Apology*. I had hoped to meet him, if I had the chance. Since I did not, I sent him my greetings by letter,

---

Busleiden built a magnificent mansion (now the town museum), beautifully decorated and furnished and with a large library of printed books and illuminated manuscripts. He left the Netherlands on 24 June 1517 to accompany Charles, King of Castile, on his journey to Spain after his accession. Before departure he made his will, leaving his fortune to establish a trilingual college at Louvain, which, on the advice of Erasmus, he grafted on the earlier foundation, the College of St. Donatian. At Bordeaux he contracted pleurisy, epidemic there, and died on 27 August. His body was taken home for burial in St. Rombaut's in Mechlin.

17. Peter Gilles, born c. 1486 of an old Antwerp family, was the son of the town treasurer. He was given an excellent education in Antwerp schools, and then became a corrector in Thierry Martens' press. In 1521 he became chief secretary of the town, but continued his humanistic studies, and his work for the press. Because of his three interests, his acquaintance with scholars and writers of his day was very broad. He was a close friend of Erasmus, More, Tunstal, Dorp, Jerome de Busleiden, John Louis Vives, Conrad Goclenius, to mention only those who appear in More's correspondence. He married Cornelia Sanders in 1514. She died in 1526, leaving several children. He remarried, but soon lost his second wife. He resigned his office in 1532, and died in November 1533.

18. Beatus Rhenanus (1485–1547) was born at Sélestat and educated there, and at Paris under Lefèvre d'Étaples. In 1511 he settled at Basel, engaged in work for the Froben press, and knew Erasmus well. In 1526 he went again to Sélestat and spent the rest of his life there. He wrote *Rerum Germanicarum Lib. III,* and edited Tacitus and Livy. More puns on the meaning of his first name with the phrase "a man truly blessed."

just a brief laconic note, as I did not have time for a longer one. I could not pass the fellow by without some word of greeting, as I find him curiously attractive because of his extraordinary scholarliness and for many other reasons too, not the least of which is the fact that his criticism of the *Folly* provided you with the opportunity for penning your *Apology*.

I am glad that your works on Jerome and the New Testament are coming along so well. It is remarkable, how eagerly those editions are anticipated by everybody. You can be sure, Erasmus, that Linacre [19] has a very high opinion of you and talks about you everywhere. I recently learned this from some men who were dining with him at the King's table, where he spoke of you in very fond and lavish terms; the King's response, in the course of the conversation, was such as to give my informants the clear impression that you were soon to be the recipient of some unusual bit of good luck. May such be the will of Heaven!

Farewell, my dearest Erasmus, and give my regards to Rhenanus and Lystrius,[20] who, because of your recommendation and their own writings, are dearer and even more intimately known to me than are many of the people with whom I have daily contact. My wife sends you her regards, and so does Clement, whose daily progress in Latin and Greek arouses no little hope in me that one day he will be an honor to his country and to letters.

Again, farewell, and let this one letter satisfy you for several months. In writing this letter, I have tried to mimic a stingy person who seldom entertains, but when he does invite guests to his table, he prepares a banquet that lasts indefinitely, so that the one meal will save him the expense of entertaining every day. For the third time, farewell.

The Bishop of Durham [21] was most gratified by the dedica-

19. Erasmus had long doubted his friendship (Allen, *1*, 478; *2*, 139, 198, 420).

20. Gerard Lister of Rhenen in Utrecht, who wrote a commentary on the *Praise of Folly*.

21. Thomas Ruthall (d. 4 February 1522/3) was born at Cirencester; he was educated at Oxford, was D.D. there, and was incorporated D.D. at Cambridge. He was Bishop of Durham 1509. He had much duty at

tion of your edition of Seneca. Notice how quick I am to copy your habits; this letter has been written to you just as your recent letter to me was, with the help of a secretary; and I copy you so closely, I would not even write these few words in my own hand except that I want to assure you that this letter is from me.[22]

6

[20, Allen, 2, 461] To Erasmus.

London

3 September ⟨1516⟩

MORE SENDS HIS VERY BEST GREETINGS TO MASTER ERASMUS.

I am sending you my "*Nowhere*," [1] which is nowhere well written. I have added a prefatory epistle to my friend, Peter. I know from experience that I do not have to tell you to give proper attention to everything else. I have delivered your letter to the Venetian ambassador,[2] who, it appears, was very

---

court under Henry VII and Henry VIII, as royal secretary, and also in diplomacy, assisting Cardinal Wolsey. Sebastian Giustinian, the Venetian ambassador, regarded him as "singing treble to the Cardinal's bass," and as "one and the same thing as the right reverend Cardinal." In 1506 More had dedicated to him his translation of three of Lucian's dialogues.

Erasmus dedicated his *Senecae Lucubrationes* to Ruthall, 7 March 1515 (Allen, 2, Ep. 325). The volume did not reach Ruthall then and he was annoyed. It was still delayed and Erasmus hoped that Ruthall could find it in July 1516 (ibid., Ep. 437).

22. Erasmus' answer to this letter was written at Brussels, c. 3 June 1516 (Allen, 2, 412). He wrote of a dangerous journey from Basel, as the party had met "crowds of soldiers" at Kaisersperg in the Vosges, near Colmar. Plans had been changed, and at Cologne they had met an Italian embassy, joined them and were then nearly eighty horsemen. "Nor in this number did we make the journey without danger."

He spoke of the friends he met in Brussels, including the Bishop of Chieti (John Peter Caraffa, later Pope Paul IV), Tunstal, and Mountjoy. If his appointment as Councilor to Prince Charles of Castile (Ep. 370, line 18 and note) should not prove satisfactory, he would return immediately to Basel, where he had been valued. He had dined that day with Tunstal, "most like you."

1. More's first choice of title for the *Utopia*. The latter comes from Greek οὐ, no, and τόπος, place. It was dedicated to Peter Gilles; see my *Correspondence*, Ep. 25.

2. Sebastian Giustinian, ambassador in England from February 1515 to September 1519.

well disposed to receive your New Testament, which was intercepted by a Carmelite.[3] He is completely devoted to sacred learning and has finished reading almost all the authors who treat of petty questions; he attributes so much importance to them that not even Dorp could outdo him in that. We conferred with one another like candidates campaigning for votes; we tickled one another with set speeches and lengthy encomia. But, to be honest, I like him very much. Apparently, he is very sincere and very competent in the things of man, and now he is completely dedicating himself to learning the things of God; and last, but not least, he is very interested in you.

I have no news as yet from the Archbishop of Canterbury about the situation. Colet has not had a conference with him about that business of yours,[4] but he did have one with the Archbishop of York and says that he found him so much in your favor and so lavish in his praises of you that all he wants now is to have the Archbishop match his brilliant words with deeds. I expect him to do that soon, with open-handed generosity. The money you left with me will be delivered to Gilles by my John,[5] at Michaelmas; he will not reach Antwerp before that feast. If you publish my *Epigrams,* give some thought to the propriety of printing my remarks about Brixius,[6] as some of them are rather caustic, although it might well seem that I had provocation from his insulting comments about my country. In any case, as I said, examine

3. Peter de Brescia Carmelianus, luteplayer to the King.
4. Evidently these sentences refer to hopes of patronage for Erasmus.
5. His brother, who acted as secretary to More.
6. Germain de Brie's poem *Chordigerae nauis conflagratio,* published in 1513, commemorated an engagement with the English on 10 August 1512, honored the French commander, and attacked the English. More was injured in his national pride and replied in epigrams which scorned Brixius' work. Brixius replied in his *Antimwrus,* published in 1519 in spite of Erasmus' protests. More's letter to Brixius is Ep. 86 in the *Correspondence,* and other letters in the controversy are in Allen, passim. The epigrams in Latin and English translation are printed by Bradner and Lynch, and discussed by them and by the late Hoyt Hopewell Hudson, *The Epigram in the English Renaissance.* It was through Erasmus' fault that the Epigrams concerning the *Chordigera* were included in More's printed volume, Froben, Basel, 1518. More bought up copies to end the circulation.

those expressions carefully and, in general, anything else that
seems to you spiteful. As for any silly remarks, handle them
all as you know will be for my own good. Quintilian [7] regrets
that Seneca did not follow someone else's judgment in using
his own ability as a writer; however, it were better for me,
when writing, not only to follow someone else's judgment,
but also to use someone else's ability. Farewell, and give my
regards to Master Tunstal and Master Busleiden. Hurriedly,
from London, September 3.

7

[22, Allen, 2, 467] To Erasmus.

⟨London
c. 20 September 1516⟩

MORE SENDS HIS VERY BEST GREETINGS TO ERASMUS.

I received your letter from Calais, and am happy to hear
that you had a pleasant voyage. The Provost of Cassel,[1] now
on a diplomatic mission to our country, told me that you
had arrived safe at Brussels before he left home. Not long ago
I encountered Maruffo,[2] who was moaning that, because of
some slip, your money was paid, but to his loss. I have also
recently sent you another money draft of his, to the amount
of twenty English pounds, from the Archbishop. I expect that
you will have the same good luck in cashing this draft, if you
act quickly before he issues a countermand to his agents,
which seems to be exactly what he has in mind. The bearer
of this letter will pay to Gilles the twenty pounds you left
with me, which, at the rate of exchange, amounts to thirty
pounds in your money.

Not long ago I talked with Urswick [3] about the horse for

7. *Inst.* 10.1.130.
1. George of Theimseke, Provost of Cassel and member of Mechlin
Parliament and of the Privy Council, who was often sent on embassies.
2. See above, Letter 5.
3. Christopher Urswick (1448–1522), probably educated at Cambridge,
was chaplain to the Lady Margaret Beaufort. He accompanied Henry
Earl of Richmond when he came to claim the throne in 1485, and received much preferment in reward, becoming dean of York in 1488 and
dean of Windsor 1495. He also served on embassies abroad. He gave

you. He says he will arrange for you to have one soon, but right now he does not have any he would care to send to you. Some time ago I sent you my *Nowhere;* I am most anxious to have it published soon and also that it be handsomely set off with the highest of recommendations, if possible, from several people, both intellectuals and distinguished statesmen. I want this principally because of one individual,[4] whose name, I think, will occur to you even without my mentioning it, and who, for some strange motive, which you can also guess, regrets that the work is being published before the lapse of nine years. Handle this matter as you think is for my own good. I am also anxious to know if you have shown it to Tunstal, or at least described it to him, as I think you have done, and which I do prefer. For then he will gain a twofold delight; your account will make the work appear to have a more elegant style than it really has, and also you will save him the job of reading it himself. Farewell.

8

[23, Allen, 2, 468] To Erasmus.

London

⟨22 September 1516⟩

THOMAS MORE SENDS HIS VERY BEST GREETINGS TO ERASMUS.

Greetings, my dearest Erasmus. The lord Archbishop of Canterbury has arranged to have twenty English pounds transmitted to you. So, I have sent you Maruffo's [1] draft, plus the letter I received from the Archbishop; thus you can understand that he is generous with his own money and I am by no means a stingy administrator of other people's money;

Erasmus a horse "which thrice carried him safely to and from Basel" (*L.P., 2,* 3339; see below, Letter 9). When the horse died, Erasmus hoped for another in return for the gift of a copy of the Greek New Testament, but in vain.

4. More refers to Jerome Busleiden, who was a statesman as well as a scholar. Erasmus made the request of Busleiden, who sent More a congratulatory letter for the first edition of the *Utopia* (see *Correspondence,* Ep. 27), accompanied by a letter to Erasmus, who had "commanded" it (see Allen, 2, Ep. 484).

1. See above, notes to Letter 5.

you can also promptly inform the Archbishop that you have received the money, so that Maruffo can be reimbursed. I have written to one of our countrymen who is to receive the money from me at your exchange market; he can then turn over thirty Flemish pounds to Gilles so that he can vouch, in your name, for the payment of the twenty English pounds which you had recently left with me.

I have forwarded your letter to Latimer,[2] along with a letter of my own about the Bishop of Rochester; but as yet no word from him, nor from the Bishop. Colet is working strenuously on his Greek, with the solicited help of my boy Clement. I do believe he will persevere until he masters the subject, especially if you keep spurring him on from Louvain; and yet, it might be better to let him follow his own impulse. As you know, he has the habit of disagreeing with suggestions given him, just to have an argument, even when those suggestions correspond with his own ideas. I went to see Urswick; he says he has not forgotten about your horse and will soon arrange for you to have one. When he does, I shall let you know, so you will not be taken in by a fraudulent exchange.

Hurriedly, from London, on the morrow of Saint Matthew the Apostle.[3]

2. William Latimer (1460?–1545) B.A. Oxford, was Fellow of All Souls College. He had traveled in Italy for six years, studied Greek at Padua, and taken his master's degree. On his return to England he spent some years in London, but later went back to Oxford and incorporated M.A. He was a great friend of More and Pace. Erasmus sought his aid in revising his edition of the Greek New Testament, but in vain (Allen, 2, Ep. 520, Latimer to Erasmus. See below, Letter 9).

3. The letters of c. 20 September and 22 September were answered by Erasmus from Antwerp 2 October. He continued to have difficulty with the transfer of his money, and hoped More could send it by someone. He wrote, "I have emptied all my pocketbooks to buy clothes. Believe me, my More, I have squandered over four hundred florins. The danger now is that in my fine clothes I shall die of starvation." He wrote that the edition of St. Jerome would come within two days, and that he had arranged that copies of it should be sent first to Warham, Colet, Fisher, Urswick, and More (Allen, 2, Ep. 474).

9

[26, Allen, 2, 481] To Erasmus.

London

31 October ⟨1516⟩

THOMAS MORE SENDS GREETINGS TO HIS FRIEND, MASTER ERASMUS.

My answer, dear Erasmus, is a little tardy, because I was anxious to get some definite information to send on to you from Urswick about that horse for you; but that has been impossible, since he is gone on a business trip several miles from London and has not as yet returned. I expect him any day now, and as soon as he gets back, the matter will be taken care of. The money you had left with me, I am sure, has been paid over to our friend, Gilles, as I have received a communication from my agent in Antwerp, saying that he would make prompt payment. I could not entrust this bearer with the letters from Basel, which you sent me some time ago to peruse; but I will send them shortly, as soon as I hit upon someone to burden with a large bundle. Bedill [1] showed me the letter from the Bishop of Basel to the Archbishop of Canterbury, and also the Archbishop's response; both were the original copies. The latter, however, was much too much the original; it was so smeared with words struck out or written in as to be not at all legible except to the one who wrote it, and perhaps not even to him.

Our two letters encouraging Latimer to spend a month or two with the Bishop of Rochester reached him too late; he had already made up his mind to go to Oxford and could not possibly be persuaded to postpone his trip for the time being. You know how these philosophers regard their own decisions as immutable laws; I suppose from a love of consistency. He does like your rendering of the New Testament very much, although you are too punctilious to suit him. He does not like the fact that you have retained the word "Sabbath," and other similar points, which you did not think necessary to change, or did not dare to do so. However, he does not admit

---

1. Thomas Bedill was secretary to Archbishop Warham.

of any word at all that would be foreign to Roman ears. I approved of his criticism insofar as Hebrew customs and practices would permit. However, I urged him to note down the various words for which he prefers a different rendering and to send them on to you, along with his criticism; and I think he will do that. This interest of his, I know, will make you very happy.

There are other people, though, my dearest Erasmus, who have formed a conspiracy here in our country to read through your writings from quite a different point of view; and I find their dreadful plot disturbing. Therefore, do not be in a rush to publish a second edition of your works, as the time is ripe to take stock. Out of my loyalty and my anxiety for you I urge you, and I beg you to do at least this much—to revise and correct everything promptly so as to leave the very least opportunity for slander in any passage. Some very sharp-minded men have set their hearts upon making a careful search for such opportunities and will snap them up greedily. You want to know who these people are? I am reluctant, of course, to mention any names, for fear that your spirit be crushed by the frightening thought of such powerful enemies. However, I shall tell you anyhow, to put you more on your guard. The top-ranking Franciscan theologian, whom you know and to whom you gave honorable mention in your edition of Jerome, has picked a group of men who are of the same Order and made of the same stuff, and has hatched a plot with them, aimed at refuting any errors of yours he can find. To make this operation easier and more effective, they devised a scheme whereby they would divide up your works among themselves, read through each one with a critical eye, and then understand absolutely nothing of it all. So you see what a crisis is hanging over your head! You have got to work hard to condition your troops for facing this monstrous peril You can be sure, Erasmus, this decision was reached at a council meeting of the elders, late at night, when they were well soaked. But the morning after, as I am told, with the effects of the wine slept off, they forgot, I guess, all about their resolution; since the decree was written in wine, it was now blotted out of their memory, and so they abandoned their proposal, and instead of reading, they went back to their begging, which experience had taught them to be a far more profitable enterprise.

It is worth noting how much everybody enjoys the *Epistolae Obscurorum Virorum;* the educated take it as a joke, while the uneducated take it seriously and think that our laughter is caused by the style alone. While not defending the style, they do maintain that it is offset by the weighty contents, and under the crude scabbard lies a very handsome blade. It is unfortunate that the work does not have a different title! Then not even in a hundred years would the silly fools realize that the authors were sneering at them with a snout more obtrusive than that of a rhinoceros.

I am happy that my *Nowhere* meets the approval of my friend, Peter; if such men like it, I shall begin to like it myself. I am anxious to find out if it meets with the approval of Tunstal, and Busleiden, and your Chancellor; [2] but their approval is more than I could wish for, since they are so fortunate as to be top-ranking officials in their own governments, although they might be won over by the fact that in this commonwealth of mine the ruling class would be completely made up of such men as are distinguished for learning and virtue. No matter how powerful those men are in their present governments—and, true, they are very powerful—still they have some high and mighty clowns as their equals, if not their superiors, in authority and influence. I do not think that men of this caliber are swayed by the fact that they would not have many under them as subjects, as the term is now used by kings to refer to their people, who are really worse off than slaves; for it is a much higher honor to rule over free people; and good men, such as they, are far removed from that spiteful feeling which desires others to suffer while they are well off themselves. I expect, therefore, that those men will also give

2. John le Sauvage (1455–1518) was a member and then President of the Council of Flanders, President of the Privy Council, and from 1509 Chancellor of Brabant. Under young Charles of Austria he became Great Chancellor of Burgundy and in 1516, Chancellor of Castile. He negotiated with the English ambassadors who had come to Bruges in May 1515.

their approval to my work, and I am very anxious to have it. However, if a deep conviction to the contrary has been implanted in their minds by satisfaction with their present good fortune, then your one vote will be more than adequate to influence my decision. To my way of thinking, we two are a crowd, and I think I could be happy with you in any forsaken spot.

Farewell, dearest Erasmus, more precious to me than my own eyes!

I have succeeded in getting a more favorable letter from Maruffo; that seemed to me to be more convenient and more prudent than to bother the Bishop [3] again about the same matter. Not that he would be unwilling to listen to anything, as long as it concerned you; but I do prefer to approach him with matters of greater import.

Hurriedly, from London, before dawn, All Hallows Eve.

10

[28] To Cuthbert Tunstal.

Cuthbert Tunstal (1474–1559) was educated at Oxford and Cambridge and later spent about six years (from 1499) at the University of Padua, taking his LL.D. there. Besides Roman and Canon law, he was very learned in theology, Greek, Hebrew, and mathematics. The years in Italy gave him an international circle of friends. On his return to England, he was appointed Chancellor to Warham, Archbishop of Canterbury, just before the accession of Henry VIII. From then on, he received many valuable church preferments, usually as rewards for state services. The King employed him on many embassies from 1515 to 1529. More—who had perhaps known him from Oxford days on—was associated with him several times, in 1515, 1516, in the Low Countries, and in negotiating the Treaty of Cambrai in 1529.

Tunstal was made Dean of Salisbury 1521, Bishop of London 1522, Bishop of Durham 1530. He opposed Royal Supremacy in the Convocation of York, but accepted it in the end, perhaps hoping that the King would use his power for the reform of the church and without encroaching on sacerdotal functions. Later developments under Edward VI and Elizabeth made him change his opinion, and he was deprived of his bishopric under both.

3. Warham, Archbishop of Canterbury.

<London
c. November 1516>

Although all the letters I receive from you, my honored
friend, are pleasing to me, yet the one you last wrote is the
most pleasing; for besides its eloquence and its friendliness—
all your letters abound with these commendations—it gave
me especial satisfaction by its praise of my *Commonwealth*
(would that it were as true as it is favorable). I asked our
friend Erasmus to describe to you in conversation its theme,
but forbade him to urge you to read the book. Not that I
did not wish you to read it (nothing would have pleased me
more) but I was mindful of your wise resolution not to take in
hand any modern authors until you had sated yourself with
reading the ancients—a task which, measured by the profit
you have derived from them, is fully accomplished, but,
measured by the love you bear them, will never come to an
end. I feared that when the learned works of so many other
authors could not engage your attention, you would never
willingly descend to my trifles. Nor would you have done so,
surely, unless you had been moved rather by your love of me
than by the subject of the book. Wherefore, for having so
carefully read through the *Utopia*, for having undertaken so
heavy a labor for friendship's sake, I give you the deepest
thanks, not diminished by your having found pleasure in the
work. For this, too, I attribute to your friendship which has
obviously influenced your judgment more than strict rules of
criticism. However that may be, I cannot express my delight
that your judgment is so favorable. For I have almost succeeded
in convincing myself that you say what you think, for I know
that you are far from all deceit, and I am not important
enough to be flattered, and I love you too much to deserve
mockery. So that if you have objectively seen the truth, I am
overjoyed at your verdict; or if in reading you were blinded
by your affection for me, I am no less delighted with your
love, for vehement indeed must that love be if it can deprive
Tunstal of his judgment.

11

[29, Allen, 2, 499] To Erasmus.

⟨London
c. 4 December 1516⟩

MORE SENDS HIS SPECIAL GREETINGS TO ERASMUS.

I have conferred with Urswick about that horse for you. He insists that he still does not have a horse which he considers suitable to send to you, but is definitely going to send you one by the next market day, if not before. I recently dispatched to you Maruffo's money draft, along with his letter containing more favorable terms. At least, so he says; but I was unable to decipher it; neither could our friend, Lily,[1] although he knows Italian very well. The money you had left with me has been in the hands of our friend Gilles for some time now; my agent, who has returned, told me he had made the payment to him.

Our friend Master Palsgrave,[2] who, as you are aware, has long been very much attached to you, is going to Louvain to

1. William Lily (1468?–1522) took a degree at Oxford, and then went on pilgrimage to Jerusalem. On his return he spent some time in Rhodes, to acquire Greek; he continued his studies in Italy and became a good Greek scholar. Colet appointed him the first high master of St. Paul's School. He wrote two books on Latin grammar for the school, and in combined form, they served English schoolboys (including Shakespeare) for more than a century.

2. John Palsgrave (1485?–1554) was a native of London and perhaps belonged to the Pagrave family of Pagrave in Norfolk. He was at Corpus Christi College, Cambridge and took a B.A. degree in 1504. He was schoolmaster to the Lady Princess (Mary Tudor, b. 1496) at least a year before her marriage to Louis XII in October 1514. Palsgrave was well known to More and with the introduction contained in this letter went to Louvain to study law and classics. He wrote a French grammar, *L'Éclaircissement de la langue française*, contracted for publication by Pynson in 1523, but not ready to appear until July 1530. Meanwhile, he held several livings to which he was preferred by More. From July 1525 he was schoolmaster to Henry Fitzroy, Duke of Richmond, the King's natural son, nominal head of the Council of the North, and Palsgrave was a member of the Council, with responsibility for the education of the young Duke (*Correspondence*, Ep. 168, which should be redated). As tutor, he was replaced by Dr. Richard Croke by February 1526.

study law. But he will retain his devotion to the classics of
Latin and Greek literature. He has heard that you will be living there, and while he might expect absolutely anything from
you since he is an old friend of yours, still he earnestly begged
me for a letter of recommendation to increase the favor which,
he believes, he by himself already enjoys with you. Notice
how people think I have great influence with you; for me this
is as much a triumph as is the friendship of kings, which is
the boast of other men. Palsgrave would like to have your
advice and assistance, so as to make progress in his studies. I
realize, my dear Erasmus, that there is no need of many words
when one asks you to help in his studies a person who has
a love for intellectual things, who is already a well known
scholar, with a great future before him, whose great progress
is also known to you, and who, moreover, is your friend and
my friend, which means, he is twice your friend. Years ago,
you took upon yourself the special task of spending the days
and nights of your whole life in advancing the intellectual
life of all men. And, if this involves even a further request,
I also ask you to be openhanded in bestowing upon our friend,
Palsgrave, that which you refuse to no man. I have given him,
to deliver to you, all the letters which you received long
ago from your friends in Basel and which I had in my possession for some time. This is a fortunate coincidence; you
could not find a more reliable letter carrier, nor could he
want anything that would assure him a warmer reception
than a large bundle of erudite letters written by dear friends
of yours, letters which you had missed a long time and had
almost despaired of recovering. I have told him, however, not
to hand them over to you until you sign the contract and agree
to receive him as if every single one of them were a letter of
recommendation for him.

Each day I stand by, waiting with eager ears, for news about
that business of yours in Sicily.[3] Please God, it may have a
happy ending. Master Tunstal recently wrote me a most
friendly letter. Bless my soul, but his frank and complimen-
tary criticism of my commonwealth has given me more cheer

3. Perhaps Erasmus had had the promise of the next suitable vacancy
in Sicily (Allen, 2, 355, note 4).

than would an Attic talent. You have no idea how thrilled
I am; I feel so expanded, and I hold my head high. For in my
daydreams I have been marked out by my Utopians to be their
king forever; I can see myself now marching along, crowned
with a diadem of wheat, very striking in my Franciscan frock,
carrying a handful of wheat as my sacred scepter, thronged
by a distinguished retinue of Amaurotians, and, with this
huge entourage, giving audience to foreign ambassadors and
sovereigns; wretched creatures they are, in comparison with
us, as they stupidly pride themselves on appearing in childish
garb and feminine finery, laced with that despicable gold, and
ludicrous in their purple and jewels and other empty baubles.
Yet, I would not want either you or our friend, Tunstal, to
judge me by other men, whose character shifts with fortune.
Even if heaven has decreed to waft me from my lowly estate to
this soaring pinnacle which, I think, defies comparison with
that of kings, still you will never find me forgetful of that old
friendship I had with you when I was but a private citizen.
And if you do not mind making the short trip to visit me in
Utopia, I shall definitely see to it that all mortals governed
by my kindly rule will show you the honor due to those who,
they know, are very dear to the heart of their king.

I was going to continue with this fascinating vision, but the
rising Dawn has shattered my dream—poor me!—and shaken
me off my throne and summons me back to the drudgery of
the courts. But at least this thought gives me consolation:
real kingdoms do not last much longer.

Farewell, dearest Erasmus.

12

[30, Allen, 2, 502] To Erasmus.

London
15 December ⟨1516⟩

THOMAS MORE TO MASTER ERASMUS, BEST GREETINGS.

I am sure, dearest Erasmus, that you have received my
letter, which I gave Palsgrave to deliver to you, along with

the letters from your friends in Basel.[1] I am glad that Dorp
has come back to his senses;[2] obviously, his feelings were
salved by stern language, after soothing words had only ex-
asperated him. That is the way some people are; if you show
them a little deference, they become bullies; if you treat them
somewhat scornfully, they are crushed and flattened. I am
desperately anxious to read the correspondence carried on
between the two of you, if that can be conveniently arranged.

Lupset[3] has handed over to me several manuscripts of
yours, which had been in his possession for some time. Among
them are the *Iulii Genius*[4] and two declamations, one on the

1. See above, Letter 11, and notes.
2. See above, Letter 4, which helped to change Dorp's mind, and below, Letter 25, which congratulated him.
3. Thomas Lupset (c. 1495–1530), a Londoner, was in boyhood a member of Dean Colet's household, was taught by him, and attended the
grammar school attached to St. Paul's and later Colet's new foundation.
He began Greek there under William Lily. He was at Cambridge for a
short time and assisted Erasmus in the collating of manuscripts for the
printing of the Greek New Testament and St. Jerome's Works. Probably
at this time the manuscripts mentioned here came into his hands. He
seems to have been so indiscreet as to lend the papers, but then wrote
a humble letter of apology to Erasmus (Allen, *3*, Ep. 664), which Erasmus
answered most pleasantly (ibid., Ep. 690).
In late December 1516 Lupset went to Paris to supervise the printing
of Linacre's translations from Galen and the second edition of More's
Utopia. He studied in the university about two years but did not take a
degree. He returned home and spent several years at Corpus Christi
College, Oxford, first as student and then as lecturer in Greek and Latin,
succeeding John Clement by early 1520. He was B.A. and proceeded M.A.
1521. In the spring of 1523, he went to Padua as tutor to Thomas Winter, Wolsey's natural son, was a member of Reginald Pole's household
and a warm friend of Richard Pace. In 1525 he assisted at the Aldine
Press in the first edition of Galen in Greek.
It is difficult to date his travels and visits. Around March 1527/8 he
was again tutor to Winter, this time in Paris. He returned to England
finally in 1529. He published three English treatises, *A treatise of charitie,
An exhortation to young men*, and *A Compendious Treatise . . . of
Dieyng Well*. Lupset died of consumption in his mother's home, 27 December 1530.
4. Iulii Genius was one of the three characters in the *Iulius Exclusus e
Coelo*, probably written in 1513 or 1514, soon after the death of Pope
Julius II. It was circulated in manuscript among Erasmus' friends. A
printed version is first mentioned at the beginning of 1517. Erasmus did
not admit that he had written it, and resorted to equivocation, but not
literal mendacity (see Allen, *2*, 419 f., Ep. 908; Ferguson, pp. 35–124).

education of children from infancy, the other a consolation; they are entirely in your own handwriting, but only the first draft, and the text is incomplete. Except for this material, he swears that he has nothing else that belongs to you, which you are trying to recover. If you want these sheets forwarded, please let me know.

Right after Christmas Linacre is going to send his translation of Galen to Paris for printing. Lupset will accompany the manuscript and then stay on to correct the proof. You have no idea how happy you made him by mentioning his books in your recent letter [5] to me; believe me, he is all yours, heart and soul. The Bishop of Winchester,[6] who is, as you are aware, a very discreet person, was present at a large gathering of prominent people when the conversation turned upon you and your laborious publications; he testified, to the approval of all, that your rendering of the New Testament was as valuable for him as ten commentaries, for it shed so much light on the subject; he also said that here was a Latin translation that avoided Greek turns of expression, even apart from any other alteration that had to be made in the text of the Vulgate. Your letter has aroused my hopes, which I greedily seize upon; and from day to day I look forward to my *Utopia* with the feelings of a mother waiting for her son to return from abroad. Farewell, dearest Erasmus.

Hurriedly, from London, December 15.

I have forwarded your letter to Latimer; [7] I am sure he will comply with your wishes, and will be glad to do so. My wife [8] sends you a thousand greetings, and also thanks you for the

5. Not extant.
6. Richard Fox (c. 1446/7–1528) was present at Bosworth Field and became one of Henry VII's most trusted advisers for the next thirty years. He was rewarded with four bishoprics—Exeter, Bath and Wells, Durham, and Winchester. The first two he never had time to visit. At seventy he retired from state duties and served his dioceses. He became interested in the new classical education and founded Corpus Christi College, Oxford, in 1517, endowing it most generously, building beautifully, collecting books for its library, and choosing the President and Fellows. (See P. S. and H. M. Allen, *Letters of Richard Fox 1486–1527*).
7. See above, Letter 5, and note 19.
8. Dame Alice More.

very thoughtful wish that she may enjoy a long life; she craves
that all the more, as she says, so as to have a longer time to
pester me.

13

[31] To William Warham.

William Warham (c. 1447–1532) was educated at Winchester and
New College, Oxford, of which he was a Fellow for thirteen years.
He was LL.D. of Oxford 1488, of Cambridge 1500. In 1488 he went
to London to practise as an advocate in the Court of Arches. From
1490 on, he served often on foreign embassies, and in 1493 he received the subdiaconate and soon his first ecclesiastical preferment
(Hughes, p. 76). He was appointed Master of the Rolls 1494, Bishop
of London 1501, and Keeper of the Great Seal 1502. In 1504 he ex-
changed that office for the Chancellorship, which he resigned 22
December 1515. In 1504 also he became Archbishop of Canterbury.

He was munificent in gifts to scholars, especially to Erasmus. Because of this and much building for the church, he died very poor,
having only £30 a few days before his death, saying, "It is enough
for the journey."

The parenthetical glosses in this letter are Stapleton's, from
whose *Life of More* the text is taken.

⟨London
January 1517⟩

I ever judged your Paternity happy in the way you exercised your office of Chancellor, but I esteem you much happier
now that you have laid it down and entered on that most
desirable leisure, in which you can live for yourself and for
God. Such leisure, in my opinion, is not only more pleasant
than the labors, but more honorable than all your honors. To
be a judge is the lot of many, and sometimes of very bad
men. But you possessed that supreme office which, when re-
linquished, is as much exposed to calumny as it formerly
conferred authority and independence; and to give this up
willingly as your Paternity has with great difficulty obtained
permission to do, is what none but a moderate-minded man
would wish, and none but an innocent man dare.

I do not know which to admire the most, your modesty in
willingly laying down an office of such dignity and power,

your unworldliness in being able to despise it, or your integrity in having no fear of resignation; but in any case together with many other men I give to your action my most cordial approval as most excellent and wise. Indeed I can hardly say how heartily I congratulate you on your singular good fortune and how I rejoice in it for your sake, for I see your Paternity retiring far away from secular affairs and the bustle of the courts, and enjoying a rare glory by the honorable repute of your tenure of the Judgeship and your resignation from it. Happy in the consciousness of duty well done, you will pass the rest of your life gently and peacefully in literature and philosophy. This happy state of yours my own wretchedness makes daily more brightly attractive; for although I have no business worth mentioning (yet he was at this time a member of the Royal Council,[1] Under-treasurer of the realm, and often employed in legations) yet since feeble powers are readily oppressed by paltry affairs, I am always so distraught that I have not a free moment in which to visit your Paternity or excuse my remissness in writing—indeed I have scarcely been able to get ready this present letter.

Herewith I would beg your Lordship to accept a none too witty little book (the *Utopia*). It was written in undue haste, but a friend of mine, a citizen of Antwerp (Peter Gilles) allowed his affection to outweigh his judgment, thought it worthy of publication, and without my knowledge had it printed. Although I know it is unworthy of your high rank, your wide experience, or your learning, yet I venture to send it, relying on the generosity with which you habitually encourage all men's literary endeavors, and trusting to the favor I have always experienced from you. Thus I hope that even if the book pleases you but little, yet your good will may be extended to the Author. Farewell, my lord Archbishop.

1. More was called Councilor in the pension grant of 1516, but his actual introduction to the Privy Council seems to have been delayed to the summer of 1518.

14

[32] To a Member of the Royal Court.

⟨London
January 1517⟩

I had had it in mind to betroth my *Utopia* to Cardinal Wolsey alone (if my friend Peter [1] had not, without my knowledge, as you know, ravished her of the first flower of her maidenhood), if indeed I should betroth her to anyone and not rather keep her with me ever unwed, or perhaps consecrate her to Vesta and initiate her into Vesta's sacred fires.

15

[34] To Antonio ⟨?Bonvisi⟩.

Antonio Bonvisi came of a distinguished merchant family of Lucca in Italy, which had settled in England. Bonvisi imported wool and jewels and by 1513 had established his fortune. He was also a banker for the English government and sent money and letters to ambassadors abroad.

He was a patron of men of letters and a close friend of More's. In 1524, More sold to him Crosby Place, which he had owned for only six months. See also below, Letter 65.

⟨London
January 1517?⟩

That you have any such esteem of me issues, I suspect, from affection rather than judgment. For love, generally, when it settles deep in men, spreads darkness over their thinking. Which I see has happened to you, especially since my *Utopia* has pleased you so much, a book which I think clearly deserves to hide itself away forever in its own island.

16

[37] To Cuthbert Tunstal.

The text of this letter consists of two extracts made by Stapleton from a single and longer letter.

1. Peter Gilles of Antwerp had sent the *Utopia* to Th. Martens of Louvain for publication.

⟨London
1517?⟩

That in your letter you thank me so carefully for my services
on behalf of your friends is a mark of your great courtesy.
What I did was quite trifling: it is only your goodness that
exaggerates it. But you scarcely do justice to our friendship,
for you seem to think that what I may do puts you under an
obligation, whereas you should rather claim it as your own
and service due you. . . .

The amber which you sent me,[1] a precious sepulcher for
flies, was most acceptable on many counts. For the material in
color and brilliance can challenge any gem, and the form is
all the more excellent in that it represents a heart, a sort of
symbol of your love for me. For thus do I interpret your
meaning: as the fly, winged like Cupid and as fickle, is so shut
up and entangled in the substance of the amber that it cannot fly away, so embalmed in the aromatic juice that it cannot
perish, so your love will never fly away and always remain
unchanged.

That I have nothing to give you in return does not greatly
trouble me. For I know you do not look for an interchange
of gifts and I am quite willing to remain in your debt. But
yet I am somewhat distressed that so slender are my small
means, I cannot bear myself so dutifully as to appear not unworthy of such proofs of your friendship. Wherefore, since
I cannot prove myself to others, I must needs be content with
our joint understanding, yours and mine.

17

[43] To his Daughters and to Margaret Gyge.

More's children were by his first marriage to Jane Colt, the eldest
daughter of John Colt, a gentleman of Netherhall, Essex. Margaret,
born c. 1 October 1505, was most like her father, and was most beloved by him. She was one of the most learned women of her day,
trained in the classics, philosophy, and science. Her emendation of
Cyprian (Epistle 30.3) *neruos sinceritatis* for *nisi vos sinceritatis* was

1. Tunstal was abroad in 1517, and would probably have purchased
the amber on the Continent.

adopted by Erasmus. She translated Erasmus' *Precatio Dominica in Septem Portiones Distributa* into English in 1524, and an introduction to it was written by Richard Herde, once a tutor to the children, defending the higher education of women. She wrote a devotional treatise, *De Quattuor Nouissimis*. She also imitated the style of Quintilian, and translated Eusebius from Greek into Latin. She is portrayed as Magdalia in Erasmus' colloquy, *The Abbot and the Learned Woman*, and she and her sisters, the "Moricae," are commended.

Elizabeth, 1506, Cecily, 1507, and John, born c. 1509, were also educated in Latin, Greek, and science. John was not as gifted as his sisters, but was very well read and studious. He is evidently the "pupil" spoken of at the end of this letter and if "a bit too lazy" this time, is praised in Letter 32. Margaret Gyge was the same age as Margaret More and was perhaps the daughter of Margaret's wet-nurse. She was her equal in learning and later was proficient in medicine. She assisted More in dispensing alms and visiting the poor.

This letter seems very formal and labored. The explanation is probably that More is writing a "dialectic exercise" to answer those of the children, and thus makes it as artificial and rhetorical as theirs.

⟨1517?⟩

THOMAS MORE TO MARGARET, ELIZABETH, CECILIA, HIS DARLING DAUGHTERS, AND TO MARGARET GYGE EQUALLY DEAR, BEST GREETINGS.

I cannot adequately express, my delightful daughters, how greatly pleased I am by your charming letters and no less by the fact, as I notice, that though you are on the road moving from place to place, you yet abandon none of your habit either of dialectic exercises or writing themes or composing verse. This fully convinces me that you love me as you ought, since I observe you feel so much concern in my absence that you practise zealously what you know gives me pleasure when I am with you. When I return I shall make you realize that disposition toward me is as profitable to yourselves as I realize it is pleasurable to me. For believe me truly there is nothing which refreshes me so much in the midst of this bothersome business as reading what comes from you. Whereby I perceive the truth of what your affectionate teacher writes so affectionately that if your own letters did not declare your extraordinary devotion to literature he might appear to have indulged his affection rather than the truth. But now by what you write you win him trust and I credit the truth of his almost incredible boastings about you, the beauty and discernment of your discourses. And so I long with all my heart to hasten home so as to match my pupil in competitive audition with you; he is a bit too lazy in the matter, because he cannot give up the hope that he may find you fall short of your teacher's promise. But I harbor the hope (knowing that you are persistent) that shortly you will surpass even your teacher, if not in discourse at least in not abandoning the suit. Farewell, my darlings.

18

[57] To John Fisher.

John Fisher was born in Beverley, Yorkshire, in 1469. The son of a mercer, he was educated by his parents at the school attached to the Minster and at Michaelhouse, Cambridge. He was B.A. 1488, M.A. and Fellow of Michaelhouse 1491, and was ordained priest in that year by papal dispensation, for he was under canonical age. He was chosen Senior Proctor 1494 (an administrative officer of the university), and was elected Master of Michaelhouse in 1497. He became chaplain and confessor to Lady Margaret Beaufort, mother of Henry VII, c. 1501, and when she founded Readerships in divinity at the two universities, Fisher was the first appointed at Cambridge. He became very interested in preaching from the Bible, with quotations and illustrations. He was Vice-Chancellor twice and in 1504 was made Chancellor. In the same year he was appointed Bishop of Rochester, the smallest of the English dioceses.

Fisher assisted the Lady Margaret in the foundation of Christ's College, developed from Godshouse 1505, and wrote its Statutes. He was president of Queens' College 1505–08, and built the president's Lodge with first floor rooms for the Lady Margaret, and in her absence for Fisher. He knew Erasmus from 1505 on, particularly when he returned as Lecturer in Greek at Cambridge. He was so interested in the edition of the Greek New Testament that he began the study of Greek during a ten-day visit from Erasmus in 1516, and continued it. He also learned Hebrew.

The Lady Margaret's will provided for the foundation of St. John's College, using the old hospital of St. John the Evangelist, and Fisher gave 1500 acres of the lands bequeathed to him in her will, and £500. The emphasis on theology was strengthened by prescribed Greek and Hebrew.

Fisher was an admirable bishop, residing much in his diocese, caring for the poor and holding ordinations, duties left usually to suffragans. He wrote much in the controversies of the day. His *Of One Magdalene* was written against Lefèvre, who thought the church wrong in applying to one woman what the Gospels had said of three: the converted sinner, the sister of Martha and Lazarus, Mary of Magdala out of whom Christ cast seven devils. He answered Ulrich Velene of Minden, who thought St. Peter could not have been at Rome, so that the popes could not be his successors. He wrote *A Defence of the Assertions of the King of England against Luther's Babylonian Captivity* and answered Luther's *On the Abrogation of the Mass* by writing *The Defence of the Priesthood*. Like More, Fisher was involved in the affair of the Nun of Kent, and refused to take the Oath to the Act of Succession. His martyrdom, after long and very severe imprisonment, was on 22 June 1535.

⟨c. 1517–1518⟩

Much against my will did I come to Court (as everyone knows, and as the King himself in joke sometimes likes to reproach me). So far I keep my place there as precariously as an unaccustomed rider in his saddle. But the King (whose special favor I am far from enjoying) is so courteous and kindly to all that everyone (who is in any way hopeful) finds a ground for imagining that he is in the King's good graces, like the London wives who, as they pray before the image of the Virgin Mother of God which stands near the Tower, gaze upon it so fixedly that they imagine it smiles upon them. But I am not so fortunate as to perceive such signs of favor, nor so despondent as to imagine them. But the King has virtue and learning and makes great progress in both with almost daily renewed zeal, so that the more I see His Majesty increase in all the good and really kingly qualities, the less burdensome do I feel this life of the Court.

19

[60] To Oxford University.

Erasmus in a long letter to Mosellanus (Allen, *3*, Ep. 948, lines 182–219) gives the occasion of the letter to the University. "England has two universities, hardly anywhere uncelebrated, Cambridge and Oxford. Greek literature is taught in both, but quietly in Cambridge, because its chancellor is the Reverend Father John Fisher, Bishop of Rochester, a man theological not only in erudition but in life. But at Oxford where a young man of no ordinary learning happily teaches Greek, a barbarous preacher in a public sermon began to rage against Greek learning in great and violent abuse. But the King, who was in the neighborhood, who is himself not unlearned and is a patron of learning, having heard it from More and Pace, gave orders that those wishing and approving it should embrace Greek letters."

The parenthetical glosses in this letter are those of the translator, Prof. T. S. K. Scott-Craig.

Abingdon

29 March ⟨1518⟩

THOMAS MORE TO THE REVEREND FATHERS, THE COMMISSARY,[1]
PROCTORS, AND OTHERS OF THE GUILD OF MASTERS OF THE UNIVERSITY OF OXFORD, GREETING.

I have been wondering, gentlemen, whether I might be permitted to communicate to scholars of your distinction certain conclusions to which I have recently come. Yet I have hesitated in approaching so brilliant a group, not so much on the ground of my style as on that of seeming to give an exhibition of pride and arrogance. Who am I, the possessor of little prudence and less practice, a scholar of mediocre proportions, to arrogate to myself the right to advise you in anything? And how can I dare to offer advice in the field of letters especially, when any one of you is fitted by his wisdom and erudition to give advice in that field to thousands?

At first sight, Venerable Fathers, I was therefore deterred by your unique wisdom. But, on second thought, I was encouraged; for it occurred to me that only ignorant and arrogant fools would disdain to give a man a hearing, and that the wiser and more learned you were, the less likely you would be to think highly of yourselves or to scorn the advice of others. I was further emboldened by the thought that no one was ever harmed by just judges, such as you are above all, simply on the ground that he offered advice without thinking of the consequences. On the contrary, loyal and affectionate

1. The Commissary was the Chancellor's Deputy; now called the Vice-Chancellor.

advice, even if imprudent, has always deserved praise and thanks.

Finally, when I consider that, with God's help, I ought to offer you whatever slight learning I have acquired, since it was at your University that my education began, it seems the duty of a loyal friend not to pass over in silence what I deem it serviceable to bring to your attention. Since, then, the only danger in putting my pen to paper seemed to lie in the fact that a few might deem me too audacious, while I know that my silence would be condemned by many as ingratitude, I have preferred that the whole world should condemn my audacity rather than that anyone should have the chance to say that I showed myself ungrateful to your University, the honor of which I feel myself bound to defend to the uttermost. Moreover, no situation has, I believe, arisen in recent years, which, if you desire to maintain the honor of that institution, more urgently requires your serious attention.

The matter is as follows: when I was in London recently, I rather frequently heard that some members of your teaching body, either because they despised Greek or were simply devoted to other disciplines, or most likely because they possessed a perverse sense of humor, had proceeded to form a society named after the Trojans. The senior sage christened himself Priam; others called themselves Hector, Paris, and so forth; the idea, whether as a joke or a piece of anti-Greek academic politics, being to pour ridicule on those devoted to the study of Greek. And I hear that things have come to such a pass that no one can admit in public or private that he enjoys Greek, without being subjected to the jeers of these ludicrous "Trojans," who think Greek is a joke for the simple reason that they don't know what good literature is. To these modern "Trojans" applies the old saw, "Trojans always learn too late."

The affair aroused much comment, all very critical; and I myself felt somewhat bitter that even a few academics among you had nothing better to do in their spare time than to cast slurs on their colleagues' subjects. But I kept in mind that one could not expect the whole crowd of academics to possess wisdom, temperance, and humility; and so I began to dismiss the matter as a triviality. However, since I have been here in Abingdon in attendance at the court of His Victorious Majesty (Henry VIII), I have found that the silliness is developing into a form of insanity. For one of the "Trojans," a scholar in his own estimation, a wit of the first water in that of his friends, though slightly deranged in that of anyone observing his actions, has chosen during Lent to babble in a sermon against not only Greek but Roman literature, and finally against all polite learning, liberally berating all the liberal arts.

His whole performance was of a piece. Perhaps such a body of nonsense could not be preached on the basis of any sensible text; in any case, he followed neither the old custom of elucidating a whole passage of Scripture, nor the recent one of expounding some few words of Scripture; instead he elaborated on some stupid British proverbs. So I have no doubt that his frivolous sermon very deeply disturbed those who heard it; since I see that all who have heard fragmentary reports of it are unfavorably impressed.

What man in the audience, in whose breast burned even a spark of Christianity, would not groan at the degradation of the royal office of sacred preaching, which gained the world for Christ—above all at the hands of those whose supreme duty it was to protect it with the authority of their office? Who could possibly have devised a more outrageous insult than for an avowed preacher, during the most solemn season of the Church's year, in the presence of a large Christian congregation, in the sanctuary itself, from the elevation of the pulpit (as it were from the throne of Christ), and in view of the Sacred Body of Christ, to turn a Lenten sermon into Bacchanalian ravings? What a look must have been on the faces of the audience, who had come to hear spiritual wisdom, and saw the laughable pantomime he put on in the pulpit! They had expected to listen in reverence to the Word of Life; when they departed, all they could record they had heard was an attack on humane letters and a defamation of the preaching office by a fatuous preacher.

It would have been no reproach to secular learning if some good man, who had retired from the world to monastic life, suddenly returned and used this speaker's phrases: "much in watchings, much in prayer" or "the path to be trod by those who seek for heaven" or "other matters, like humanistic education, trivial if not a positive hindrance to the spiritual life," or "simple country folk, and the unlettered, flying quicker to heaven," etc., etc. All this could have been borne from such a man. His simplicity would have been pardoned by his audience. They would have generously admitted his saintliness, and given serious consideration to his piety, devotion, and righteousness. But when they saw a man with the academic ermine over his shoulders, step on to the platform in the midst of a gathering composed solely of academics, and calmly proceed to rant against all humane learning, one would have had to be stone blind not to notice a signal pride and wickedness, a positive hatred of the higher arts. Many must have wondered indeed how such a man could get the idea that he had to preach either about Latin, of which he did not know much, or about the liberal arts, of which he knew less, or about Greek —in which he could not even grunt that it was "all Greek" to him!

If such an abundance of material had been supplied by the seven deadly sins, an altogether suitable theme for sermons, who would have believed him totally inexperienced therein! Though, as a matter of fact, what is it but sloth, when one is in the habit of denouncing rather than of learning that of which one is ignorant? And what is it but hatred, when one defames those who know what one deprecates but does not comprehend? And what is it but supreme pride, when he wishes no kind of knowledge to be prized save what he has falsely persuaded himself that he knows, and when he even—not from modesty, as might be the case with other people—arrogates more praise to himself for his ignorance than for his knowledge?

Now as to the question of humanistic education being secular. No one has ever claimed that a man needed Greek and Latin, or indeed any education in order to be saved. Still, this education which he calls secular does train the soul in virtue. In any event, few will question that humanistic education is the chief, almost the sole reason why men come to

Oxford; children can receive a good education at home from their mothers, all except cultivation and book learning. Moreover, even if men come to Oxford to study theology, they do not start with that discipline. They must first study the laws of human nature and conduct, a thing not useless to theologians; without such study they might possibly preach a sermon acceptable to an academic group, without it they would certainly fail to reach the common man. And from whom could they acquire such skill better than from the poets, orators, and historians?

Moreover, there are some who through knowledge of things natural (i.e. rational) construct a ladder by which to rise to the contemplation of things supernatural; they build a path to theology through philosophy and the liberal arts, which this man condemns as secular; they adorn the queen of heaven with the spoils of the Egyptians! This fellow declares that only theology should be studied; but if he admits even that, I don't see how he can accomplish his aim without some knowledge of languages, whether Hebrew or Greek or Latin; unless, of course, the elegant gentleman has convinced himself that there is enough theology written in English or that all theology can be squeezed into the limits of those (late scholastic) "questions" which he likes to pose and answer, for which a modicum of Latin would, I admit, suffice.

But really, I cannot admit that theology, that august queen of heaven, can be thus confined. Does she not dwell and abide in Holy Scripture? Does she not pursue her pilgrim way through the cells of the holy Fathers: Augustine and Jerome; Ambrose and Cyprian; Chrysostom, Gregory, Basil, and their like? The study of theology has been solidly based on these now despised expositors of fundamental truth during all the Christian centuries until the invention of these petty and meretricious "questions" which alone are today glibly tossed back and forth. Anyone who boasts that he can understand the works of the Fathers without an uncommon acquaintance with the languages of each and all of them will in his ignorance boast for a long time before the learned trust his judgment.

But if this foolish preacher pretends that he was not con-

demning humanistic education in general but only an immoderate thirst for it, I can't see that this desire was such a
sin that he had to deal with it in a public assembly, as if it
were causing society to rush headlong to ruin. I haven't heard
that many have gone so far in such studies that they will soon
be overstepping the golden mean. Further, this fellow, just
to show how immoderate *he* could be in a sermon, specifically
called students of Greek "heretics," teachers of Greek "chief
devils," and pupils in Greek "lesser devils" or, more modestly
and facetiously as he thought, "little *devils*"; and the zeal of
this holy man drove him to call by the name of devil one whom
everybody knows the Devil himself could hardly bear to see
occupy a pulpit. He did everything but name that one (D. Erasmus), as everybody realized just as clearly as they realized the
folly of the speaker.

Joking aside—I have no desire to pose as the sole defender
of Greek learning; for I know how obvious it must be to
scholars of your eminence that the study of Greek is tried and
true. To whom is it *not* obvious that to the Greeks we owe all
our precision in the liberal arts generally and in theology particularly; for the Greeks either made the great discoveries
themselves or passed them on as part of their heritage. Take
philosophy, for example. If you leave out Cicero and Seneca,
the Romans wrote their philosophy in Greek or translated it
from Greek.

I need hardly mention that the New Testament is in Greek,
or that the best New Testament scholars were Greeks and
wrote in Greek. I am but repeating the consensus of scholarship when I say: however much was translated of old from
Greek, and however much more has been recently and better
translated, not half of Greek learning has yet been made available to the West; and, however good the translations have
been, the text of the original still remains a surer and more
convincing presentation. For that very reason all the Doctors
of the Latin Church—Jerome, Augustine, Bede, and a host
of others—assiduously gave themselves to learning Greek; and
even though many works had already been translated, they
were much more accustomed to reading them in the original
than are many of our contemporaries who claim to be erudite;

nor did they merely learn it themselves, but counseled those among their successors who wanted to be theologians above all to do the same.

So it is not as if I were just giving your Worships good advice about preserving the study of Greek. I am rather exhorting you to do your duty. You should not allow anyone in your university to be frightened away from the study of Greek, either by public assemblies or private inanities, since Greek is a subject required in every place of learning by the Church Universal. Common sense is surely enough to convince you that not all of your number who give themselves to the study of Greek can be blockheads; in fact, it is in part from these studies that your university had acquired its pedagogical prestige both at home and abroad.

There seems to be an increasing number of cases where Oxford has benefited from the presence of men nominally studying Greek only, but really taking the whole liberal arts course. It will be a wonder if their enthusiasm for you does not evaporate when they realize that so serious an enterprise is held in such contempt. Just think, too, what they are doing at Cambridge, which you have always outshone; those who are *not* studying Greek are so moved by common interest in their university that they are actually making large individual contributions to the salary of the Greek professor!

You see what I mean; and much more could be said to the point by men with better minds than mine. All I am doing is warning you of what others are saying and thinking, not telling you what it behooves you to do. You see much better than I that, if wicked factions are not suppressed at birth, a contagious disease will spread, and the better half be slowly absorbed by the worse, and that outsiders will be forced to take a hand in helping the good and wise among you. Any former student of the university takes its welfare as much to heart as you who are its living members. And I am sure that the Reverend Father in Christ who occupies the See of Canterbury (William Warham), who is the Primate of all our Clergy, and who is also the Chancellor of your university will not fail to do his part. Whether for the clergy's sake or yours, he rightly feels interested in preventing the decay of learning; and learn-

Lincoln Christian College

ing will perish if the university continues to suffer from the
contentions of lazy idiots, and the liberal arts are allowed to
be made sport of with impunity. And what about the Reverend Father in Christ, the Cardinal of York (Thomas Wolsey),
who is both a patron of learning and himself the most learned
of the episcopate? Would he endure patiently if aspersions
were cast in your university on the liberal arts and the study
of languages? Will he not rather aim the shafts of his learning,
virtue, and authority at these witless detractors from the arts?

Last but not least: what of our Most Christian King? His
Sacred Majesty has cultivated all the liberal arts as much as
ever a king did; indeed, he possesses greater erudition and
judgment than any previous monarch. Will his wisdom and
piety suffer him to allow the liberal arts to fail—through the
interests of evil and lazy men—in a place where his most illustrious ancestors wished that there be an illustrious seat of
letters, a place which is an ancient nursery of learning, whose
products have been an ornament not only to England but to
the whole Church, a place which possesses so many colleges
that have perpetual endowments specially designated for the
support of students (in which respect there is no university
outside the kingdom that can compare with Oxford), a place
in which the aim of all its colleges and the purpose of all its
endowments is none other than that a great body of academics,
delivered from the necessity of earning their daily bread,
might there pursue the liberal arts?

I have no doubt that you yourselves will easily in your
wisdom find a way to end this dispute and quiet these stupid
factions; that you will see to it not only that all the liberal
arts may be free from derision and contempt but that they
shall be held in dignity and honor. By such diligence in intellectual pursuits you will reap benefit for yourselves; and
it can hardly be said how much you will gain favor with our
Illustrious Prince and with the above-mentioned Reverend
Fathers in Christ. You will forge an almost miraculous bond
between yourselves and myself, who have thought that all this
had to be written now in my own hand out of my deep personal affection for you. You know that my services are at the
disposal of each and all of you. May God preserve your

glorious seat of learning unharmed; and may He grant that
it flourish continually in virtue and in all the liberal arts.
Abingdon *29th March* ⟨1518⟩

THOMAS MORE

20

[63] To William Gonell.

William Gonell (d. 28 August 1560) was probably a schoolmaster
at Landbeach in Cambridgeshire when Erasmus first knew him. He
was recommended by Erasmus to More, who chose him as tutor to
his children. He was also a member of the household of Cardinal
Wolsey. West, the Bishop of Ely, appointed him to the living of
Conington in Huntingdonshire 6 September 1517, but he evidently
remained some time longer as tutor in More's family.

Other tutors were John Clement, "Master Drew," Nicholas Kratzer the astronomer, and Richard Herde, who died on a mission to
Spain in 1528 (*L.P. 4*, 4090, 4103).

At Court

22 May ⟨1518?⟩

I have received, my dear Gonell, your letter, elegant and
full of affection as always. Your devotion to my children I
perceive from your letter, your diligence from theirs. Everyone's letter pleased me greatly, but above all that I notice
Elizabeth shows a modesty of character in the absence of her
mother, which not every girl would show in her mother's
presence. Let her understand that such conduct delights me
more than all the learning in the world. Though I prefer
learning joined with virtue to all the treasures of kings, yet
renown for learning, if you take away moral probity, brings
nothing else but notorious and noteworthy infamy, especially
in a woman. Since erudition in women is a new thing and a
reproach to the sloth of men, many will gladly assail it, and
impute to learning what is really the fault of nature, thinking from the vices of the learned to get their own ignorance
esteemed as virtue. On the other hand, if a woman (and this
I desire and hope with you as their teacher for all my daughters) to eminent virtue of mind should add even moderate
skill in learning, I think she will gain more real good than

if she obtain the riches of Croesus and the beauty of Helen. Not because that learning will be a glory to her, though learning will accompany virtue as a shadow does a body, but because the reward of wisdom is too solid to be lost with riches or to perish with beauty, since it depends on the inner knowledge of what is right, not on the talk of men, than which nothing is more foolish or mischievous.

For as it becomes a good man to avoid infamy, so to lay oneself out for renown is the sign of a man who is not only arrogant, but ridiculous and miserable. A mind must be uneasy which ever wavers between joy and sadness because of other men's opinions. Among all the benefits that learning bestows on men, I think there is none more excellent than that by study we are taught to seek in that very study not praise, but utility. Such has been the teaching of the most learned men, especially of philosophers, who are the guides of human life, although some may have abused learning, like other good things, simply to court empty glory and popular renown.

I have written at length on not pursuing glory, my dear Gonell, because of what you say in your letter, that Margaret's lofty and exalted character of mind should not be debased. In this judgment I quite agree with you; but to me, and, no doubt, to you also, that man would seem to debase a generous character of mind who would accustom it to admire what is vain and low. He, on the contrary, raises it who rises to virtue and true goods, and who looks down with contempt from the contemplation of the sublime, on those shadows of good things which almost all mortals, through ignorance of truth, greedily snatch at as if they were true goods.

Therefore, my dearest Gonell, since I thought we must walk by this road, I have often begged not you only, who, out of your exceptional affection for all my family, would do it of your own accord, nor only my wife, who is sufficiently urged by her truly maternal love for them, which has been proved to me in many ways, but absolutely all my friends, continually to warn my children to avoid as it were the precipices of pride and haughtiness, and to walk in the pleasant meadows of modesty: not to be dazzled at the sight of gold; not to lament the lack of what they erroneously admire in others; not to think more of themselves for gaudy trappings, nor less for the want of them; not to deform the beauty that nature has given them by neglect, nor to try to heighten it by artifice; to put virtue in the first place among goods, learning in the second; and in their studies to esteem most whatever may teach them piety towards God, charity to all, and modesty and Christian humility in themselves. By such means they will receive from God the reward of an innocent life, and in the assured expectation of it will view death without dread, and meanwhile possessing solid joy will neither be puffed up by the empty praise of men, nor dejected by evil tongues. These I consider the real and genuine fruits of learning, and though I admit that all literary men do not possess them, I would maintain that those who give themselves to study with such intent will easily attain their end and become perfect.

Nor do I think that the harvest is much affected whether it is a man or a woman who does the sowing. They both have the name of human being whose nature reason differentiates from that of beasts; both, I say, are equally suited for the knowledge of learning by which reason is cultivated, and, like plowed land, germinates a crop when the seeds of good precepts have been sown. But if the soil of a woman be naturally bad, and apter to bear fern than grain, by which saying many keep women from study, I think, on the contrary, that a woman's wit is the more diligently to be cultivated, so that nature's defect may be redressed by industry. This was the opinion of the ancients, both the wisest and the most saintly. Not to speak of the rest, Jerome and Augustine not only exhorted excellent matrons and honorable virgins to study, but also, in order to assist them, diligently explained the abstruse meanings of the Scriptures, and wrote for tender girls letters replete with so much erudition that nowadays old men who call themselves doctors of sacred literature can scarcely read them correctly, much less understand them. Do you, my learned Gonell, have the kindness to see that my daughters thoroughly learn these works of saintly men. From them they will learn in particular what goal they should set for their studies, and the whole fruit of their endeavors should consist in the testimony of God and a good conscience. Thus they will be inwardly calm and at peace and neither stirred by praise of flatterers nor stung by the follies of unlearned mockers of learning.

But I fancy that I now hear you object that these precepts, though true, are beyond the tender years of my daughters, since you will scarcely find a man, however old and advanced in study, whose mind is so fixed and firm as not to be tickled sometimes with desire of glory. But, dear Gonell, the more do I see the difficulty of getting rid of this pest of pride, the more do I see the necessity of getting to work at it from childhood. For I find no other reason why this inescapable evil so clings to our hearts, than that almost as soon as we are born, it is sown in the tender minds of children by their nurses, it is cultivated by their teachers, it is nourished and brought to maturity by their parents; while no one teaches anything, even the good, without bidding them always to expect praise as the recompense and prize of virtue. Thus long accustomed to magnify praise, they strive to please the greater number (that is, the worse) and end by being ashamed to be good. That this plague of vainglory may be banished far from my children, may you, my dear Gonell, and their mother and all their friends, sing this song to them, and repeat it, and beat it into their heads, that vainglory is despicable, and to be spit upon, and that there is nothing more sublime than that humble modesty so often praised by Christ; and this your prudent charity will so enforce as to teach virtue rather than reprove vice, and make them love good advice instead of hating it. To this purpose nothing will more conduce than to read to them the lessons of the ancient Fathers, who, they know, cannot be angry with them; and, as they honor them for their sanctity, they must needs be much moved by their authority. If you will read something of this sort, besides their reading of Sallust—to Margaret and Elizabeth, who are more mature than John and Cecily—you will bind me and them, already in your debt, still more to you. And besides you will make my children who are dear to me first by the law of nature, and then dearer by learning and virtue, most dear by such advancement in knowledge and good character. Farewell.

From the Court, on the vigil of Pentecost.

21

[65] To William Budaeus.

Guillaume Budé, born in Paris 26 January 1467, went to his parish school and then to the University of Orléans to study for the practice of law. He came of a family of state officials and his father was able to secure his appointment as a royal secretary, but he resigned soon after the accession of Louis XII. He devoted himself to the serious study of Latin and Greek and became the most distinguished Greek scholar in Europe. After the death of his parents he had a small competence adequate for his scholar's life. c. 1505–06 he married Roberte Le Lieur, aged fifteen. He said that Philology would give him a posterity of books which would assure the memory of his name, but life gave him more children than books. Six sons were born and then a daughter, whom he said he loved best of all, and later a seventh son and a second daughter. Six sons and a daughter survived.

He established his reputation as a scholar by the publication in 1508 of *Annotations on the Pandects,* which discarded the old glosses and restored the text by study of the manuscripts. In March 1515 he published *Concerning the As,* the Roman measure and coin, originally a pound weight of uncoined copper. It was a book of 800 pages, addressed "to all men of good faith who are students of liberal arts and philosophy." The work was original, and was of importance to scholars in every field of the study of ancient times. The meaning of the words used in Greek and Latin with regard to wealth had been completely lost. Budé tried to find the exact sense which the different names of money and measures had for the ancients and to determine their absolute value so as to be able to make comparisons between Roman times and the sixteenth century. He weighed Roman coins of different periods and saw that gold content was gradually diminished. Surprised at Pliny's statement concerning the value of a pearl in Cleopatra's possession, he went to a jeweler, saw a fine pearl, and thought Pliny's value not impossible. His quotations from many ancient writers, and his own digressions on Roman wealth and extravagance were of great value to sixteenth-century scholarship. He published a Greek lexicon in 1529. His last work, *Of the Transition from Hellenism to Christianity,* appeared in 1535.

He was influential with Jean du Bellay, Bishop of Narbonne, in

persuading Francis I to found a Trilingual College (later the Col-
lège de France) and the Library at Fontainebleau (now one of the
collections in the Bibliothèque Nationale). He was suspected of
Protestantism, and after his death in 1540 his widow professed that
faith at Geneva.

Budé wrote to More 9 September 1518, thanking him for a pair
of English dogs which More had sent in gratitude for Budé's recommendation of the *Utopia*. He spoke of the recent birth of his seventh
son—which child he lost.

He introduced Nicholas Bérault of Orléans to More, as he set
out on an embassy with Stephen Poncher, Bishop of Paris, to England. I have corrected "Beroaldus" (for Philip Beroaldus, died 30
August 1518), whose career was in Italy, to "Beraldus," Nicholas
Bérault, c. 1470 – c. 1545, the distinguished French scholar of Latin
and Greek (see introduction to Ep. 42 in *Correspondence*, and
Allen, *3*, 503–04). More wrote Budé, "I have hardly ever met a more
learned man or a more pleasant companion."

⟨c. August 1518⟩

I never skim any of your works, but study them seriously
as works of the first importance. To your treatise, however,
on Roman Measures I gave a very special attention such as I
have given to no ancient author. For that it cannot be understood in any cursory way, you have provided by your careful
choice of words, your well-balanced sentences, the studied
gravity of your diction, and not least by the serious and difficult nature of the matters you treat of—matters almost lost
in antiquity, and requiring the deepest research. But yet if
anyone will turn his eyes to what you have written and give
it careful and continued attention, he will find that the light
you have thrown upon your subject brings the dead past to
life again. Whilst he ponders your words, he will live in
imagination through all the past ages, and will be able to
gaze upon, to count and almost to take into his hands, the
hoarded wealth of all kings, tyrants and nations, which is
almost more than any misers have been able to do.

I can hardly enumerate the multitude of reasons for which
I am attached to you, my dear Budaeus. You are so exceed-
ingly good to me: whomsoever I love, you, by good fortune,
love also: you possess so many excellent virtues: your tem-
perament, as I judge, hardly differs from mine: you have

earned the gratitude of all men for your useful literary labors:
though a married man you have happily acquired a degree
of learning that was once the exclusive possession of the
clergy. Indeed I am hardly content to call you a layman when
by your splendid gifts you are so highly raised beyond the
level of the laity.

22

[69] To Margaret More.

⟨1518⟩

I was delighted to receive your letter, my dearest Margaret,
informing me of Shaw's [1] condition. Later letters will be even
more delightful if they have told me of the studies you and
your brother are engaged in, of your daily reading, your
pleasant discussions, your essays, of the swift passage of the
days made joyous by literary pursuits. For although everything you write gives me pleasure, yet the most exquisite
delight of all comes from reading what none but you and
your brother could have written. (And the letter concludes:) [2]
I beg you, Margaret, tell me about the progress you are all
making in your studies. For I assure you that, rather than
allow my children to be idle and slothful, I would make a
sacrifice of wealth, and bid adieu to other cares and business,
to attend to my children and my family, amongst whom none
is more dear to me than yourself, my beloved daughter.
Farewell.

23

[70] To Margaret More.

⟨1518⟩

You are too bashful and timid in your request for money,
from a father who wants to give it and when you have greeted
me with a letter such that I would not only repay each line of

1. Shai (genitive). The English form of the name was probably Shaw,
but we have no clue as to who he was.
2. The parenthetical comment is Stapleton's.

it with a gold Philippeus (as Alexander did with Choerilos),[1] but, if my means were as great as my desire, I would reward each syllable with two ounces of gold. As it is, I send only what you have asked, but would have added more, except that as I am eager to give, so I like to be asked and coaxed by my daughter, especially by you, whom virtue and learning have made so dear to my heart. So the sooner you spend this money well, as you always do, and the sooner you ask for more, the more will you be sure of pleasing your father. Farewell, my dearest daughter.

24

[72, Allen, 3, 907] To Erasmus.

John Clement was one of the first pupils in Dean Colet's new school. From there he went to More's household, continued the study of Greek and was tutor to the More children. He accompanied More to the Low Countries in 1515, met Peter Gilles in Antwerp, and is represented in the *Utopia* as having heard the account of that commonwealth by Raphael Hythloday. In the prefatory letter to Gilles, More reported Clement's progress in Latin and Greek.

In 1518 he entered the service of Cardinal Wolsey, and Erasmus advised him to learn to write when standing in his position as gentleman-in-waiting. In 1519 he was Lecturer in Rhetoric and Reader in Greek at Cardinal College. He resigned the next year to devote all his time to the study of medicine and was succeeded by Lupset. He seems first to have gone to Louvain and later to Italy, where he studied several years and was promoted M.D. at Siena, 30 March 1525. He worked with Lupset on the Aldine edition of Galen's works in Greek. He was in royal service from 1525 and the King's physician from 1528. In 1526 probably, he married Margaret Gyge, More's very learned foster-daughter. He was elected in 1544 to the presidency of the Royal College of Physicians.

The Clement family remained loyal to the Catholic faith. Probably the More circle was protected by the sympathy of Bishop Bonner until the passing of the first Act of Uniformity in 1549. Clement fled overseas in July, and Margaret joined him in October, after making an inventory of their books and other possessions. Under Mary they were able to return to England, and through litigation regained their property or were compensated for what they had lost. Under Elizabeth they were again forced into exile and lived in Mechlin. Margaret died in 1570, Dr. Clement in 1572.

1. Choerilos was a worthless Greek poet, whom Alexander thus rewarded beyond his merits.

⟨London?
1518?⟩

My Clement lectures at Oxford to an audience larger
than has ever gathered to any other lecturer. It is astonishing
how universal is the approbation and the love he gains. Even
those to whom classical literature was almost anathema now
show attachment to him, attend his lectures, and gradually
modify their opposition. Linacre, who, as you know, never
praises anyone extravagantly, cannot contain his admiration
for his learning, so that, although I love Clement so much,
I am almost tempted to envy him for the high praises heaped
upon him.

25

[82] To Martin Dorp.

After More's letter (No. 4) to him, Dorp changed his point of
view entirely. In July 1516 he began lectures on the Epistles of St.
Paul and in the important *Oratio* which preceded them avowed his
faith in humanism. He admitted that any deep study of St. Paul's
letters required a thorough knowledge of Greek and, as he did not
have it, said he was glad to use the learned writings of Valla, Lefèvre, and, most important of all, Erasmus.

Erasmus immediately heard the good news in Brussels from
Paludanus, who gave him an account of the lecture. Erasmus' edition of the Greek New Testament had been published 27 April,
and had caused great anxiety to the conservatives. As the supporter
of Erasmus, Dorp was refused permission to lecture during the
academic year beginning 1 October. The reproof was doubly unpleasant as he was president of the College of the Holy Ghost, for
students of theology only.

Dorp then shocked Erasmus and his friends by a second change
to complete disagreement. This irked Erasmus greatly and he showed
it in a number of his letters, speaking of Dorp as "that egregious
N." Dorp's reversal was evidently caused by the appearance of the
Greek New Testament, but even those who disagreed with Erasmus'
critical annotations were annoyed at Dorp's second shift of opinion.
Erasmus soon came to see, however, that Dorp hurt him less than
he did his own reputation.

Erasmus wrote two severe letters to Dorp in November 1516.
Mutual friends thought these brought repentance, but Dorp's reply
showed vanity much more than penitence. Vanity was his recurring
fault. He enjoyed the adulation of the theological faculty.

Erasmus needed the support of the University of Louvain, as he worked on a second edition of his "Novum Instrumentum." He hoped to renew the life of the Church by methodical study of the Bible, and he rejoiced in the encouragement of being co-opted by the theologians on 30 September 1517, evidently solemn approval of his work on the New Testament.

Outside Louvain, Dorp was unfortunately known for his defection from, rather than for his usual support of, Erasmus. He was humiliated by this criticism and fearful of a war of pamphlets against him. To break with his late allies, the theologians, he decided to publish his *Oratio* of 1516. It appeared in Antwerp, 27 September 1519, dedicated to Beatus Rhenanus, since he most feared opposition from Basel or that neighborhood. Probably about mid-October Dorp left for a visit to Holland, and during his absence heard news of Erasmus' difficulties in the university. When Dorp returned to Louvain, he was "ejected" from his college room and resigned his presidency of the College of the Holy Ghost. He asked to continue university lecturing. The ejection from the college is probably the "opprobrium" to which More refers.

Dorp asked Erasmus to mention him in letters, especially to More, Pace, Rhenanus, Ulrich von Hutten, and Budé. This Erasmus did. More's letter was written in most generous spirit. It must have been composed between the publication of the *Oratio* in September 1519 and the reconciliation of scholars with Dorp in March 1520.

The text consists of two extracts made by Stapleton.

〈London

1519〉

I easily foresaw that you would one day think otherwise than then you thought. But really that you would not only become wiser, but even in a most elaborate address testify that you had changed, and that so openly, genuinely, and categorically, this indeed went far beyond not only my expectation, but also the hopes and almost prayers of all, for your action manifested incredible probity and utter self-restraint. For though nothing indeed is more usual than to change one's opinion about a matter, yet nothing is anywhere more rare than, after you have once declared your view and then confirmed it by assertion, and then defended it with vehemence, after all that to reverse course upon realizing the truth and return once again to the harbor from which you sailed, as though your voyage had been vain. Believe me, my dear Dorp, what you have done with such great humility, you would have asked in vain of those whom the world nowadays considers most humble. Men are almost all so foolish in their misdirected shame that they prefer to proclaim that they are fools now, than own that they ever were. How much more virtuously have you acted, my dear Dorp. Although you are so keen-witted, so learned and so eloquent that if you pleased to defend anything, even what appeared improbable or absolutely paradoxical, you could yet prove it to your readers, yet in your love of truth rather than shams you have preferred to declare to all men that you were once deceived, rather than go on deceiving.

But what am I to say of the further act of modesty by which you have surpassed that exceptional modesty? Although it was due to your own happy talent that you saw the truth, yet you chose to ascribe it to the admonitions of others, and even to mine. Thus although the first rank in wisdom is yours by right, and is given to you by all men's votes, yet you alone thrust yourself down to the second rank. Learned men must thrust you back into first rank, with their elbows if necessary. For that letter of mine was wordy rather than convincing; and when I compare it with your address, so eloquent, so full of close-packed and cogent arguments, I see quite clearly, my dear Dorp, and to my shame that my letter had no power to change you, although out of courtesy or modesty you now yield to it praise which belongs to you and which, the more you avoid it, will all the more surely follow you. So, my very dear Dorp, you must consider that the rarer the occurrence of an act like yours, the more it has gained for you of true glory, which will never die.

If they go on boldly in the path they have chosen, attempting to suppress good learning and to drive it from the schools, in a very short time I expect to see a marvelous change. Learned men will arise everywhere. Those teachers in the public academies who now look on such studies with indifference will themselves be accounted but indifferently learned. It vexes me, my dear Dorp, to think of these things, because I cannot help feeling a certain pity for those who by the action of a few bigoted partisans are undeservedly compromised.

But the praise that will be your portion is a far more agreeable thought to me than their opprobrium.

26

[83] To a Monk.

Dom David Knowles has identified More's correspondent for the first time. He was evidently John Batmanson, the only English monk who attacked Erasmus' edition of the Greek New Testament. He was probably the son of John Batmanson, Doctor of Laws of Seville, by his first wife Margaret. He was ordained deacon by the Bishop of London, Fitzjames, on 31 March 1510, when he would have been about twenty-two. He was Prior of Hinton 1523–29 and of the London Charterhouse 1529–31. See *The Religious Orders in England, 3* (Cambridge, 1959), 469.

He wrote *Contra Annotationes Erasmi Roterodami* and other books, which were not printed and which are not found in English collections of manuscripts. His name does not appear in degree lists of Oxford or Cambridge. The youthfulness of More's correspondent and the statement that he was self-taught agree with the facts we know of John Batmanson's life. A *Retractatio* of some of his writings is the last in a list of his books. He died at the Charterhouse 16 November 1531, and was buried in the monastery.

Only the second part of this letter (lines 693–1555 in *Correspondence*) is reprinted in this edition. The first section deals in great detail with the monk's criticisms of Erasmus' *New Testament*. More then proceeds, in the selection given here, to a more general consideration of the issues at stake.

⟨1519–20⟩

LETTER OF THE DISTINGUISHED GENTLEMAN THOMAS MORE IN WHICH HE REFUTES THE ANGRY AND ABUSIVE CHARGES OF A CERTAIN MONK WHOSE IGNORANCE WAS EQUALED BY HIS PRIDE.

And so you decide the goal of Erasmus' toil—to cause discord and bring deception. Yes, by all means, he does confuse the poor simple people who would never give a thought to his writings, were it not that certain persons, like another Cain,[1] are goaded on by jealousy when noticing with downcast countenance that the smoke rises up from their brother's sacrifice, but curves downward from their own, and make

1. Gen. 4:5.

every attempt possible to murder the innocent one by their damnable disparagement, by assaulting the known truth, and by stirring up the simple people with their cries of sedition. By holding their tongue, they might have let those people remain undisturbed, but having aroused them with lying reports, they ought to have calmed them down again by telling the truth. Besides, those are the fellows who create wild discord; realizing their inability to defend their case in the presence of intellectual men, they stand before the unlettered rabble and carp at Erasmus' labors intended for men of letters, and rudely force learned matters upon unlearned ears, and chase after the silly applause of the rabble, because they are incapable of giving satisfaction to the wise. If, however, they said nothing about such matters to the rabble or at least told the truth, there would be no discord. For why will discord arise when different translators use different words with the same meaning? On this point one could quote your own words against you, which you took from Ambrose,[2] and recently threw up to Erasmus—"The man who agrees with my meaning, agrees with my words." But you express the fear that such a principle could soon result in the production of an endless number of editions, since (you say) there are not a few men in the world equal to, or even superior to Erasmus in the knowledge of Greek. I do not know what number you consider more than a few; but if you begin to list them by name, I am positive you will find that the number of his peers is less than a few, and the number of his superiors, perhaps, less than one,[3] if you also include a scholarly study of Sacred Scripture; for, lacking that, even a thorough mastery of the language will find this field of learning beyond its strength. I have no doubt that the result of Erasmus' labors will be the eventual emergence of many new translators of the same matter; while it is very possible that some of these interpreters will, with self-assurance, grasp the meaning of one or the other passage with greater accuracy, still I do not anticipate anyone so learned or so brash as to

2. Ambrose, *Exposition of St. Luke* 2.42.
3. Only Budé his superior, and he not a biblical scholar.

entertain the idea that some day he will, by making a new version of the whole work which Erasmus had previously translated, produce something comparable to the effort.

Supposing there would be several editions; what harm would result? What you fear, Saint Augustine considers extremely useful; while they could not all be of equal value, still one has a more suitable translation of one passage, another of another passage. But, you object, such a situation will raise doubts in the reader's mind as to which one of the many editions he should trust most of all; that is a valid objection, if the reader is such an absolute blockhead as to lack both brains and judgment. If, on the other hand, he has intelligence, it will be all the easier for him, as Augustine says, to choose from the various versions the accurate rendering. Now tell me, why do you fear that a great risk is involved in a variety of versions even at variance with one another, since you take no offense at all in reading the manifold explanations of the commentators, who, in commenting on the identical text, come to no agreement at all on the meaning of the text, and very often those discrepancies have a value in that they provide an opportunity for scholars to think and judge for themselves? To conclude this point, at least the Psalms with their different versions and variant readings, offer clear evidence of the value of having a variety of editions, and also of the fact that no confusion results in the Church; nor will anything else be of greater assistance to one who decides to apply himself diligently to a thorough study of the Psalms, unless he is so foolish as to think it is enough to have read the decrees of the Council of Vienne.[4]

I almost overlooked a point which in your opinion is very strong, but in mine so flabby and weak as to be bowled over with a single breath. As I notice that you consider it the most impregnable point of your defense, I have decided to quote your own words, so you cannot complain I am distorting your arguments in reporting them. Your words are: "I am

4. See the *Catholic Encyclopedia*, *"Commentaries"* on the importance of the decree of the Council of Vienne, 1311, which ordained that chairs of Hebrew, Chaldean, and Arabic be established at Paris, Oxford, Bologna, and Salamanca.

completely puzzled by the blindness of many people who think that anything traceable back to Greek or Hebrew manuscripts has been well done, since it is clear to all that, as an effect of the faithlessness of the Jews and the various aberrations of the Greeks, their manuscript copies would likewise be extraordinarily distorted and replete with the dregs of their manifold errors. Furthermore, because of their great antiquity, these manuscripts are necessarily more defective than ours. At present I shall omit the testimony given by Saint Jerome that even in his day the Latin copies were in a better state of preservation than the Greek or Hebrew." What causes you to be so puzzled, I am thoroughly at a loss to imagine; you ought easily to understand that ages ago all these same objections were made to Saint Jerome and completely refuted. First of all, he considers it silly to believe that an entire nation could plot a falsification of absolutely all the books. Not to speak of other drawbacks involved in that explanation, the conspirators could never entertain the slightest hope that their deed would remain hidden indefinitely, and, once the plot was revealed, they could be sure their case was lost on their own evidence, since it would be a known fact that they had supported a suit defensible, on their own admission, only through a distortion of the texts. The impossibility of maintaining the secrecy of a plot known to all the people is perceptible, I imagine, even to you. A further point, which I think you also realize: Since apostasy from the Hebrews to the Christians, and with equal eagerness from the Greeks to the Latins was a daily occurrence, such a falsification of the texts would have come to light immediately. Besides, since books in both languages not only were in the hands of the pagans, but also were readily available to those of the true faith, one must conclude that the latter either, as a favor to the former, distorted the text of their own copies, or, with the help of their genuine copies, refuted their deception. And furthermore, in matters of controversy between ourselves and the Greeks, or the Hebrews, their texts are in accord with the Latin texts; almost never has there been any question about the text, always about the meaning and interpretation. One can readily conclude, then, that there was no intention of tampering with the text in passages not relevant to the controversy, if they left the text intact in those passages where a change would have been very much to their advantage.

Now your objection that our manuscript copies are more accurate than the Greek ones. If so, why does Augustine recommend having recourse to the Greek manuscripts when the reading of the Latin ones is doubtful? Your preference, however, is to go along with Jerome, who, on your word, states that in his day the Greek manuscript copies were more accurate than the Hebrew, and the Latin more so than the Greek. All the other arguments you had compiled, I must say, were very simple. Upon reading this one, I confess being somewhat shaken. To me, Jerome is on every point an imposing authority, on this point particularly imposing, and rightly so. If he had admitted the Greek writings were in a better state of preservation than the Hebrew, and the Latin writings better than the Greek, others perhaps could find a loophole; for me there was no escape. Then I began to wonder if Jerome ever made such a statement. Of one thing I was positive; he could have made no statement more contrary to his own policy. I could not recall the exact reference of this remark, since he was not likely to make it at all. While giving the matter closer thought, I finally began to recall, through the haze, of having read something of the sort long ago in the codex of Pontifical Decretals. I grabbed the book, hoping to catch you red-handed in error; I could almost surmise you had taken the passage from that work, and I was hoping you had misinterpreted it. When I found the place, my heart fell, my hopes were almost dashed to the ground; true, the notes of the codex said exactly what you did. Although I was not so cowed by the learning of the man, whoever he was, who produced this note, as to lose all hope that a misinterpretation of Jerome was possible, still I shuddered when thinking of what I had been convinced was a most careful surveillance in compiling only what was thoroughly understood in this sacred volume of decrees, which prescribes absolutely inflexible laws upon the entire world. However, while reflecting on Jerome's good sense, I was distracted by another thought.

Jerome, after pleading the defects of the Greek manuscripts, had decided to purge the text of the Old Testament and restore it to harmony with the accurate Hebrew text, and also to correct the flaws which had gathered in the Latin text of the New Testament by having recourse to the prime source in the Greek manuscripts. He could not, I was sure, have been so stupid as to do all of this and still admit that the Greek copies were more accurate than the Hebrew, and the Latin more than the Greek. What statement or what notion could be more directly opposed to his policy? With these reflections, my mind gradually veered away from a suspicion of Jerome's good sense and toward a suspicion of the accuracy of the note. So I turned to the passage; it occurs at the end of the letter of which the initial words are *Desiderii mei*.[5] Good heavens! what an awful slip the editor of the note had made! The passage in Jerome reads as follows: "It is another matter if they have proved that later conflicting evidence was acquired from the Apostles, and if the Latin manuscripts are in a better state of preservation than the Greek, and the Greek than the Hebrew." After answering other objections which Jerome thought his rivals would make, he points out that those men are undeserving of a reply who could be so extraordinarily stupid as to think the Greek manuscripts were more accurate than the Hebrew, and the Latin more than the Greek. Without grasping this manner of speaking, that editor lopped off several words upon which depends the whole force of the sentence, and quoted the rest, thereby making Jerome say the very thing he thought no man could be so stupid as to say. Go on and trust those compilers of digests; their word is trusted so much nowadays that the authors of the original sources of those compilations are considered as almost superfluous.

After demolishing the citadel of his translation and annotations, you then make a vigorous attack on some of the smaller towns, like one in search of plunder. You direct your attack especially against the *Folly*, which is really a large metropolis. As the supreme power is in the hands of a woman accustomed to govern by whim and arbitrarily, not according

5. Jerome, *Preface to the Pentateuch* (Migne, 22, 152A).

to measures of military strategy, you expect to subdue it with little opposition. But just a minute! I warn you; it is not as easy to subdue as you think. First of all, as Solomon says,[6] "The number of fools is infinite"; and secondly, where intelligence is lacking, foolhardiness supplies. They will admit you as a fellow citizen, if you make the effort to be enrolled; still they will never put up with you as their conqueror, for they would sacrifice even their lives rather than be subject to any man. However, to put all joking aside, this *Folly* contains less folly and even more true piety than do the vast majority of those works which some of your friends—but I had better hold my tongue; even so, I shall go ahead and say it—than do certain hymns which some of your friends think place all the Saints under their obligation. These songs in honor of the Saints are such silly ditties, no clown could ridicule them with sillier ones, try as he would; yet, in our day some of this trash has crept into the churches and is gradually assuming such a prominent position, particularly because of the accompanying music, that we have become much less inclined to listen to the serious and solemn prayers arranged long ago by the holy Fathers. As a matter of great concern to Christianity, the Popes should ban all that sort of nonsense, as I am sure some day they will; or the cunning enemy may prevail upon Christ's flock, which He desired to be simple, but also prudent, gradually to take to its heart foolishness instead of true piety.

I shall not undertake a defense of the *Folly*, as it needs no defense. For some time now the book has received favorable criticism from all the most competent men, and several years ago it was vindicated, with a defense of Erasmus, against the slanderous attacks of the envious. In their name Dorp,[7] himself outstanding in sacred and profane learning, had compiled every flight of fancy those men were capable of, and, to avoid giving it the appearance of a sham accusation had written it all up in a polished, eloquent style; as a result it has been difficult for you to offer an objection not already refuted. One brand new discovery you did make to add to the collec-

6. Ecclesiasticus 1:15.
7. Cf. above, Letter 4, More to Dorp.

tion is your remark that Erasmus in his *Folly* is playing the
role of a Moschus.[8] I cannot refute, I admit, that insulting
charge, since I have not the slightest idea what your remark
means, or who that fellow Moschus was. Nor am I so stupidly
proud as to pretend to be more learned than I really am.
I have often heard of a certain Momus; [9] whether his family
name happened to be Moschus, I am not sure.

Concerning the *Dialogue of Julius*,[10] I have never been very
interested in discovering the name of the author or the type
of work it is, although I have heard different views on both
points. Of this one thing I am sure; immediately upon the
death of Julius, a play on the same theme was staged publicly
in Paris. As many people know, the Reverend Father Poncher,
Bishop of Paris and former Legate to our country, has ascribed
the work to Faustus.[11] The fact that Erasmus, who was an acquaintance of Faustus, had a copy of the book in his possession even before it was published does not contradict that
ascription. When you base your argument on the style, which
you maintain is Erasmus' own peculiar style, I cannot hold
back a laugh as I recall that you, utterly incapable of telling
what style or language is, deny to Erasmus, universally known
to be thoroughly conversant with all the niceties of speech,
the right to make any criticism with regard to style in Jerome's
works; yet, you take it upon yourself to determine what is
typical of Erasmus' style, although a huge throng of writers
are doing their best to imitate Erasmus' manner of writing.

8. A rhetorician of Pergamus.

9. Momus, the son of Night in Greek mythology, was the personifica-
tion of censoriousness.

10. The *Dialogus, Iulius Exclusus e Coelis* was quite certainly written
by Erasmus, probably in 1513 or 1514 soon after Julius II's death. Erasmus
always tried to give the impression that he had not written it, but there
is evidence of a manuscript copy of it in Erasmus' handwriting (cf. above,
Letter 12; Allen, 2, 502 and intro.; Ferguson, *Erasmi Opuscula*, pp.
38–124, for the dialogue itself and intro.). Ferguson shows that it was
not by Faustus Andrelinus.

11. The fact that Stephen Poncher attributed the dialogue to Faustus
Andrelinus does not necessarily mean that More agreed (Allen, 2, 420).
Ferguson (pp. 44–45) shows how circumstances had changed after the
writing of the dialogue. Erasmus had now published his edition of the
Greek New Testament, dedicated to Leo X, and such an attack on his
predecessor was published at a most inopportune time.

Well, suppose the book is his; suppose the man is opposed
to wars, and that he was angered at the troublesome times,
and under the impulse of strong emotion he went further
than he wished he had, once peace was restored and emotions
were calm. First of all, the charge should have been made
not against him but against those responsible for the un-
timely publication of a timely book. Secondly, tell me, was it
proper for a monk to ferret out a brother's mistake, when
duty demands that he sit in solitude and weep over his own
sins, rather than expose the sins of others? However, if the
work has offended any people, I think you will find yourself
in great disfavor with them for assigning the satire to Erasmus,
since it would be more to their advantage for the work
to remain anonymous than to have it valued from an ap-
praisal of its author.

The kind of writings Luther has produced is a problem for
those who have the time. As for Erasmus, I am sure that all
his works have been written in a manner proper to a good
man. You give no indication of having anything definite to
say; and until that time comes, you cannot hold back your
insults, I suppose, so as not to be deprived of the gratification
of making that neat quip, "a lid like a saucer." Apparently
you were lured on by the charm of this one remark to mention the name of Erasmus along with Luther. Strange how
you are always trying to appear a little clever. I am surprised
at the unusual amount of time you have to spend on schismatical and heretical books—that is, if you are telling the truth;
perhaps the great shortage of good books necessitates your
spending a little time on the worst ones. But if the books
are good, why do you condemn them? If bad, why read them?
You have no chance to become proficient in refuting errors
and warning the world, since you gave up interest in the
world by shutting yourself up in the cloister. Then what else
do you accomplish in reading what is evil except to learn
about it?

I do not quite understand your spending good hours on
bad books; perhaps you are even wasting much time on gos-
sipy conversations and chitchat, which is still worse than
reading bad books; for I notice that every single bit of gossip
or slander or scandal is carried straight to your cell. Yet, books

tell us there once were monks so completely withdrawn from the world, they did not even allow themselves to read letters from friends, to avoid taking so much as a glance back at the Sodom they had left behind.[12] The monks of today, though, I see, read through heretical and schismatical works and huge volumes crammed with sheer drivel. The cunning enemy now smuggles into their place of retreat and shoves into their cells all the things they dreaded hearing out in the world and which they tried to escape by fleeing to the cloister. Their unusual manner of life serves merely to facilitate their deception of the unwary; their leisure serves merely to allow more time for dressing up their abuses; their seclusion merely makes them blush at nothing, being withdrawn from the gaze of men; the secrecy of their cells merely permits greater freedom in slandering others. The first act upon entering a cell is the recitation of the Lord's Prayer, to call down God's blessing upon their conversation and to make it holy and beneficial. But what is the point of saying the Lord's Prayer at the beginning of scandalous and slanderous gossip? If that is not taking the name of God in vain, what is? [13] Undoubtedly your strongest argument against Erasmus is your quotation from the Gospels. Yet, not everyone who says to God, "Lord, Lord," will enter into the kingdom of Heaven.[14] I look at this letter of yours, crammed full of reproaches, insults, slander, and jeers, and then I think back upon the charming simplicity and truly lovable qualities you had as a youth, when you were as far removed from such defects as could reasonably be expected in one of your age and state of life. If I judged your whole character in the light of this letter, I would surely be reminded of the passage in Ovid,[15] where Deianira gives this reprimand to Hercules:

Your start was better than your finish: the ending falls
Far short of the beginning; how different the man from the
    boy.

However, I am not so unfair as to appraise you from just one letter. I would tend rather to think that the better and holier you are in the rest of your character, so much the more

12. Gen. 19:17.　　　　13. Exod. 20:7.　　　　14. Matt. 7:21.
15. *Heroides* 9.23–24.

violently does some demon grudge you your virtues; he darts
forth from his lurking place and, setting aside his other
methods of deception, he is making a vicious attempt to
snare you with just one very treacherous trap and to drag
you to himself; thus he transforms himself into a dazzling
angel of light, so that seeing, we do not see,[16] and to our dazed
eyes black is white and white is black, the virtue of others
appears sordid, our own defects glitter attractively, while an
assault upon another's reputation is termed brotherly admonition; bad temper and jealousy are taken for fervor and zeal
for God; ignorance is called simplicity, and boorishness, holiness; arrogance and stubbornness are called strength and un-
swerving firmness of character; in a word, we are ever blind
to the progress of others, but humor our own passions, and
those usually the worst.

Such is the method you use in this letter of yours; while
seeming to admonish me, you are disparaging Erasmus. Yet,
none of your bitter charges strike home; several of them re-
bound directly upon yourself. You criticize his style as affected; your own solecisms reek more of the study lamp than
do his finished phrases. You charge him with using caustic
language, you shout that he gnaws on everything with a
cur's fang; in this one letter you gnaw more on him than he
has ever done on anyone. If one pages through all his books,
all his letters, everything that ever came from his pen—and
the number of volumes from his pen are endless—and if one
selects from all these works and piles together all his un-
kindly remarks, even his remarks that mention no names,
some of which might well have been considerably more bitter, still that pile would be much smaller than your huge
mass, outsoaring the pyramids, of insult upon insult heaped
on the head of Erasmus, and by name too. Yet his writings
have never given any offense to you; they have even been a
help to your studies and a service to you beyond repayment.

Your cry is that he is arrogant, for daring to censure other
people's mistakes; you, of course, in your own eyes, are modest
in criticizing him when he is right, and in finding fault with
him where he is praised by those who regard loud-mouthed
carping as a sign of extraordinary lack of modesty. I could

16. Luke 8:10.

mention the names of several of such men, who are highly distinguished for moral and intellectual qualities, men of every nation who are trying to outdo one another in thank-ing Erasmus for the great value his work has meant to them. However, I shall omit those from foreign lands; as they are strangers to you, their importance will probably escape you. I shall name one or two of our own countrymen whom it would be insolent to contradict. In my list the place of honor goes to the Reverend Father in Christ, John, Bishop of Rochester,[17] distinguished for virtue as well as for learning, qualities in which he has no superior among living men. I shall mention Colet, the equal of any of our countrymen in scholarliness and in holiness for many, many centuries. We have letters from these men written not only to Erasmus, in which their gratitude is clearly expressed (unless, of course, they are incapable of any gratitude and would lie just to harm others); but there are also letters from them to other men, containing every encouragement to read through Erasmus' translation thoughtfully, with the prospect of deriving much good from it. Doctor John Longland, Dean of Salisbury,[18] to sum up his merits in a single phrase, is another Colet, either in his speaking ability or in his purity of life; he repeatedly admits that Erasmus' works on the New Testament have added more to his understanding than practically all the other commentaries in his possession. There is no reason to continue the list, if you credit the word of these men; still less reason is there, if you do not. Whose word would you accept, if not theirs?

You are taking upon yourself quite a task in condemning mightily what these men praise so highly. Besides, has not the Supreme Pontiff,[19] on two occasions, given definite approba-

17. For Bishop Fisher's praise of Erasmus' edition of the New Testa-ment, cf. Allen, 2, 432. Colet's letter to Erasmus is found ibid., p. 423, but More evidently quotes a letter of Colet to some other correspondent.

18. John Longland (1473–1543) was educated at Magdalen College, Oxford, and was later principal of Magdalen Hall. He was ordained priest, proceeded doctor of divinity, and in 1514 was made dean of Salisbury, which preferment he held until his consecration as Bishop of Lincoln in 1521. He was very severe in putting down heresy, but sup-ported royal supremacy and, for a time, the King's divorce.

19. Cf. Allen, 2, 519, from Leo X, praising Erasmus' erudition, and 3, 864, which speaks particularly of the edition of the Greek New Testa-ment.

tion to what you condemn? That which the Vicar of Christ, as the mouthpiece of God, has declared to be useful, thou, child, prophet of the Most High, dost augur to be harmful. That which the High Prince of the Christian world from the fortress of religion honors with his support you, a poor little monk, unlearned and unknown, from the burrow of your tiny cell defile with your fetid tongue. You, of all people, ought to follow the advice you give to Erasmus, to aspire after prudence, not after that which is beyond you. Are you not doing the very thing you criticize in Erasmus, disregarding the law of God and setting up your own? For that which the Supreme Pontiff has respectfully recommended, time and again, to all scholars, you do not hesitate to condemn with insolence.

The fundamental argument you posit is that Erasmus is completely ignorant of the Scriptures, while you, of course, are all-knowing, though he has spent almost as many years studying the Scriptures as you have lived. Whether you are his superior in talent or studiousness is not the point of my consideration; this I do know, and I can say it without any insult to you: you are not so far superior to him as to be able to accomplish in a much shorter time what he is incapable of doing in a much longer time. Yet, oddly, while he has grown gray in the study of Scripture, you, a self-taught young fellow, who never really had the opportunity for an education, disrespectfully play the tutor to an old man; oddly, too, you look upon yourself as a savant when dealing with such arguments as prove your ignorance of the subject. To crown it all, you think you really have done something remarkable in ridiculing him with bits of quotations scraped together hither and yon from the Sacred Books; you jest with the words of Sacred Scripture like the parasites in the comedies playing with clever quips. This is altogether improper, yet it is the easiest thing in the world to do.

For instance, recently some clown staged an impersonation of a friar preaching and mimicked his garb, words, facial expressions, and gestures; and, in the course of the sermon, which was indecent but humorous, and completely a patchwork of quotations from Scripture, he introduced an anecdote

involving the practice of some friars; it was a lewd story about
a poor friar who wooed and violated a woman. The tale,
though coarse and obscene, was completely pieced together
by the clown from Scriptural phrases, so that every single
word was borrowed from the text of Scripture, as it told of
the poor friar making the proposition, the adulterous woman
being violated, the discovery of the affair by the arrival of the
husband, and how the fellow was caught red-handed, seized,
and castrated. All those phrases from Scripture were so cleverly
applied to a matter quite different from that intended that
no one could be so strait-laced as to hold back a smile. Yet,
no one was so amused as not to resent having Holy Writ used
as a plaything for such a filthy sport. Some people, however,
remarked that it was by some mysterious providence of God
that, since many of the friars had long been accustomed to
prostitute the Word of God, there should finally appear on
the scene "Friar-mimes" to out-friar the friars and embarrass
them with a picture of themselves and foil them with their
own devices.

If it is sinful, as it certainly is, to misuse Scripture for lewd
purposes, it is still more sinful to misuse it, as you are doing,
to defame another person. The fact of your writing to me,
whom you know to be a friend of his, does not render your
action any more excusable; in fact, that is a still greater sin.
For if you had mentioned all of this to one who hated
Erasmus, you would only have widened the split between men
already far apart. In the present circumstances you have tried
with might and main to separate one very closely attached to
him. Therefore, as I said above, when I thought back upon
the gentle and modest behavior of your youth, I could not
help feeling very sad and also very puzzled at the lack of
modesty that has sprung up in your more mature years, not
to mention any more serious defect, and this in a state of
life which absolutely professes humility and contempt of self.
As I quietly try to solve this puzzle, I begin to realize that,
over and above the universal enemy of mankind, who is the
secret source from which flow, as from a polluted spring, practically all sins—over and above some of his henchmen, who,
I notice, have spoiled your simple candor with the foul stench

of their jealousy—a large portion of this poison takes its
origin from a passion within you that is no stranger to mankind; and yet no other passion has brought more terrible
woes into the lives of men. I mean the passion which causes
almost every person, through some secret attachment to himself, to be so prejudiced in favor of his own group that he is
incapable of either seeing its defects or tolerating one who
points them out. You have been stunned by this very passion,
I notice, and goaded on by a misguided zeal to revile, because
of your party feeling for religious orders, the man who has
done great service to all religious orders, and never a greater
one than this service which you, by your slander, are trying
to subject to hateful and hostile feelings. "How often," you
say, "he snaps out criticisms at the sacred practices of religious life, at the pious observances of religious, at their strict
way of life, at their holy seclusion, in a word, at everything
that clashes with his own vagrant mode of life." [20] When reading these words of yours, I quickly detected the goad that
spurs you on; it is the zeal for your own religious order. I,
for my part, have no doubt that every good person cherishes
and values all religious orders most dearly; whom I too have
always loved and held in great respect, preferring to honor
one who is very poor but outstanding in virtue, rather than
one who is famous for his wealth or illustrious for his high
birth. On the one hand, it is my sincere desire that all other
men bestow upon you and your religious orders an extraordinary degree of love; indeed, because of your services, you
have a right to it, as I believe your spiritual support lightens
the sorrows of this world considerably. (For if the constant
prayer of a good man has much value,[21] how much must be
the value of the unrelenting prayers of thousands upon thousands?) Yet, on the other hand, I do not like to see you favor
yourselves with so misdirected a zeal that, if anyone touches
your interests, you strain to distort what he has said well, by
your way of relating it, or to pervert what he meant well, by
your misinterpreting it.

20. For Erasmus' opinion of monasticism, cf. his letter to Lambertus
Grunnius (Allen, 2, 447, trans. Mangan, *Erasmus of Rotterdam, 1*, 9–28).
21. James 5:16.

I fail to grasp why you find his words so unsavory, but of this I am sure; I do not know of any person who has interpreted his writings as a criticism of the observances of members of religious orders, rather as a criticism of those religious who make a superstitious use of them, or dangerously overestimate them, and, relying upon their own stupidity, convert a thing not bad in itself into a cause of disaster. However much inclined you may be to favor your own people, you will admit, I think, that there are altogether too many of this type. No matter how sacred a thing is, the cunning enemy is forever at work trying to spoil it with some wily device; being God's adversary in all things, he endeavors to make evil of our good works, just as God accomplishes good out of evil works. How many religious do you find who place more importance on the observances of their own group than even on the divine commandments! And could you not find whole orders who contend fiercely with other orders in defense of their own customs? Meanwhile their common aim is not to be, but to seem, holier, and this in matters of observance that are peculiar to each order and often not very essential, while sometimes in matters that are important and more pertinent and upon which there is complete agreement the observance is not taken very seriously. Into what factions and cliques does the same order split up! And what internal battles! What tragic situations arise over the change of color of the habit or of the type of cincture or of some other local custom! Perhaps such situations are not altogether contemptible; at least they are are not so important as to outlaw charity. And the very worst thing of all—how many, with complete reliance on their religious state, are so conceited in their hearts that they imagine themselves strolling about in the heavens and, enthroned on the rays of the sun, looking down from their lofty pinnacle upon the people, crawling like ants along the ground, and not only upon the lay people, but upon all priests outside the fold of the cloister! Yes, to many of them nothing is holy except what they do themselves.

God foresaw many problems in decreeing that all things were to be a matter of common interest; so too did Christ when He in turn endeavored to urge men to turn away from provincial interests back to universal interests. To be sure, He realized that our fallen human nature was desperately in love with its own private pursuits to the detriment of the common cause; that fact is everywhere obvious. Everyone loves his own premises, his own money; everyone is interested only in his own profession, or his own corporation; anything at all which we can call our own attracts our attentions to itself and away from common interests. So too we prefer our own private fasts to the general fasts. If we choose some patron saint for ourselves, we often give more honor to him than to ten more prominent saints, just because he is ours, while the other saints belong to everybody. Now if anyone censures such behavior, he is not condemning the piety of the ordinary people, only warning them for fear impiety may creep in under the cloak of piety. For example, no one would find fault with a nation that bestows honor upon some saint individually for a worthy reason; yet some perhaps will think it an excessive display of piety on the part of those who, out of a narrow devotion to their own saint, pull down and drag out of church the patron saint of an enemy nation, and fling it into the mud. Such religious practices and private devotions sometimes end up badly with us laymen; so, I imagine, with you religious too they do not always end well. The more personal a thing is, in the eyes of many of you, the more valuable it is. As a result, many treasure their own private devotions more highly than those of the monastery; those of the monastery more highly than those of the order; those peculiar to their own order more highly than those common to all orders; and those which belong to all religious they regard much more highly than the lowly, humble things, not exclusively their own, but possessed in common with absolutely all Christians, such as the ordinary virtues of faith, hope, and charity, fear of God, humility, and the like.

This is nothing new. Long ago Christ made this reproach to the chosen people: "Why do you also transgress the commandments of God out of preference for your own traditions?" [22] Men who do that very thing today, I am sure, will deny it. Who is such an idiot as to admit he considers

22. Matt. 15:3.

his own religious practices more important than the commandments of God? He knows, if he fails to obey them, that his own practices are worthless. If the question is put to them, undoubtedly they will answer with the right words; but their actions belie their words. Call me a liar, if there are not some poor religious in certain places who are so set on keeping silence that you could not bribe them with a great deal of money to utter just one little whisper in those cloister walks; but remove them just an inch from the cloister, and they will not hesitate to boom out with dreadful insults. There are some who would be scared the devil was coming to take them off to hell alive if they were to make the slightest change in their type of habit; but they are not at all disturbed at piling up cash, or opposing the abbot and then overthrowing him. Do you think there are just a few who would consider it a crime deserving of many tears to omit merely a verse in saying their office, while they do not have the slightest scruple in soiling themselves with the most destructive, slanderous gossip, that goes on longer than even their longest prayers? Yes, they crush a gnat and swallow an elephant whole.[23]

Indeed, there are many more than I would like to see who merely because of their title of religious imagine they soar far above the lot of mortal men. A good part of these, however, are lunatics, not malicious, and so delightfully insane that they promptly accept as a divine inspiration every suggestion of their silly minds; and then they fancy they are being swept off to the third heaven,[24] when really they have suffered a seizure of delirium to the third degree. Even more frightening is the frenzy of those men who are so terribly haughty and who appear to themselves as such little saints that they condemn, as well as contemn, all the rest of mortal men in comparison with themselves, and mainly because of a superstitious excessive attachment to their own religious practices and because of a pride in their own little observances; and some imagine that these observances even provide perfect protection as they don this armor of theirs and go forth to commit any and every outrage.

23. Matt. 23:24—*camelum autem glutientes*.   24. 2 Cor. 12:2.

I know a religious belonging to an institute that today has the reputation, and, I am certain, a genuine reputation, for a very good religious spirit. This person had spent many years after his novitiate in the observance of his rule with such fidelity that he was put in charge of the monastery; being, however, more devoted to monastic practices than to God's commandments, he fell into one vice after another, and went so far as to plot a most awful and unbelievably abominable crime; not just a single criminal act, but one teeming with crime upon crime, for he had resolved to commit murder and parricide and even sacrilege. Being unable to accomplish all these outrages by himself, he enlisted the aid of killers and hatchetmen, who carried out the most monstrous deed ever to come to my attention. They were caught and jailed. However, it has not been my intention to give all the details, and I shall not name the guilty ones, for fear some of the ill-feeling, which has died out, might be revived against the order, which is guiltless. My reason for relating the incident is this: those criminal assassins told me personally that, whenever they came to the cell of that poor religious, they began their shameful business only after first being led to his private chapel and kneeling down, as is the rule, and begging the blessing of the Holy Virgin by reciting the "Hail, Mary." Only upon completing that act according to the rule did they, now spotless and pious, arise from their knees to tackle their unspeakable crime. What I have just referred to was a most awful crime; what I am now going to tell you, though seemingly a much less serious crime, was perhaps in actual fact almost as scandalous; certainly the harm it did was much more widespread.

There was at Coventry a friar belonging to the group of Franciscans not as yet reformed according to the Rule of Saint Francis. He went about preaching in the city, in the suburbs, in the adjacent areas, in the hamlets scattered about, and taught that anyone who daily recited the Psalter of the Blessed Virgin could not lose his soul. This preaching was listened to with favorable ears and readily believed, since it opened up an easy way to heaven. The local pastor, a virtuous and learned man, considered it a senseless doctrine; yet, for some time he concealed his feelings on the matter, thinking it innocuous; he believed the people would become holier as a result of a greater devotion to the Blessed Virgin. But, finally, upon examining his fold, he noticed that his flock was suffering a severe infection from this mange, and that the very worst sinners among them were the most pious in the recitation of the Psalter, only because they had assured themselves of the permission to do anything at all without perturbation; there was no good reason to feel uncertain about heaven, for that had been promised to them with strong assurance by a prominent authority, a friar direct from heaven. Then at last the pastor began to warn his people that they could have just as much assurance of heaven, if they chanted the Psalter, even ten times a day; but if they recited it well, they would certainly do well, provided it was not recited with that cocksureness already noticeable in some of them; otherwise, it would be better to omit the prayers altogether, provided they also called a halt to the sins being committed with too much reliance upon the protection of those prayers. As he spoke these words from the pulpit, they stormed upon him with violent indignation; they hissed and booed him out of the pulpit, and exposed him everywhere to public ridicule as the enemy of Mary. The next day, the friar mounted the pulpit and, intending to deal the pastor a sharp slap, he opened with the text, "Deem me worthy of praising thee, O hallowed Virgin; grant me strength against thy enemies." According to the story, Scotus [25] used this same text in beginning his disputation at Paris on the Immaculate Conception of the Virgin; the report adds falsely that he had been transported more than three hundred miles in a flash,

25. The doctrine of the Immaculate Conception was denied by Bernard of Clairvaux, Thomas Aquinas, and Bonaventura, but the arguments advanced in its favor by Duns Scotus gradually prevailed. The bull *Ineffabilis Deus* of Pope Pius IX in 1854 stated: "The doctrine which holds that the Blessed Virgin Mary, from the first instant of her conception, was, by a most singular grace and privilege of Almighty God, in view of the merits of Jesus Christ, the Redeemer of the human race, preserved from all stain of Original Sin, is a doctrine revealed by God, and therefore to be firmly and steadfastly believed by all the faithful."

to preserve the honor of the Blessed Virgin. What need to
speak at length? With ease the friar convinced his ready listeners their pastor was a fool and a blasphemer.

Just when the situation was red hot, I happened to go to
Coventry to visit my sister there. I had hardly dismounted
when the question was put to me, "Could a person who daily
recited the Psalter of the Blessed Virgin lose his soul?" My
answer to the silly question was a laugh. I was promptly
warned, that sort of answer was a dangerous thing, for a very
holy and learned Father was preaching quite the opposite. I
shrugged off the whole affair as none of my business. I was
at once invited to dinner; I accepted and went. And, of all
things, in came an old friar, cadaverous, stern, and gloomy;
a boy behind him was carrying a stack of books. I saw at a
glance I was in for a battle. We sat down at table, and, so as
not to lose a moment, the topic was promptly broached by the
host. The friar put forth exactly what he had been preaching.
I did not say a word myself. I do not like to get involved in
arguments that are unpleasant and sterile. At last they asked
for my opinion too. Since I now had to say something, I
gave a statement of my views; but I was brief and casual.
Then the friar launched out on a speech that was carefully
prepared and tedious; for the length of almost two sermons
he babbled on and on at table. The main point of his discussion was completely based on miracles, many of which,
as he chattered on, he quoted to us from a *Mariale,* some
too from other books full of the same stuff, which he had
ordered brought to the table to give his words added authority. At long last he drew his speech to a conclusion. Then I
calmly remarked, there was not in his entire lecture a single
convincing argument for those who would deny the miracles
he had recounted, and such denial was reconcilable with the
Christian Faith; and even if those miracles were authentic,
they were not sufficient proof for the point at hand; true, one
could readily find a sovereign who on occasion would pardon
even an enemy in answer to his mother's pleas; but no one
is so foolhardy as to promulgate a law that would challenge
his subjects to insolent disobedience, by the promise of im-

punity to all disloyal citizens who obliged his mother by a specific act of homage. Much was said on both sides, but the final result of my efforts was that he was lauded to the skies and I was laughed at as a fool. In fact, thanks to the misguided zeal of men who gaze through the mask of piety with a kindly eye upon their own sins, the situation eventually became so bad that it was brought under control only through the most strenuous efforts of the bishop.

I have not mentioned this incident with any intention of belittling religious life by recounting the crimes of some religious, since wholesome as well as poisonous herbs grow in the same soil, nor with the intention of condemning the practice of frequent recitation of the "Hail, Mary," which is a most wholesome practice; but because some people rely so much upon devotions as to use them primarily as a guarantee for the commission of sin. These and similar practices are what Erasmus judges worthy of censure; one who is furious with him should also be enraged at Saint Jerome, and likewise at the other very saintly Fathers, who present a much more detailed account of the defects of religious and inveigh against them with much more bitterness. How cunning the old serpent is! How he always smears honey over aconite, so no one will be alarmed by the poison! How he spoils our taste and makes us vomit when we are given an antidote! People who gaze admiringly at us and applaud everything we do and tell us we are wonderful and holy—in other words, people who delude us and convert our stupidity into insanity— such people, of course, are honest and friendly; and, in turn, we tell them they are good and pious. However, the people who do us a much more worth-while service, those who tell us just exactly what we really are, they are dogs—growling, gnawing, vicious, green-eyed dogs. Such names are given to those who criticize faults, though not the faults of any man in detail; and those names are given by men who splatter their own filth over other people, without any reserve.

I notice, then, that the saying of the comic poet [26] is valid for the cloister as well as for other places: "Flattery breeds

26. Terence, *Andria* 1.1.41.

friends, the truth breeds bitter enemies." A slanderer named
Rufinus once derided Jerome [27] for telling the truth, while
all good and honest readers were highly satisfied with the
truth. Erasmus not only wrote the truth, but did so with such
an attractive style that letters expressive of deep gratitude
have come to him from all parts, from religious of every order,
especially from your own; but this is the very object of your
attack, in a manner rather silly and haughty, with slanders
and insults, although your whole profession is based on
humility; clearly, you praise your own and all religious orders
because of their humble manner of life, as exemplified in
their sacred practices, their seclusion from the world, their
pious observances, their vigils, the severity of their life, and
their fasts. Yet you boot him like a cur, making of him a
growling stray dog. When I read words like this coming from
the pen of a religious, they sound to me almost like the
humble prayer of the holy Pharisee, "I give Thee thanks, O
Lord, because I am not like the rest of men, as is this publi-
can." [28]

Although, in my opinion, singing the praises of good men
is a somewhat holier act than uttering calumnies against
them, still my present purpose is not to pen an encomium
of Erasmus. First of all, I am not equal to the task; secondly,
outstanding scholars the world over are vigorously competing
with one another in their attempts, which some day will succeed, to win for him an appreciation even among those now
blear-eyed with envy and so blinded by his brilliance they
cannot face him. Suppose these scholars held their tongues;
even so his services, valuable for all men, are in his lifetime
winning the acclaim of good men, and after his death, which
I pray may be deferred for many years, when envy will pass
with his life, those services will win for him the acclaim of all
men. Since good men have no need to hear his praises, I
shall temper my remarks, for fear of causing a surge of envy
among those monstrous creatures who find nourishment in
any bit of slander, but starvation in the praises bestowed
upon the good.

I think I can at least make this statement, without giving

27. Jerome Ep. 81, to Rufinus.   28. Luke 18:9–14.

any offense to such men. If one reflects upon Erasmus' constant preoccupation with study and upon the size and number of volumes he alone has published, the mere writing of which would seem too great a task for one person, I believe he will quickly conclude that, even if Erasmus were not absorbed in the pursuit of virtue, he would have very little time to spend on vice. Then, if one, with impartial eyes, takes a closer view of his works and studies their value and, in that light, considers the testimony of those whose own intellectual life has been illumined or whose spirit has been fired by those works, such a man will surely understand that a heart from which leaps up a flame that ignites the souls of other men is not very likely to be cold-blooded itself. No man will niggardly begrudge Erasmus these words of praise, which, in my opinion, are not so generous as to excite envy. Even so, I would never have brought them up except for your peevishness, which prevents me from stopping even at this point, but pushes me on even further. For who has the patience to tolerate your peevish insults, when you reproachfully describe him as a vagrant, because he occasionally changes residence, which he almost never does unless the common good demands it? As if to reside forever in the same spot and, like a clam or a sponge, to cling eternally to the same rock were the ultimate of sanctity! If that be true, then there was no justification for founding the Order of Friars Minor, which, unless I am wrong, is the equal of any order in sanctity; and yet many of its members are, with good reason, world travelers. Then Jerome, too, was wrong for making trips between Rome and Jerusalem. The holy Apostles, too, failed to meet your demands for sanctity; while you were situated in one spot, or, rather, before you were even situated, they were traveling over the face of the globe. In making that remark, I do not mean to compare Erasmus with the Apostles, to forestall any slanderous quibbling; I merely want to point out that a change of residence does not necessarily involve a defect, nor is there any special virtue in residing forever in the same spot.

But to get down to Erasmus. No matter what his other characteristics may be, and they are splendid, as for his habit of roaming, which is the object of your rude attack, I would definitely not hesitate to prefer it to any one of your virtues, even one in which you take the greatest pride. I imagine that one who has a penchant for relaxation and shudders at hard work would rather squat with you than roam with him. If one looks at his hard work, he sometimes does more work in one day than your people do in several months; if one judges the value of his work, he sometimes has done more for the whole Church in one month than you have in several years, unless you suppose that anybody's fastings or pious prayers have as deep and wide an influence as his brilliant works, which are educating the entire world to the meaning of true holiness; or unless you suppose he is enjoying himself as he defies stormy seas and savage skies and all the scourges of land travel, provided it furthers the common cause. Possibly, it is not a pleasant experience to endure seasickness and the tortures of tossing waves and the threat of a deadly storm, and to stare at the ever-present menace of shipwreck. Possibly, it is not a keen delight to plod along through dense forests and wild woodland, over rugged hilltops and steep mountains, along roads beset with bandits, or to be battered by the winds, spattered with mud, drenched by rains, weary of traveling, exhausted from hardships, and then to receive a shabby welcome and be refused the sort of food and bed you are enjoying; and especially since all these many, many troubles, which would soon tire a healthy, sturdy young man, must be encountered and endured with a poor body that is growing old and has lost its strength from hard study and toil; and therefore, it is quite obvious that he would have had to succumb long ago to all these difficulties, had not God ("Who makes His sun to rise upon the good and the bad") [29] preserved him for the benefit even of ungrateful people. No matter where his journeys take him, he always comes back loaded with wonderful gifts for everyone else, while the only returns for him are his shattered health and the insults from wicked men which have been occasioned by his kindly gifts.

Therefore these expeditions are so dear to his heart that he would be quick to drop them only at the demand of his

29. Matt. 5:45.

studies, that is, for the cause of the common good, which he
very often purchases at great expense to himself. On these
trips, which are the target of your criticisms, he spends his
time only with those men approved for learning and goodness, and, as a result, his mind is ever nurturing some unborn
idea, which eventually will be brought forth to the general
profit of scholarship; but if he had preferred his own personal
comfort, he would now be much healthier in body and also
much richer in money, because rulers and leaders all over the
world have been competing with one another to win him
with their extraordinary offers. Since, wherever he is, he
scatters abroad, as the sun its rays, his wonderful riches, it
was only a matter of justice that comparable returns be made
to him from all sides. Because he dedicates himself completely
to the service of others and expects no personal reward in this
life, I am sure that the all-kind God will repay him in that
place where he would rather receive his reward; and when I
compare you with him, who is the object of your contempt, and
when I contrast your services with his, then, to the extent that
a human being may make a conjecture from that comparison,
I feel confident that when the day dawns on which the merits
of each of you will be recompensed, while I hope your reward
will be high and pray it will be extremely high, God, however, the just dispenser for both of you, will prefer his traveling to your squatting, and this He will do without any offense
to you, in fact, in keeping with your disposition then, even
with your compliance; I feel confident too that, since all things
work together unto good,[30] God will prefer his use of the
tongue to your silence, his silence to your prayers, his eating
to your fasting, his sleeping to your vigils, and, in a word,
everything you haughtily disdain in him, God will esteem
much more than all the things that fascinate you in your way
of life.

I am positive, though it embarrasses me to admit it, that
you could never have criticized anyone with such arrogance
without taking great pride in a strong conviction of your
own sanctity, which is the one most disastrous attitude in a
religious; and, by my love for you, I want you to rid yourself

30. Rom. 8:28.

of it completely. For it would help me and others in the same
condition, tossed as we are on the waves of an unhappy world,
to look up to you religious and to marvel at your orders as
models of angelic life, so that, while we admire the virtue in
others, our own way of life may seem all the more worthless.
On the other hand, it would be of little use to you to disdain
and condemn the way of life of other men, which in some
instances is holier than your own. Rather learn to respect
even a lower level of life as led by other men, and to develop
a modest attitude toward your own state, and, furthermore
to be apprehensive of everything, and ever to live in trem-
bling, and, though hopeful, still very fearful not only of the
possibility of falling in the future, according to the saying,
"He who stands, let him take heed lest he fall," [31] but also of
the possibility of having fallen in the past, yes, even at the
very moment you thought you were advancing the most,
namely, at your entrance into religion. In saying this, I do not
mean to doubt that Mary chose the better part; [32] I mean that
all our just acts are like a soiled menstrual cloth,[33] and therefore every man should rightly be suspicious even of his good
acts. Perhaps then you would be doing a wholesome thing, to
begin to doubt and to be worried whether you really are living Mary's part, or were wrong in choosing Mary's part, when
preferring her role, which Christ did think better than
Martha's lot, to the lot of the Apostles; or whether you only
lightly examined your motives and thought you were fleeing
into a holy retreat and withdrawing from dangerous pleasures,
but, in the hidden presence of God, Who sees deeply within
us, Who pierces the secrets of our hearts more than we do
ourselves,[34] and to Whose view our imperfections are obvious,
perhaps you are clearly exposed as a shirker and a fugitive
from hard work, while using the cloak of piety to gain the
luxury of idleness and a shelter from troubles, and while
wrapping in a handkerchief the talent entrusted to you,[35]
only to waste it within the cloister rather than fling it away
out in the world.

Thoughts like these will have at least this much value for

31. 1 Cor. 10:12.   32. Luke 10:42.   33. Isaiah 64:6 (Vulgate).
34. Ps. 138:1 (Vulgate).   35. Luke 19:20.

you; they can provide a motive for not priding yourself on
your own order (than which nothing is more pernicious), for
not putting too much reliance on private observances, for
placing your hope in the religion of Christ, not in your own,
and for depending not on those things which you can do by
yourself, but on those which you can do only with God's help.
You can fast by yourself, you can keep vigils by yourself, you
can pray by yourself, in fact you can do these things even with
the help of the devil. But truly Christian faith, through
which the name of Jesus Christ is spoken truly in the Spirit,
truly Christian hope, which distrusts its own good works and
places its trust only in God's loving kindness, and truly Christian love, which is not puffed up,[36] is not angered, does not
seek its own honor—all are absolutely unattainable except by
the grace of God alone, which is the free gift of His good will.
The more confidence you put in those universal virtues of
Christianity, the less trust you will have in private observances,
either those of your order, or of your own; and the less trust
you place in those observances, the more beneficial they will
be for you. Not until you look upon yourself as an unprofit-
able servant will God look upon you as a faithful one.[37] This
we can certainly do with all justice, even when we do everything of which we are capable; and I pray to God that both
of us may eventually do just that, and Erasmus too; and not
only that, but a good deal more; and if we succeed in accom-
plishing much, that we still may look upon ourselves as having
done absolutely nothing. This is the path that leads, above
all others, to the goal where the virtue of others will never
cause us anguish and where the love that others receive will
never draw a tear from eyes inflamed with envy.

At the end of your letter you suggest that it would be
modest on my part not to show your letter to anyone else;
however, I fail to see how this relates to modesty on my part;
it would have been a mark either of modesty or certainly of
discretion for you not to show it to so many people—of
modesty, if it were as good as you thought it was, discretion,
if you too thought it as bad as it really is. But you have a
strange concept of modesty; first, you demand silence from me,

36. 1 Cor. 13:4 f.   37. Luke 17:10.

as if you were displeased with your letter, or were shunning
applause; then, eagerly itching for a smattering of glory, you
promptly looked around for others who suffer from the same
tickling mange, so as to feel the delightful sensation of scratch-
ing one another. I have been told by various sources that
these friends of yours boasted that your elegantly written
letter, inspired by the Holy Spirit, affected me so much that
I discarded the writings of Erasmus; and therefore, I decided
that my response should be in the form of a public letter, to
silence either the stupidity of those men if they believed their
own words, or their malice if they trumped up the story. I
am in no position to judge what effect your letter had on them,
since, as the proverb says, thistles delight the palate of a jack-
ass; at any rate, nothing in it struck me as being so brilliant as
to blind me completely and make me think white was not
still white.

And so, that absolutely inane boast made by you or your
friends has forced my decision to air my views on the matter;
yet, I was determined ever to keep in mind your reputation
and not to make any mention in my letter of your name,
which otherwise is very dear to me, and to blot out your name
from your own letter, or at least from the copy in my possession.
Consequently, no matter what people will say or think about
this action of yours (and undoubtedly educated men will say
and think some dreadful things about it), at least no stain of
disgrace or embarrassment will touch your name. I was very
much delighted to note that, after you had had your fill of rev-
elry, you recovered your senses and were quite calm at the end
of your letter, giving a glimpse of hope that your fury with
Erasmus could be appeased on terms not so difficult to meet.
You say as follows: "All in all, my animosity toward Erasmus
is not such that I could not easily be reconciled with him,
provided he corrects his slight errors." Splendid! You have
made the fellow happy; otherwise he was dangerously close to
tearing out his heart with misery if he was to be completely
deprived of any hope of ever enjoying the good will of one
obviously so important as yourself. But since you do offer
such easy terms of peace, with demands that are very just, I
am sure that he will eagerly comply with them and will

promptly correct his mistakes, as soon as you point them out. Up to now you have only pointed out your own. Still, those slight errors you refer to, such as the use of *verriculum* instead of *sagena*, *remitte* instead of *dimitte*, *discumbentibus* instead of *discumbentium*,[38] and other similar errors, such as his substitution of a Latin word for a foreign one, or an idiomatic phrase for a solecism, or a precise expression for an ambiguous one, or his correction of a wrong translation, or of an error made by the copyist, or his rendering of a Greek idiom by an expression peculiar to Latin—all these errors, I say, he will revise rather than have you as his enemy; and the entire loot, consisting of all the barbarisms, all the solecisms, all the obscurities, every phrase rendered sleepily, and every defect of the copyist will be conscientiously restored to the sanctuary by Erasmus, since, in stealing them from the church, as I observe, he was guilty of theft, and also of sacrilege. He will not at all be deterred by the prospect of alienating all good scholars, whose friendship had been secured by this service of his; for their affections will be replaced by his reconciliation with you and with that tall teller of tales—that is to say, the rank and file will be replaced in his affections by the top-ranking chiefs, the two officials in charge of all intellectuals.

But to become serious; this one act of yours was really honorable and good, and therefore I truly and sincerely praise you for admitting that there are only some small errors requiring correction; though you make this admission shyly, as suits your modesty, still it is made with the sincere intention of ridding yourself of a terrible falsehood, for it implies that the earlier charges, which you made in the heat of passion, of his being a heretic, a schismatic, and the herald of anti-Christ were all completely false. For, in my eyes, your case is not so hopeless nor is my opinion of you so low that I would take your words "insignificant little errors" to refer to heresy and schism and being the herald of the anti-Christ; the hideousness of such crimes surpasses any mass of evil. Since I see you have revoked your serious charges, I do not intend to argue with you over trifling matters. Let everything said on both sides be considered unsaid; let all the hubbub, which started over

38. These were discussed in the first part of the letter.

nothing, tail off to nothing, and may this tragedy at last end in
a comedy. Farewell, and if you do not want to live the sheltered
life of the cloister in vain, give yourself up to peace of spirit,
not to these wrangling squabbles.

27

[96] To William Budaeus.

Henry VIII and Francis I, each accompanied by his Queen, met
on 7 June 1520 at a tilting ground in the open field between Guis-
nes and Ardres. Temporary buildings were erected and made
magnificent by the hanging of tapestries. Each King was suspicious
of the other. Henry VIII had received Charles V at Dover on 27
May, and after leaving Francis I, saw the young Emperor again,
with his aunt and regent, Margaret of Austria-Savoy, at Gravelines
on 10 July. France had hoped to recover Calais and was greatly
disappointed to hear of this evidence of continued Anglo-Bur-
gundian good will. Budé had returned to Court in 1519, at the
summons of Francis I.

⟨Calais
c. June 1520⟩

If it were not for the vehemence of my desires, I would not
dare to ask you to lessen the pain of your absence by writing
to me. For I fear that engaged as you are in the affairs of the
Most Christian King, you will not enjoy much leisure, and
for my part I am only too conscious of my remissness in this
kind of duty, when letters ought to be answered. It is not
only my lack of eloquence, my dear Budaeus, that keeps me
from writing to you, but still more my respect for your learning. Shame would even have forbidden me to write this letter,
unless another kind of shame had wrung it from me. This is
the fear lest the letters that you have received from me should
be published along with yours. If they should go forth to the
world alone, their defects would be abundantly clear, but if
they were side by side with yours their shameful poverty would
be exposed as by a light of fierce and unpitying brilliance.
For I remember that in our conversation mention was made
of the letters that I had formerly sent you, which you had it in
your mind to publish if you thought I would raise no objection. It was only a passing suggestion, and I forget what reply

I gave. But now, as I think the matter over, I see that it would be safer if you would wait a while, at least until I revise my letters. It is not only that I fear there may be passages where the Latin is faulty, but also in my remarks upon peace and war, upon morality, marriage, the clergy, the people, etc., perhaps what I have written has not always been so cautious and guarded that it would be wise to expose it to captious critics.

28

[97] To William Budaeus.

⟨Calais
c. June 1520⟩

I doubt, my dear Budaeus, whether it is good ever to possess things which are pleasing and dear unless you can keep them. For I thought I would be completely happy if I had the good fortune ever to see Budaeus face to face (of whom reading had drawn me a very beautiful image), and after I got my wish I thought I was happier than happiness itself. But when our duties prevented our meeting often enough to satisfy my longing for conversation with you, and within a few days (as our Kings were called away by affairs of state) our association only just begun was at once broken off; and we (who had each to follow his own prince) were drawn in opposite directions, perhaps never to see each other again; the happier our meeting had been, the greater was the sadness which assailed me at our parting. This you can somewhat lighten if you will deign sometimes to visit me by letter, which, however, but that eager longing urges me, I would not dare ask.

29

[101] To his School.

More's "School" included others than his own children: Alice Middleton, his step-daughter; Ann Cresacre, his ward and then daughter-in-law; Margaret à Barrow, who later married Thomas Elyot; and others.

At Court
23 March ⟨1521⟩

THOMAS MORE TO HIS WHOLE SCHOOL GREETING.

See what a compendious salutation I have found, to save
both time and paper, which would otherwise have been wasted
in listing the names of each one of you in salutation, and my
labor would have been to no purpose, since, though each of
you is dear to me by some special title, of which I could have
omitted none in an ingratiating salutation, no one is dearer
to me by any title than each of you by that of scholar. Your
zeal for knowledge binds me to you almost more closely than
the ties of blood. I rejoice that Master Drew [1] has returned
safe, for I was anxious, as you know, about him. If I did not
love you so much I should be really envious of your happiness
in having so many and such excellent tutors. But I think you
have no longer any need of Master Nicholas,[2] since you have
learned whatever he had to teach you about astronomy. I hear
you are so far advanced in that science that you can not only
point out the polar star or the dog star, or any of the ordinary
stars, but are able also—which requires the skill of an absolute
Astronomer—among the special and principal heavenly bodies,
to distinguish the sun from the moon! Onward then in that
new and admirable science by which you ascend to the stars!
But while you gaze on them assiduously, consider that this
holy time of Lent warns you, and that beautiful and holy poem
of Boethius [3] keeps singing in your ears, teaching you to raise
your mind also to heaven, lest the soul look downwards to

1. Drew is not mentioned in the lists of young tutors given by Roper,
Cresacre More, or Erasmus. Perhaps he is the Roger Drew (Drewe or
Drewys), B.A. Oxford, 1512, M.A. 1514, Fellow of All Souls from 1512.
A Roger Drewe received a prebend in St. Stephen's, Westminster, 1523,
and the Church of Highbray in the diocese of Exeter in May 1524.

2. Nicholas Kratzer (1486/7–3 August 1550) of Munich, B.A. Cologne
1509, and also of Wittenberg, went to England late in 1517, became
Astronomer to the King in 1519, and held the office for many years. In
1523 he went to Oxford to lecture on astronomy and geography as one
of Wolsey's Readers and was incorporated M.A. in the University. He
married in 1535. A magnificent portrait of him by Holbein, 1528, is in
the Louvre.

3. Boëthius, 5, Metrum v.

the earth, after the manner of brutes, while the body is raised
aloft.

Farewell, all my dearest.

From Court, the 23rd March.

30

[105] To John Fisher.

Roper (pp. 21–22) tells us of More's visits to the universities, of
his interest in their disputations, and of students resorting to him,
but there is no other mention of the relations described here.

⟨1521⟩

As to this priest, Reverend Father, of whom you write that
he will soon obtain a prebend if he can obtain a vigorous advocate with the King's majesty, I think I have so wrought that
our Prince will raise no obstacle . . .

Whatever influence I have with the King (it is certainly
very little) but such as it is, is as freely available to your
Paternity and all your scholars as his own house to any man.
I owe your students constant gratitude for the heartfelt affection of which their letters to me are the token. Farewell,
best and most learned of Bishops, and continue your affection
for me.

31

[106] To Margaret Roper.

Margaret More was married in July 1521 to William Roper
(1498–1578) of Eltham in Kent and of Canterbury, a graduate of
one of the universities and later prothonotary or clerk of the pleas
of the court of the King's Bench for fifty-four years. He seems to
have been a member of More's household as early as 1518, when he
became a member of the Society of Lincoln's Inn. He was called to
the Bar 1525 and to the Bench 1535. Roper was M.P. for Bramber
in Sussex, 1529; for Rochester, 1554; and for Canterbury, 1555 and
1558.

He was at one time interested in the Lutheran doctrine of justification by faith and was charged with heresy before Wolsey, but
was "with a friendly warning discharged." He was ever thereafter
loyal to the Catholic Church, suffered imprisonment in the Tower

in 1542, and under Elizabeth was summoned before the Privy Council because of aid to exiles for religion who had printed books
against the government. He entered into a bond to be of good behavior, and then remained unmolested.

Roper's *Life of More* was written c. 1556 as notes to be used by
Nicholas Harpsfield for his biography of More.

⟨1521?⟩

THOMAS MORE TO HIS MOST DEAR DAUGHTER MARGARET:

There was no reason, my darling daughter, why you should
have put off writing me for a single day, because in your great
self-distrust you feared that your letters would be such that I
could not read them without distaste. Even had they not been
perfect, yet the honor of your sex would have gained you
pardon from anyone, while to a father even a blemish will
seem beautiful in the face of a child. But indeed, my dear
Margaret, your letters were so elegant and polished and gave
so little cause for you to dread the indulgent judgment of a
parent, that you might have despised the censorship of an
angry Momus.

You tell me that Nicholas, who is fond of us and so learned
in astronomy, has begun again with you the system of the
heavenly bodies. I am grateful to him, and I congratulate you
on your good fortune; for in the space of one month, with only
slight labor, you will thus learn thoroughly these sublime won-
ders of the Eternal Workman, which so many men of illustrious
and almost superhuman intellect have discovered only with
hot toil and study, or rather with cold shiverings and nightly
vigils in the open air in the course of many ages.

I am, therefore, delighted to read that you have made up
your mind to give yourself so diligently to philosophy as to
make up by your earnestness in future what you have lost in
the past by neglect. My darling Margaret, I indeed have never
found you idling—and your unusual learning in almost every
kind of literature shows that you have been making active
progress—so I take your words as an example of the great
modesty that makes you prefer to accuse yourself falsely of
sloth rather than to boast truly of your diligence; unless your
meaning is that you will give yourself so earnestly to study

that your past industry will seem like indolence by comparison. If this is your meaning, my Margaret, and I think it really is, nothing could be more delightful to me, or more fortunate, my sweetest daughter, for you.

Though I earnestly hope that you will devote the rest of your life to medical science and sacred literature, so that you may be well furnished for the whole scope of human life, (which is to have a sound mind in a sound body), and I know that you have already laid the foundations of these studies, and there will be always opportunity to continue the building; yet I am of opinion that you may with great advantage give some years of your yet flourishing youth to humane letters and so-called liberal studies. And this both because youth is more fitted for a struggle with difficulties and because it is uncertain whether you will ever in the future have the benefit of so sedulous, affectionate, and learned a teacher. I need not say that by such studies a good judgment is formed or perfected.

It would be a delight, my dear Margaret, to me to converse long with you on these matters: but I have just been interrupted and called away by the servants, who have brought in supper. I must have regard to others, else to sup is not so sweet as to talk with you.

Farewell, my dearest child, and salute for me my beloved son, your husband. I am extremely glad that he is following the same course of study as yourself. I am ever wont to persuade you to yield in everything to your husband; now, on the contrary, I give you full leave to strive to surpass him in the knowledge of the celestial system. Farewell again. Salute your whole company, but especially your tutor.

32

[107] To his Children and Margaret Gyge.

John More was born c. 1509, and was scarcely two years old when his mother, Jane Colt More, died. She was still living on 19 May 1511 when Ammonius wrote of her to Erasmus as More's "very gracious wife," but died soon after, as More had married Dame Alice Middleton before 27 October, and Ammonius had fled the

house to avoid "the crooked-beaked harpy." To the children, however, Dame Alice was as devoted "as very few mothers are to their
own children."

John More did not have as great intellectual gifts as his sisters,
but was very well read and studious. Erasmus dedicated to him his
edition of *Aristotle* (*Correspondence,* Ep. 183) and Simon Grynaeus,
the later Protestant Reformer, his *Plato* (ibid., Ep. 196).

At Court

3 September ⟨1522?⟩

THOMAS MORE TO HIS DEAREST CHILDREN AND TO MARGARET
GYGE, WHOM HE NUMBERS AMONG HIS CHILDREN, GREETING.

The Bristol merchant brought me your letters the day after
he left you, with which I was extremely delighted. Nothing
can come from your workshop, however rude and unfinished,
that will not give me more pleasure than the most meticulous
writing of anyone else. So much does my affection for you
commend whatever you write to me. Indeed, without any
recommendation, your letters are capable of pleasing by their
own merits, the charm and pure Latinity of their style. There
has not been one of your letters that did not please me extremely. But to confess ingenuously what I feel, the letter from
my son John pleased me the best, both because it was longer
than the others and because he seems to have given it a bit
more labor and study. For he not only put out his matter
prettily and composed in fairly polished language, but he plays
with me both pleasantly and cleverly, and turns my jokes on
myself wittily enough. And this he does not only merrily, but
with due moderation, showing that he does not forget that he
is joking with his father, whom he is eager to delight and yet
is cautious not to give offense.

Now I expect from each of you a letter almost every day. I
will not admit excuses (for John makes none) such as want of
time, sudden departure of the letter carrier, or want of something to write about. No one hinders you from writing, but,
on the contrary, all are urging you to it. And that you may not
keep the letter carrier waiting, why not anticipate his coming,
and have your letter written and sealed, ready two days before a carrier is available? How can a subject be wanting when
you write to me, who am glad to hear of your studies or of

your games, and whom you will please most if, when there is
nothing to write about, you write just that at great length.
Nothing can be easier for you, especially for girls, loquacious
by nature and always doing it.

One thing, however, I admonish you, whether you write
serious matters or the merest trifles, it is my wish that you
write everything diligently and thoughtfully. It will do no harm
if you first write the whole in English, for then you will have
much less trouble and labor in turning it into Latin; not having
to look for the matter, your mind will be intent only on the
language. That, however, I leave to your own choice, whereas
I strictly enjoin you that whatever you have composed you
carefully examine before writing it out clean; and in this examination first scrutinize the whole sentence and then every
part of it. Thus, if any solecisms have escaped you, you will
easily detect them. Correct these, write out the whole letter
again, and even then do not grudge to examine it once more,
for sometimes, in rewriting, faults slip in again that one had
expunged. By this diligence you will soon make your little
trifles seem serious matters; for while there is nothing so neat
and witty that will not be made insipid by silly and careless
loquacity, so also there is nothing in itself so insipid that you
cannot season it with grace and wit if you give a little thought
to it. Farewell, my dearest children.

From the Court, the 3rd September.

33

[108] To Margaret ⟨Roper⟩.

John Veysey or Voysey (?1465–1554) was consecrated Bishop of
Exeter by Archbishop Warham on 6 November 1519. He served
later as President of Wales, but was not a capable administrator.

At Court
11 September   ⟨1522?⟩

THOMAS MORE TO HIS DEAREST DAUGHTER MARGARET, GREETING.

I need not express the extreme pleasure your letter gave me,
my darling daughter. You will be able to judge better how
much it pleased your father when you learn what delight it

caused to a stranger. I happened this evening to be in the company of the Reverend Father, John, Bishop of Exeter, a man of deep learning and of a wide reputation for holiness. Whilst we were talking I took out of my pocket a paper that bore on our business and by accident your letter appeared. He took it into his hand with pleasure and began to examine it. When he saw from the signature that it was the letter of a lady, his surprise led him to read it more eagerly. When he had finished, he said he would never have believed it to be your work unless I had assured him of the fact, and he began to praise it in the highest terms (why should I hide what he said?) for its pure Latinity, its correctness, its erudition, and its expressions of tender affection. Seeing how delighted he was, I showed him your speech. He read it, as also your poems, with a pleasure so far beyond what he had hoped that although he praised you most effusively, yet his countenance showed that his words were all too poor to express what he felt. He took out at once from his pocket a portague [1] which you will find enclosed in this letter. I tried in every possible way to decline it, but was unable to refuse to take it to send to you as a pledge and token of his good will towards you. This hindered me from showing him the letters of your sisters, for I feared that it would seem as though I had shown them to obtain for the others too a gift which it embarrassed me to have to accept for you. But, as I have said, he is so good that it is a joy to have pleased him. Write him your thanks carefully in the nicest letter you can. You will one day be glad to have given pleasure to such a man. Farewell.

From the Court, just before mid-night, September 11th.

34

[113] To Conrad Goclenius.

Erasmus had introduced Goclenius to More in July 1521, when More was expected in the Netherlands. Perhaps Goclenius had asked for the introduction. Erasmus recommended him as "made

1. A portague was a Portuguese gold coin, the great "crusado" bearing the figure of a cross struck under Alfonso V c. 1457, when Pope Calixtus III urged a crusade against the Turks. Its value ranged between £3. 5s. and £4. 10s.

for friendship" and praised his teaching and scholarship (Allen, 4, 1220).

Conrad Wackers (called Goclenius, from his second name, Gockelen or von Gockel), born in late 1489 or early 1490, was a pupil in Deventer and a student in the universities of Cologne and Louvain, taking his master's degree at the latter in 1515. In December 1519 he was appointed Professor of Latin in the Collegium Trilingue founded by Jerome Busleiden at Louvain. By October 1520 the college had been formally installed in its own buildings, with President, Professors of Latin, Greek, and Hebrew, and ten "adolescents" as scholars. The Latin professor was to receive only half what the others were paid, and the executors soon felt it necessary to increase the stipend. When Goclenius had offers elsewhere, Erasmus advocated a further increase, and twelve Rhine florins were secretly paid (to avoid envy) by the President every year "to a certain person by order of the executors" (Allen, 3, 691, intro.; 4, 1221).

Goclenius was admitted to the Council of the University in 1524. He was a Canon of Antwerp from 1533. His success in teaching was extraordinary, and because of it he wrote little. He translated Lucian's *Hermotimus* in 1522 and dedicated it to More "as a remembrance of a new friend, who will yield to no one of your older friends in duty, love, and respect." More's charming reply was accompanied by the gift of a cup full of gold coins. Goclenius died on 25 January 1539 and was buried in St. Peter's, Louvain (de Vocht, *Literae Virorum ad Craneveldium,* pp. 245–49; *Collegium Trilingue, 1,* 484–87).

London

⟨c. November 1522⟩

Some little time ago my good friend Peter Gilles sent me Lucian's *Hermotimus,* translated by you, most learned Goclenius, and dedicated to me. When I received it I was indeed very greatly pleased both by your kindness to me and by the charm of the work, together with the elegance of its style; in it you seem to me to compete most happily even with the Greek. So our mutual friend Erasmus was quite right—whose frequent enthusiastic statements of your ability and learning made you dear to me before I knew you. And now really since this additional pledge, so to call it, of your affection and good will toward me in turn, although I loved you so much before that I thought I could not love you more, yet somehow or other, to that earlier love for you I feel a considerable increase has accrued. And so by showing your learned essays also to

many others among us, I have seen to it that you have here
many more friends and admirers of your talents. And if there
should occur anything in which I can gratify or serve you or
any of yours, I shall make clear ⟨by return⟩ how good and
kind has been your service to me. Farewell, my very dear friend;
all my friends here in London send their most cordial greetings.

Your (in whatever way I may serve you)

THOMAS MORE

To the very learned professor of Latin, Conrad Goclenius, at
Louvain.

35

[128] To Margaret Roper.

Reginald Pole, B.A. Oxford 1515 (at fifteen years of age) was sent
by the King, his kinsman, to Italy to study in February 1521. He
had his own house with a large household in Padua, and studied assiduously. He returned to England early in 1527.
Stapleton put two extracts together as contemporary, but we
cannot reconcile their dates. The first must be before February
1521 when Pole went abroad. The second is dated by the mention
of the approaching birth of Margaret's first child.

⟨Woodstock?
Autumn 1523⟩

I cannot put down on paper, indeed I can hardly express
in my own mind, the deep pleasure that I received from your
most charming letter, my dearest Margaret. As I read it there
was with me a young man of the noblest rank and of the widest
attainments in literature—one, too, who is as conspicuous for
his virtue as he is for his learning, Reginald Pole. He thought
your letter nothing short of marvelous, even before he understood how pressed you were for time and distracted by ill
health, while you managed to write so long a letter. I could
scarce make him believe that you had not been helped by a
teacher until he learned truly that there was no teacher at our
house, and that it would not be possible to find a man who
would not need your help in composing letters rather than
be able to give any assistance to you.

Meanwhile, something I once said to you in joke came back to my mind, and I realized how true it was. It was to the effect that you were to be pitied, because the incredulity of men would rob you of the praise you so richly deserved for your laborious vigils, as they would never believe, when they read what you had written, that you had not often availed yourself of another's help: whereas of all the writers you least deserved to be thus suspected. Even when a tiny child you could never endure to be decked out in another's finery. But, my sweetest Margaret, you are all the more deserving of praise on this account. Although you cannot hope for an adequate reward for your labor, yet nevertheless you continue to unite to your singular love of virtue the pursuit of literature and art. Content with the profit and pleasure of your conscience, in your modesty you do not seek for the praise of the public, nor value it overmuch even if you receive it, but because of the great love you bear us, you regard us—your husband and myself—as a sufficiently large circle of readers for all that you write.

In your letter you speak of your imminent confinement. We pray most earnestly that all may go happily and successfully with you. May God and our Blessed Lady grant you happily and safely to increase your family by a little one like to his mother in everything except sex. Yet let it by all means be a girl, if only she will make up for the inferiority of her sex by her zeal to imitate her mother's virtue and learning. Such a girl I should prefer to three boys. Good-bye, my dearest child.

36

[133] To the University of Oxford.

The Latin of University titles was mediaeval and somewhat barbarous, so this correspondence tries to use Ciceronian expressions, leaving the reader a little uncertain as to which officers and governing bodies are meant.

Thomas Lovell fought for Henry Tudor at Bosworth and in 1485 was appointed Chancellor of the Exchequer for life. He was M.P. and Speaker of the House of Commons 1485–88 and probably was in Parliament even later. He was knighted after the battle of Stoke in 1487. In 1502 he was made Treasurer of the Household, and in 1503 a Knight of the Garter. At Henry VIII's accession, he was continued as Chancellor of the Exchequer and Treasurer of the Household. He was elected High Steward of the University of Oxford c. 1504. Henry IV in 1406 had transferred to this new officer, appointed by the Chancellor, the right to try for felony and treason members of the University, privileged servants, and traders, who did not have the immunities of clerks (Sir Charles Edward Mallet, *A History of the University of Oxford*, 3 vols., *I*, 171).

Sir Thomas Lovell died 25 May 1524. The University wrote to More, offering him the position, 20 June (*Correspondence*, Ep. 132). Lovell had also been High Steward of the University of Cambridge, and this vacancy was likewise offered to More. In October, however, Hugh Latimer wrote to Dr. Greene, the Master of St. Catherine's College, that he had "learned . . . that nothing would more gratify Mr. Wingfield (Sir Richard) than to succeed to Lovell's place among us." More had been persuaded, though only at the King's intercession, to give way to him (*L.P. 4*, App. 14). More's acceptance was answered by the University c. August 1524 (*Correspondence*, Ep. 134).

London
26 July ⟨1524⟩

TO HIS VERY DEAR FRIENDS, THE CONGREGATION AND MASTERS OF THE UNIVERSITY OF OXFORD.

After the death of the distinguished Sir Thomas Lovell, who was the late High Steward and Agent of your University, your Proctor acting as your representative, most learned Gentlemen, came to me to inform me of your deep regret at the death of that eminent Gentleman, and, furthermore, that, having met to select his successor, you chose me, out of your friendliness and great love, as the best qualified candidate for that office. This office, conferred upon me with such sincere and friendly approbation, I have very gladly and happily accepted, with the realization that, out of a large group of extremely talented men whose wisdom and prestige could be of great service to you, I was the first choice to whom you would entrust the complete handling of your business affairs and law suits. This appointment has clearly indicated to me your opinion of my devotion to duty and the high value that you have ever set upon my services. Consequently, illustrious Gentlemen, while heretofore I have had from your indulgence the greatest possible pleasure, such that it seemed I could not have greater, while, on my part, I have ever regarded you with such affection that I thought I could not add to it; still, as a result of this recent kindness toward me, I am so moved by affection for you and so filled with new joy by your favor that I seem almost not to have been loved by you before nor to have loved you. For your previous favors were at all times such as can proceed only from the noblest love, and I have welcomed each one of them as such kindnesses should be welcomed by a sincere mind and grateful heart. Your most recent display of good will, how-ever, has placed the crown upon all the rest, and it brought before my mind's eye, in momentary flashes, all your previous favors; and yet the recollection of each of them stirred my heart no less than on the day they were bestowed and made me realize that I should be, as I really was, as grateful as if I were then receiving all of them for the first time. These reflections were caused, not by any desire of mine to occupy this office, but by the recurrent thought that those men before whom I have stood in awe since my youth, and whom I have respected, and whose gratitude I have always endeavored to earn, and whose affection I have prayed to win, were vying with one another in honoring me as if that were their one concern. Therefore, most esteemed and cultured Gentlemen, I extend to you all the sincerest gratitude of which I am capable. And I want you to promise yourselves and to expect from More, who is and will always be yours wholeheartedly, all that you would desire, either as a group from a most devoted patron and friend, or individually, from a very dear comrade or brother. I, for my part, will strive with all zeal, care and dili-gence so to prove myself to you—both as a group and indi-vidually—that not a single one of you may think that he has been deceived in his expectations. Farewell, most cherished Gentlemen. From London, July 26.

Entirely yours from the bottom of my heart,

THOMAS MORE

37

[136] To Wolsey.

Hertford

29 November ⟨1524⟩

It may like your good Grace to be advertised [1] that yester-night at my coming unto the King's Grace's presence, after that I had made your Grace's recommendations and his High-ness showed himself very greatly glad and joyful of your Grace's health; as I was about to declare further to his Grace what letters I had brought, his Highness perceiving letters in my hand, prevented [2] me ere [3] I could begin and said, "Ah! you have letters now by John Joachim [4] and I trow [5] some resolu-tion what they will do." "Nay verily, Sir," quoth I. "My Lord hath yet no word by John Joachim nor John Joachim, as far as my Lord knew, had yet no word himself this day in the morn-ing when I departed from his Grace." "No had?" [6] quoth he, "I much marvel thereof for John Joachim had a servant come to him two days ago." "Sir," quoth I, "if it like your Grace,[7] this morning my Lord's Grace had nothing heard thereof, for yesterday his Grace at afternoon dispatched me to your Grace with a letter sent from Master Doctor Knight [8] and the same night late his Grace sent a servant of his to my house and commanded me to be with his Grace this morning by eight of the clock, where at my coming he delivered me these other

1. informed.   2. anticipated.
3. before.
4. John Joachim de Passano, Sieur de Vaux, was secretary to Fregoso, governor of Genoa, and resident at the Court of France. John Joachim was sent to England in June 1524, representing himself as a Genoese merchant to deal with the affairs of the Luccan Antonio Bonvisi. The Bonvisi brothers often intervened in transactions between Henry VIII or Francis I with Italian bankers, and Antonio, as particularly attached to the French, helped John Joachim. Wolsey secured lodgings for him with his own confessor, Thomas Larke at Blackfriars.
5. trust.
6. A characteristic expression; it is also given by Cavendish (ed. Syl-vester, p. 84).
7. if your Grace like.
8. Dr. William Knight, ambassador at the court of Margaret of Austria-Savoy, the Emperor's aunt and regent in the Netherlands.

letters and advertisements [9] sent unto him from Master Pace,[10] commanding me that after that your Highness had seen them, I should remit [11] them to him with diligence, as well for that he would show them to other of your Grace's Council as also to John Joachim, for the contents be such as will do him little pleasure." "Marry," [12] quoth his Grace, "I am well apaid thereof." [13]

And so he fell in merrily to the reading of the letters of Master Pace and all the other abstracts and writings, whereof the contents as highly contented him as any tidings that I have seen come to him, and thanked your Grace most heartily for your good and speedy advertisement; and forthwith he declared the news and every material point, which upon the reading his Grace well noted unto the Queen's Grace and all other about him who were marvelous glad to hear it. And the Queen's Grace said that she was glad that the Spaniards had yet done somewhat in Italy in recompense [14] of their departure out of Provence.[15]

I showed his Highness that your Grace thought that the French King passed the mountains in hope to win all with a visage [16] in Italy and to find there no resistance and his sudden coming upon [17] much abashed the countries, putting each quarter in doubt of other and out of surety [18] who might be well trusted, but now since he findeth it otherwise, missing the help of money, which he hoped to have had in Milan, finding his enemies strong and the fortresses well manned and

9. notifications.

10. State Papers *1*, 151 n., considers this to refer to Pace's letter of 2 November, but More evidently refers to later news. The assaults on Pavia had taken place 8 and 9 November, and are reported in Pace's letters to the King and Wolsey of 19 November. I consider that More replies to the former. The posts *could* have brought it in that short time, though it is unusually quick service.

11. send back.

12. Originally, the name of the Virgin Mary, used as oath or ejaculatory invocation, in the sixteenth century probably taken as mere interjection.

13. well paid for it.   14. as an equivalent for.

15. Sampson wrote to Wolsey from Vallodolid, 13 November, that the Emperor's army, which had invaded France from Catalonia, had retreated. Pace's letter gives the encouraging news that the Imperialists in Italy have been more diligent because of their distrust of the Pope.

16. merely by showing his face.   17. attack.   18. uncertain.

furnished and at Pavia, by the expugnation [19] whereof he
thought to put all the remnant in fear and dread, being now
twice rejected [20] with loss and reproach, his estimation [21] shall
so decay and his friends fail, his enemies confirmed and encouraged, namely, such aid of the Almaignes [22] of new [23] join-
ing with them, that like as the French King before wrote and
boasted unto his mother [24] that he had of his own mind passed
into Italy, so is it likely that she shall have shortly cause to
write again to him that it had to be much better and more
wisdom for him to abide at home than to put himself there
whereas he standeth in great peril whether ever he shall get
thence. The King's Grace laughed and said that he thinketh
it will be very hard for him to get thence, and that he thinketh
the matters going thus the Pope's Holiness [25] will not be hasty
neither in peace nor truce.

Upon the reading of Master Knight's [26] letter his Grace said
not much, but that if Bewreyne [27] come to his Grace he will
be plain with him. And if he do not, but take his dispatch
there of your Grace, which thing I perceive his Highness would
be well content he did, except he desire to come to his presence,
his Grace requireth yours so to talk with him as he may know
that his Grace and yours well perceive how the matters be
handled by the Emperor's agents in the enterprise.

The King's Grace is very glad that the matters of Scotland
be in so good train [28] and would be loath that they were now
ruffled [29] by the Earl of Angwishe [30] and much his Highness

19. taking by storm.
20. repulsed. Pace reported the failure of two assaults on Pavia by
Francis I.
21. repute.   22. Germans.   23. newly.
24. Louise of Savoy was regent for Francis I.
25. The Pope had secretly given aid to Charles de Lanoy, Viceroy
of Naples. Pace considered that the Pope would favor the winning side
and this would deter him from making any truce with the French.
26. Knight's letter makes no mention of de Buren but recounts the
news from Italy. Florys d'Egmont, Count de Buren, the Emperor's lieutenant, had refused to obey the orders of Henry's lieutenant, and would
do only what was decided by mutual consent.
27. Florys d'Egmont, Lord of Iselstein, the Emperor's lieutenant; after-
wards Count de Buren.
28. order.   29. disordered.
30. Archibald Douglas, Earl of Angus, second husband of the Queen
of Scotland. Margaret (Henry's sister) made agreement with Wolsey that

alloweth the most prudent mind of your Grace, minding to use the Earl of Angwish for an instrument to wring and wrest the matters into better train if they walk awry,[31] and not to wrestle with them and break [32] them when they go right.

It may like your Grace also to be advertised [33] that I moved his Grace concerning the suit of Master Broke [34] in such wise as your Grace declared unto me your pleasure, when Master Broke and I were with your Grace on Sunday. And his Grace answered me that he would take a breath [35] therein and that he would first once speak with the young man and then his Grace departed, but I perceived by his Grace that he had taken the young man's promise not to marry without his advice, because his Grace intended to marry him to some one of the Queen's maidens. If it would like your good Grace in any letter which it should please your Grace hereafter to write hither, to make some mention and remembrance of that matter, I trust it would take good effect. And thus our Lord long preserve your good Grace in honor and health.

At Hertford the twenty-ninth day of November.

Your Grace's humble orator [36] and most bounden beadman [37]

THOMAS MORE

To my Lord Legate's good Grace

38

[148, Allen, 6, 1770] To Erasmus.

Greenwich
18 December ⟨1526⟩

Best greetings: I have received two letters [1] from you, dearest Erasmus, and have also read the one you addressed to the

---

he should return to Scotland to negotiate for the release of James V (1513–42) from the influence of the Duke of Albany, the regent. Angus was long detained by the English on the border, as the estrangement between him and the Queen interfered with the political negotiations. The Parliament of Scotland, 14 and 16 November, took the governorship from Albany, since he had remained in France, and gave the direction of affairs to the Queen and Council. "Angwish" was the Queen's nickname for her husband.

31. go perversely.   32. ruin.   33. informed.
34. *L.P.* gives nothing further of interest with regard to Master Broke.
35. respite.   36. suppliant.   37. One who prays for another.
1. Not now extant.

Reverend Father, the Bishop of London.[2] We, who are your
dear little friends, are very much disturbed to hear that the
stone disorder which gave you terrible pains for so long has
now been followed by the disease which proved fatal to Linacre;
though God's goodness and your own virtue are turning such
evils into good for you, still our joy at your spiritual blessings
does not preclude all concern, on our part, for the human
frailty of your body; our uneasiness is caused not only by concern for you personally—for whom as for ourselves we do hope
and pray for every blessing—but also, and more especially, by
concern for all of Christendom; we are afraid that this illness
will interrupt the brilliant works you have been writing to
promote Christian piety. I pray God that you may bring them
to a speedy and happy conclusion, especially the remaining
part of the *Hyperaspistes;* [3] for you could have no other work
in mind that would be more profitable for others, more satisfying to your friends, and more notable or more urgent for
your own self. You would find it hard to believe the eagerness
with which all good men are looking forward to that work;
there are, on the other hand, some wicked persons, either partisans of Luther or your jealous rivals, who apparently are glee-
ful and growing in numbers as a result of your delayed response.
However, I can sympathize with your delay, if the interruption
has been caused by your desire to complete other writings first
—as, for instance, your work on *Christian Marriage,*[4] which
her Majesty the Queen correctly regards as being of supreme
importance—and I hope that fact will shortly be brought home
to you in a concrete way. And I am very contented, too, if the
delay has been caused by your desire to handle the subject in
a leisurely, thoughtful fashion; for I am anxious to see that
part handled with the utmost care. But if, according to some
reports, the delay is due to the fact that you have been terrorized, and have lost all interest in the work, and have no courage
to go on with it, then I am thoroughly bewildered and unable

2. Cuthbert Tunstal.

3. *Defender of the Diatribe against Martin Luther's The Unfree Will.*
It was finished c. August 1527 and published in time for the Frankfort
Fair.

4. The *Institution of Christian Marriage,* August 1526, dedicated to
Queen Catherine of Aragon.

to restrain my grief. You have endured, dearest Erasmus, many, many struggles and perils and Herculean labors; you have spent all the best years of your life on exhausting work, through sleepless nights, for the profit of all the world; and God forbid that now you should so unhappily become enamored of your declining years as to be willing to abandon the cause of God rather than lose a decision.

I am not afraid that you will now throw up to me that quotation from the comic poet: "When we are well, everybody," etc., or, "If you were here, you might think differently." [5] Indeed, I am incapable of making any such promises, nor is anybody else capable of offering such prospects as the whole world is waiting with expectation to receive from you, because you have given extraordinary proof of a heart that is valiant and trusting in God. It is impossible for me to doubt that you will continue bravely to exhibit such strength of spirit right up to your dying breath, even if there were a disastrous catastrophe. For you could never fail to trust that God in His merciful kindness would intervene to calm the disturbance. Right now, as far as I can see, you are far from being terrorized; in fact, there is little cause for fear at all. If the Lutherans planned to make any threatening moves, very likely they would have made them before your reply. Then they might have forestalled any answer from you; or if they wanted to gain vengeance on you for your writings, they would have given vent to their rage at the time you published your first volume; for, in that work, you drew such a vivid description of the monster, and you pointed out so accurately the spirit that goads it on, that you displayed, for all the world to see, that fuming, hellish demon, as if you had dragged Cerberus up from the infernal regions.

At present I certainly fail to see any peril beyond that which would threaten you even if you did not write another line. You have replied to the false charges he made against you; you have stabbed him with the point of your pen; all that remains for you is a discussion of Scripture, and, by issuing, like so many promissory notes, a thousand copies of the first volume, you have solemnly promised the whole world that you would

5. Terence, *Andria* 309–10.

faithfully go through with the second volume. Therefore, not even Luther is such a fool as to hope, or such a wretch as to dare to demand, that you would now not carry out God's cause, having accomplished your own, or that you would not fulfill the promise you made publicly, especially since that would be so easy for you to do. Luther, I am sure, would rather have you say nothing, even though, in his letter to you, he pretends to have a supreme contempt for you; it is hard to tell whether that letter is marked more by boastful exaggeration or stupidity. In any case, he is fully conscious that his worthless comments, which laboriously obscure the most obvious passages of Scripture while being frigid enough in themselves, would become, under your criticism, a mass of sheer ice.

Since you, however, are present at the scene of action, while I am some distance away, if you notice that your reply involves some danger which you cannot elude and which I cannot foresee, then, please, do at least this much: write me a confidential note and have it delivered to me by a reliable carrier. Not only the Bishop of London, an absolutely honest person, as you know, and extremely devoted to you, but also I myself will conscientiously see to it that the note will never be made public, unless that can be done safely.

Your painter,[6] dearest Erasmus, is a remarkable artist; but I am afraid he will not find England as fertile and fruitful as he expected. Still, I shall do my best to see that he does not find it altogether barren. Your pamphlet was a very neat refutation of the rumor spread abroad by some malicious persons that you favored the heresy of Carlstadt;[7] you thus foiled the sly attempts of the clown who had planted that story in some German work. If God ever grants you the free time, I would like eventually to see a treatise in support of our Faith flow from that heart of yours, so perfect an instrument for defending the truth; however, right now I am very much concerned

6. Hans Holbein the Younger, who painted the portrait of More now in the Frick Collection, the sketch of Lady More now at Corsham Court, a picture of the whole family, and drawings of the group and of each member, now at Basel and Windsor.

7. Andrew Bodenstein von Carlstadt (1480–1541), the very radical Reformer at Wittenberg, whom Luther opposed, searching for slower and more conservative changes in the church.

about the *Hyperaspistes* and I would not want you to become absorbed in anything that might turn your interests elsewhere and thus prevent you from completing this work at the earliest possible date.

Farewell, Erasmus, dearest of all men; from the Court at Greenwich, December 18.

Sincerely and more than wholeheartedly yours,

THOMAS MORE

To the excellent and most learned Master Erasmus of Rotterdam.

39

[150] To the University of Oxford.

Richmond

11 March ⟨1527?⟩

RIGHT WORSHIPFUL [1] SIR IN MY MOST HEARTY WISE I RECOMMEND ME UNTO YOU.

Signifying unto you the King's pleasure is that for certain considerations moving his Highness, ye shall forthwith upon the sight of these my letters send up to me one Henry the manciple [2] of White Hall,[3] in so sure keeping that he do not escape, and that ye shall by your wisdom handle the matter so closely that there be of his apprehension [4] and sending up as little knowledge abroad as may be. And this his Grace's commandment, his high pleasure is that ye shall with all diligence and dexterity put in execution, as ye intend the continuance of his gracious favor towards you and that his University, the privileges whereof, his Grace of his blessed mind intendeth to see conserved. And for that intent his Highness hath ordered

---

1. Used in forms of address—distinguished.

2. An officer or servant chiefly concerned with provisioning.

3. Wood names nine halls of this name. The most probable one, at this date, seems to be White Hall in Cheyney Lane (now Market Street), pulled down for the building of Jesus College. We know that it had belonged to St. Frideswide's Priory since the thirteenth century and that it paid 40 shillings a year in 1524. The principal in 1527 was a Robert Woods (Anthony à Wood, *Antiquities of Oxford,* first published 1674, in Latin; ed. Clark, pp. 72, 586).

4. arrest.

that ye shall send up the said Henry to me, being Steward [5] of
this his University. And thus heartily fare ye well, at Richmond the eleventh day of March.

Assuredly your own

THOMAS MORE

40

[155] To Cranevelt.

Francis of Cranevelt (1485–1564) was educated privately and at
the College of the Falcon, Louvain University. He was Lic.A. and
M.A. 1505, ranking first among the graduates. He next studied Law,
taking the licentiate by 1506 and doctorate in 1510. As an undergrad-
uate he was much influenced by Adrian of Utrecht, later Pope Adrian
VI. As a young graduate he made many friends among scholars—of
the circle mentioned in this book he knew Martin Dorp, Peter
Gilles, Jean Luis Vives, Erasmus from July 1517, and Thomas More
from July 1520. In 1509 he married Elizabeth de Baussele, who won
the respect and deep affection of his friends. Their large family included seven daughters and four sons. Two daughters became nuns
and one son a priest.

Cranevelt's legal training prepared him for public service. In
1515 he was appointed town pensionary of Bruges and a member
of the Town Council. The trading importance of Bruges declined
with the receding of the sea, and the court then seldom resided
there, but it was still a busy place for a lawyer. In 1521 he gave the
Latin Orations which welcomed the young Emperor Charles V, the
Danish King, and the English Ambassador, Cardinal Wolsey. On 27
September 1522 the Emperor appointed Cranevelt to hold the first
of the lay seats in the Grand Council of Mechlin, the Highest Court
of Justice for the Netherlands, which met in the Old Palace (now
the Archives). Margaret of Austria-Savoy's court there was a center
of the arts and literature.

More, homesick for his own family, evidently enjoyed the Crane-
velts' hospitality and care of their little children. So he sends greetings—"farewell with your wife, mine by day, yours by night, a lady
truly shared" (de Vocht, *Epistolae . . . ad Craneveldium,* Ep. 139,
line 4) and again to "the lady your wife and likewise mine" (Ep.
142, line 15). Cranevelt evidently liked the compliment and replied humorously; in the last letter extant, More wrote, "I ask that
you greet my lady your wife (for I dare not again change the order)" (Ep. 163, lines 10–12). The last clause evidently refers to a
letter not now extant.

5. At Oxford and Cambridge a judicial officer, in whom is vested the
jurisdiction belonging to the University in cases of treason and felony.

Calais

14 July ⟨1527⟩

THOMAS MORE SENDS HIS BEST GREETINGS TO CRANEVELT, HIS
VERY DEAR FRIEND.

It would certainly be most discourteous of me, dearest Cranevelt, after receiving so many letters from you, not to reply
with even a single word, especially in the present circumstances
when I have at hand a very reliable carrier; as a result I am
completely deprived of my normal excuse, of not having a
letter bearer, which I like to use as a mask for my laziness. This
courier [1] is an employee of Erasmus, and is returning straight
to him, by whom he is recommended very highly for his trust-
worthiness and discreet silence. If you would like to send Erasmus any message which you prefer not to put in writing, you
can entrust it to him with absolute security. Whatever other
information I have for you, you will learn from this bearer.

Hurriedly, from Calais; July 14.[2]

A thousand greetings to your excellent wife. Farewell, most
honorable Sir and most dear to your friend, More!

To the most distinguished Francis Cranevelt,

Councilor to His Majesty, the Emperor,

at Mechlin.

41

[162] To John Cochlaeus.

John Dobneck (1479–1552) was born at Wendelstein in Ansbach.
He was educated at Nuremberg, was graduated M.A. at Cologne,
took his doctorate in Theology at Ferrara in 1517, and was ordained priest in Rome. For a time he was Dean of St. Mary's at

1. The letter carrier is Nicholas Cane or Cannius (1504/5–55). He was
born in Amsterdam, matriculated at Louvain 14 May 1524, and in the
summer was sent to Erasmus. He devoted himself particularly to the
study of Greek. In May 1527 he carried letters for Erasmus to England,
and returned with Wolsey's retinue to Calais, where More wrote this
introduction of him to Cranevelt. Around 1532–33 he was the spiritual
director of the Ursuline Convent in Amsterdam. He later became pastor
of the New Church there.

2. More accompanied Wolsey on the embassy to Francis I. Wolsey
landed at Calais 11 July, met Francis at Amiens 4 August, and returned
to England late in September.

Frankfort on the Main, but the spread of the Reformation caused
his flight, and he later held canonries successively in Mainz, Meissen,
Erfurt, and Breslau.

He corrected Erasmus' spelling of his name and explained, "I
write *Cochlaeus*. Certainly I do not like my name but I do not see
how I can change it. It was given to me at Cologne by the poet
Remaclus . . . The Englishman Harris called me Wendelstinus . . .
for my native place near Nuremberg is called Wendelstein—that
is, snail" (Latin *cochlaea*).

He devoted his life to work against Luther and the Reformation,
thereby losing the sympathy of many Humanists, and by his in-
discretion arousing the distrust of men in his own church. In a
desperate effort to win back the Reformers he was later ready to
demand that the clergy be allowed to marry and that the chalice
be administered to the laity. He wrote against the Disputation at
Bern and its results, using the Protestant documents relative to it,
and John Eck's account of the Catholic side, but not Thomas Mur-
ner's. Cochlaeus died at Breslau 1552, and after his death some of
his writings were put on the *Index*.

⟨1528?⟩

It is impossible, most honored Sir, to express my feelings
of debt to you for your kindness in keeping me informed on
the incidents occurring in your locale. Germany has become
our breeding ground for such things; its brood is as numerous
as that once produced by Africa, and much more monstrous.
The past centuries have not seen anything more monstrous
than the Anabaptists, or more numerous than such baneful
curses. Indeed, my dear Cochlaeus, when I view the present
situation with its rapid deterioration, from day to day, I imagine
that, in the near future, someone will rear his head and preach
the utter rejection of Christ. And if some senseless clown does
rear his head, with the present frenzied state of the masses,
there will be no lack of supporters. I have never laid eyes on
anything more foolish or more malicious than the Edict of
Bern.[1] And, I am told, they have so dignified the disputation
as to put it almost on the same level with their Edict. I wish,
my dear Cochlaeus, I had the requisite knowledge in Scripture
and theology to be able to write an effective rejoinder to those

1. The invitation to the Disputation at Bern was issued 17 November
1527, and the meeting was held 7–26 January 1528. The bishops of the
four dioceses in Canton Bern refused to attend, and the Catholic side
was not well represented. The Protestants included such leaders as
Zwingli, Œcolampadius, Bucer, Capito, and Blaurer.

baneful curses. Thanks to the goodness of God, most distinguished Sir, you do possess that knowledge, with a fullness as few other men do. Nor has God's favor proved ineffectual in your case; you have ever used the talent entrusted to you so that one day you could return it, with abundant interest.[2] This makes me very happy, and God, in His turn, has begun to manifest His pleasure with your loyal services. After all your misfortunes, including a severe personal disaster, He has begun to look upon your sorrows with sympathy. Through His inspiration, your Most Illustrious Prince has attached you to his service, to the great advantage of our Religion and to your own financial profit, and thereby he has chosen a replacement who is the perfect image of your excellent and scholarly predecessor.[3] I extend my congratulations to both of you—to your Prince for his good judgment, to you for having so noble a patron.

42

[174] To Lady More.

Dame Alice was the widow of John Middleton, of London, a mercer, and merchant of the Staple of Calais, who had died c. 4 October 1509. She was some years older than More, who ungallantly said that she was neither beautiful nor young. But Erasmus added, "And yet such as she was, being also spareful and given to profit, he so framed and fashioned her by his dexterity that he lived a sweet and pleasant life with her, and brought her to that case, that she learned to play and sing at the lute and virginals, and every day at his returning home he took a reckoning and account of the task he enjoined her touching the said exercise."

This letter, showing More's confidence that she will deal wisely and generously with their neighbor's losses, gives us another picture of Lady More. The opening paragraph of the text (before the salutation) in this and a number of the following letters is Rastell's preface from the 1557 English *Works*.

2. 1 Cor. 15:10, Matt. 25:14 ff.

3. Hieronymus Emser (1477–1527) was educated in Greek and Latin at the University of Tübingen and later studied law and theology at Basel. He became secretary to Duke George of Saxony, and was ordained in 1512. From the Disputation at Leipzig in 1519 he was Luther's literary opponent. Duke George (the "Prince" of this letter) wrote a laudatory preface to Emser's translation of the New Testament into German, and in it criticized and corrected Luther's translation.

Woodstock
3 September ⟨1529⟩

Sir Thomas More was made Lord Chancellor of England in Michaelmas [1] term in the year of our Lord 1529, and in the twenty-first year of King Henry the VIII. And in the latter end of the harvest then next before, Sir Thomas More then Chancellor of the Duchy of Lancaster being returned from Cambrai in Flanders (where he had been Ambassador for the King) rode immediately to the King to the Court at Woodstock. And while he was there with the King, part of his own dwelling house at Chelsea and all his barns there full of corn suddenly fell on fire and were burnt and all the corn [2] therein by the negligence of one of his neighbors' carts that carried the corn, and by occasion thereof were divers of his next neighbor's barns burned also. Upon which news brought unto him to the Court, he wrote to the lady his wife this letter following.

The copy of the letter.

MISTRESS ALICE, IN MY MOST HEARTY WISE I RECOMMEND [3] ME TO YOU.

And whereas I am informed by my son Heron of the loss of our barns and our neighbors' also with all the corn that was therein, albeit (saving God's pleasure) it were great pity of so much good corn lost, yet sith [4] it hath liked him [5] to send us such a chance, we must and are bounden not only to be content but also to be glad of his visitation. He sent us all that we have lost and sith he hath by such a chance taken it away again his pleasure be fulfilled; let us never grudge [6] thereat but take in good worth [7] and heartily thank him as well for adversity as for prosperity and peradventure [8] we have more cause to thank him for our loss than for our winning, for his wisdom better seeth what is good for us than we do ourselves. Therefore I pray you be of good cheer and take all the household with you to church and there thank God both for that he hath given us and for that he hath taken from us and for

1. 29 September.   2. grain.   3. commend.
4. since.   5. it has pleased God.
6. be unwilling.   7. take in good part.
8. perhaps.

that he hath left us, which if it please him he can increase when he will and if it please him to leave us yet less, at his pleasure be it.

I pray you to make some good ensearch [9] what my poor neighbors have lost and bid them take no thought therefor, for and [10] I should not leave myself a spoon there shall no poor neighbor of mine bear no loss by any chance happened in my house. I pray you be with my children and your household merry [11] in God and devise somewhat with your friends what way were the best to take for provision to be made for corn for our household and for seed this year coming, if ye think it good that we keep the ground still in our hands, and whether ye think it good that we so shall do or not, yet I think it were not best suddenly thus to leave it all up and to put away our folk off our farm, till we have somewhat advised us thereon; howbeit if we have more now than ye shall need and which can get them other masters, ye may then discharge us of them, but I would not that any man were suddenly sent away he wot nere whither.[12] At my coming hither I perceived none other but that I should tarry still with the King's Grace but now I shall, I think, because of this chance get leave this next week to come home and see you, and then shall we further devise together upon all things what order shall be best to take.

And thus as heartily fare you well with all our children as ye can wish, at Woodstock the third day of September by the hand of

Your loving husband,

THOMAS MORE kg.

43

[178, Allen, *8*, 2228] To Erasmus.

⟨Chelsea⟩
28 October ⟨1529⟩

Best Greetings. My thoughts and heart had long been set upon a life of retirement, when suddenly, without any warn-

9. search.   10. even if.   11. happy.
12. knows not where.

ing, I was tossed into a mass of vital business affairs.[1] The nature of these affairs you will discover from your man Quirinus.[2] Some people here, friends of mine, are jubilant and heap congratulations upon me. But you are usually a prudent and shrewd judge of human affairs; perhaps you will sympathize with my lot. I am adapting myself to circumstances, and I am very happy at the extraordinary favor and kindness shown me by our excellent King; lacking the talent and other gifts required for this position, I intend to try seriously to meet his optimistic expectations by making every effort I am capable of, by complete loyalty, and by utter devotedness.

The rest of the details you will get from Quirinus, as I have given him thorough instructions. The more I realize that this post involves the interests of Christendom, my dearest Erasmus, the more I hope it all turns out successfully, for your sake rather than my own. Farewell, dearest Erasmus, more than half of my soul. From my country home, October 28.

More than wholeheartedly yours,

THOMAS MORE

To the excellent and most learned Master Erasmus of Rotterdam, at Freiburg.

44

[188. Allen, *10*, 2659] To Erasmus.

The letter was delayed some months in Saxony, as Erasmus wrote Faber (Allen, *10*, 2750, lines 10–12).

Chelsea

14 June 1532

THOMAS MORE SENDS HIS GREETINGS TO ERASMUS OF ROTTERDAM.

It has been my constant wish almost since boyhood, dearest Desiderius, that some day I might enjoy the opportunity which,

1. Appointed Lord Chancellor, 25 October 1529.
2. Quirinus Talesius (1505–1573) of Haarlem, was educated in Cologne and became servant-pupil to Erasmus c. 1524 and remained seven years. He was recalled by his father to Holland, became Pensionary of Haarlem in 1532, and married. He was elected Burgomaster ten times. A devoted Catholic, he persecuted Protestants, and during the siege of Haarlem (by the Spaniards) he was hanged in reprisal, 1573.

to my happiness, you have always had, namely, of being relieved of all public duties and eventually being able to devote
some time to God alone and myself; at long last this wish
has come true,[1] Erasmus, thanks to the goodness of the Supreme and Almighty God and to the graciousness of a very
understanding Sovereign. I have not, however, attained exactly
what I had wished for. My prayer had been to reach the
crowning point of my life healthy and vigorous, no matter how
old, or at least without sickness and suffering, as far as one
could expect at that age. Perhaps that was a little too bold;
in any case, the answer to that prayer is at present in God's
hands. For some sort of chest ailment has laid hold of me; and
the discomfort and pain it causes do not bother me as much
as the worry and fear over the possible consequences. After
being troubled with this ailment continually for several
months, I consulted the doctors, who said that such a linger-
ing disease could be dangerous; in their view there was no
speedy cure possible; healing would be a long, slow process,
requiring proper diet, medicines, and rest. They did not pre-
dict the length of convalescence, nor did they even give me
assurance of a complete cure.

So, while turning these thoughts over in my mind, I realized
that I would either have to resign my office or be inefficient
in discharging it, as I would be unable to carry out the re-
sponsibilities which my position entailed, except at the risk
of my life; and in the case of death, I would have to give up
office as well as life. Therefore I decided to do without the
one rather than without both. Out of concern, then, for affairs
of state, as well as for my own health, I humbly prevailed upon
the generosity of our most noble and excellent Sovereign to
condescend to have pity on me and to relieve me of the overwhelming burden of that office, the highest in the realm, with
which, as you know, he had shown favor for me and marked
me with a distinction far beyond any merit or even ambition
or wish on my part. My prayer, then, to all the saints of Heaven
is that God, Who alone has the power, may repay adequately
these acts of fond affection shown me by our most noble King,
and, to prevent me from spending whatever time He will add

1. More had resigned 16 May 1532.

to my life in idleness and inactivity, that God may also grant me both the spirit to employ those good hours well and, in addition, strength of body to do so. For when my health is weak, I am so listless that I accomplish nothing at all.

My dear Erasmus, we are not all Erasmuses; the gracious gift which God has granted to you, practically alone of all mankind, that gift all of us must wait to receive. With the exception of yourself, who would dare to promise what you produce? Though burdened by the weight of your years and constantly suffering from illnesses that would prove exhausting and overwhelming for a healthy young man, still never all through the years of your entire life have you failed to give an account to all the world with outstanding publications, as if neither the weight of years nor ill health could in any way diminish that record. While this one fact alone is, in the judgment of all men, like a miracle, still, amazingly, the miracle is magnified by the fact that the host of brawling critics surrounding and attacking you have in no way deterred you from publishing, though apparently they had the power to crush the heart of a Hercules. Such men are constantly stirred up against you, because they are envious of your unparalleled gifts and also of your learning, which outmatches even those gifts; they readily realize that such unique qualities of native talent and hard work are far beyond their reach; still, almost bursting with envy, they cannot endure being far inferior to you; therefore, of course, they contrive together and strive with might and main by incessant personal abuse to see if they can drag your high honor down to their own shameful level.

However, all during the many years that they have been shouldering this rock of Sisyphus, what have they accomplished by their fruitless and wicked efforts except to have the rock come tumbling down again and again upon their own heads? Meanwhile you have kept surging ever upwards. And does it really matter that on occasion even good men, with a certain amount of learning, have been unsettled because, in their view, you perhaps handled some point with too little restraint? After all, every author has been guilty of that, including your own critics, who, while branding your works, could not refrain from committing the same defect—a defect, in this in-

stance, that was too obvious for men of their rank, and of too
frequent occurrence for any type of writing. There is much
less reason for excusing them, as they are surely aware of
the open confession you made before the outbreak of these
pestilential heresies, which are now spreading like wildfire
and wreaking utter havoc; you admitted that you had handled
some points with too little restraint, but, had you been able
to foresee the eventual cropping up of these treacherous enemies of religion, you would have treated those same points
more gently and more delicately. The rather strong statements
you made in those days were evoked by the defects of certain
people—defects which were quite the opposite of your own,
and which those people hugged to their bosoms as if they
were virtues. Anyone who would consider your vigorous spirit
a defect will have a difficult time trying to justify the holiest
of the ancient doctors of the Church; if those doctors had had
the same view of the modern age as they had of their own, I
am absolutely sure that some of the statements they made in
their day would have been more guarded and more carefully
modified. But they did not do that, because they were trying
to cure current evils and did not have in mind future ones. To
be sure, they suffered the same experience as you now are
suffering, in being the target for the slanderous charges of
those fellows, for the heretics that mushroomed in a later age
have boasted of their borrowings from the works of the ancients; this experience you have in common not only with
those very holy Fathers and most ancient guardians of the
orthodox Faith, but also with the Apostles and Evangelists,
and even with our own Saviour, for their words have been used
by all heretics as the chief, or almost the sole, basis upon which
they have attempted to lay the foundation of teachings utterly
false.

Congratulations, then, my dear Erasmus, on your outstanding virtuous qualities; however, if on occasion some good person is unsettled and disturbed by some point, even without
a sufficiently serious reason, still do not be chagrined at making accommodations for the pious dispositions of such men.
But as for those snapping, growling, malicious fellows, ignore
them and, without faltering, quietly continue to devote your-

self to the promotion of intellectual things and the advancement of virtue.

Concerning the person [2] whom you recommended to me for scholarly reasons, not for religious ones, I have been very prudently and politely warned by friends to be on my guard so as not to be taken in by him. I shall certainly do all I can to handle the situation. I am keenly aware of the risk involved in an open-door policy toward these newfangled erroneous sects. Even though they have been held in check up to now in our country, thanks to the vigilance of the bishops and the influence of our Sovereign, still it is remarkable what tricks they use in their first attempts to sneak into a place, and then the pertinacity with which they try to crash their way through. And one or two of our own fellow countrymen, with a steady stream of books written in our vernacular and containing mistranslations, and worse, misinterpretations of Scripture, have been sending into our land every brand of heresy from Belgium, where they have sought refuge.[3] I have written replies to several of these books, not however out of any great worry for one who would examine the works of both men thoroughly, but because some people like to give an approving eye to novel ideas, out of superficial curiosity, and to dangerous ideas, out of deviltry; and in so doing, they assent to what they read, not because they believe it is true, but because they want it to be true. However, one will never in any way succeed in satisfying that breed of humans who have a passion for wickedness. All my efforts are directed toward the protection of those men who do not deliberately desert the truth, but are seduced by the enticements of clever fellows. Farewell, most learned Erasmus, you who have been of great service to

2. Simon Gryner (Grynaeus) (c. 1494–1541), from 1529 professor of Greek at Basel and later also of exegesis of the Greek New Testament, came to England to see manuscripts. Because of his heretical views More kept him carefully under observation, to assure that he should not talk to anyone on religion (*Correspondence*, p. 479, lines 314 ff.).

3. To avoid heresy, the King forbade English books printed beyond the sea to be brought into England (*Correspondence*, p. 440, lines 6 ff.). Tyndale's translation of the New Testament was seized in the Low Countries and in England and was burned. In these years More wrote against William Tyndale, Simon Fish, Robert Barnes and John Frith, and earned the gratitude of his Church.

genuine intellectual life. From my home at Chelsea. June 14,
1532.

45

[189] To John Cochlaeus.

Chelsea

14 June ⟨1532⟩

My excellent and most affectionate Cochlaeus—our man
George [1] has returned with your letter, also with a bundle of
books including, among other things, your polemical works in
which, as a valiant champion of the Gospel and religion, you
do battle with that mighty opponent of the Church, Luther;
your learning and piety are the equal of your fighting heart.
Since George's return to England, I have received several letters from you dated at various times. The latest of them contained the information about Zwingli and Oecolampadius,[2]
and I was glad to hear the news of their deaths. Unfortunately,
however, they have left in their wake many very real reasons
for being sad, which I cannot mention without a shudder and
which are known to everybody and which pious men ought
not hear without a heavy sigh. Still, it is right for us to rejoice
that such savage enemies of the Christian faith have been removed from our midst, enemies that were so fully equipped
for the destruction of the Church and so eager for every opportunity to uproot piety.

For the past several months the condition of my health has
aroused strong feelings of fear within me, although outwardly
I have not appeared very ill. Not even since my release from
all public duties have I succeeded in shaking off this ailment.
It was a fact that I was incapable of carrying out my duties as
Chancellor effectively without aggravating the malady, and
the doctor held out no hope for my recovery unless I retired
to private life. Not even then could he give me any definite

1. Not identified.
2. Zwingli as chaplain was killed in the battle of Kappel, 11 October
1531, and his body, as a heretic's, was burned. Œcolampadius, the first
Protestant pastor at the Minster in Basel, died 24 November 1531.

assurance. My decision, then, was influenced by a desire to regain my health, but much more so by my regard for the common good, which I would hinder in many ways if, while handicapped by bad health, I would myself be a handicap to affairs of state. I have resolved to devote to intellectual things and to God the leisure graciously granted to me, at my request, by the sympathetic kindness of our Most Illustrious Sovereign. Give me your help, dearest Cochlaeus, by praying to God that this plan may turn out successfully for me. Good luck and farewell; from my home at Chelsea, June 14.

46

[191, Allen, *10*, 2831] To Erasmus.

Chelsea

⟨June? 1533⟩

THOMAS MORE SENDS GREETINGS TO ERASMUS OF ROTTERDAM.

I have received two letters [1] from you; the one was dated February 7th last; the other was delivered by Quirinus, who beside the letters also brought me some valuable information about the happenings in your locale. Many thanks for wanting me to have this information.

You can learn all details about your affairs from Quirinus, who strikes me as being honest and devoted. I am happy for your sake, and, since I love you, also for my own, that the present Archbishop of Canterbury [2] manifests as much affection for you as did Warham in days gone by; no man ever showed you greater affection, and if he appeared somewhat niggardly in his gifts toward the end of his life, it was evidently due to lack of money, not lack of heart; for he died unbelievably poor, leaving enough to cover his debts; he did not owe very much, but when all the funeral expenses were paid, there was not very much left. The Bishop of Durham [3] is surely being impoverished by this war, or rather, by the raids carried on by ourselves and the Scots; his diocese borders on Scotland and is such a distance from us that I hear as rarely from him as I do from you. There was a rumor afloat here

1. Not now extant.   2. Thomas Cranmer.
3. Cuthbert Tunstal.

that N.[4] and Melanchthon had held a lengthy clandestine conference here through the arrangements of some unnamed persons and that later they secretly parted; this rumor, however, has gradually faded away, and it has been found out that the story was absolutely false. The King appears to be more antagonistic toward heretics than even the bishops are.

The heretic Tyndale, a fellow Englishman, who is nowhere and yet everywhere an exile, wrote here recently that Melanchthon was a guest of the King of France and, on the direct word of an eyewitness, had been welcomed in Paris with a cavalcade of one hundred and fifty horse; Tyndale further expressed his fear that, if the French were to receive the word of God from Melanchthon, they would be confirmed in their belief in the Eucharist in opposition to the teaching of the Wycliffites.[5] How those people fret over this matter, as if God had commissioned them to give the whole world its fundamental instructions in the faith! Concerning the remark in your earlier letter that you were hesitant about publishing my letter in spite of motives for wanting to have it published, there is no reason, my dear Erasmus, for hesitation on your part. Some chatterboxes around here began to spread the rumor that I had resigned my office [6] unwillingly and that I had kept that detail a secret. So, after making arrangements for the construction of my tomb, I did not hesitate to make, on my Epitaph, a public declaration of the actual facts, to allow anyone a chance to refute them, if he could. As soon as those fellows noted the Epitaph, since they were unable to deny its truth, they charged it with being boastful. However, I preferred this charge rather than allow the other rumor take hold, not for any selfish reason, since I do not have a high regard for what men may say, provided I have the approval of God; but having written several pamphlets in English in defense of the Faith against some fellow countrymen who had championed rather perverse doctrines, I considered it my duty

4. N. is perhaps Grynaeus; see above, Letter 44.
5. Melanchthon's doctrine would probably be described as Consubstantiation. Wycliffe did not deny Transubstantiation, but emphasized only a spiritual Presence of the Lord's Body in the Eucharist, rather than a corporeal Presence as well.
6. His successor was Sir Thomas Audley.

to protect the integrity of my reputation; and so that you can
find out how boastful I was, you will receive a copy of my
Epitaph; you will notice, in reading it, that, out of confidence
in my own position, I do not bait those fellows at all, so as
to prevent them from making whimsical remarks about me.
After resigning my office, I waited until the opening of the
new term, and, so far, no one has advanced a complaint against
my integrity. Either my life has been so spotless or, at any
rate, I have been so circumspect that, if my rivals oppose my
boasting of the one, they are forced to let me boast of the
other. As a matter of fact, the King himself has pronounced
on this situation at various times, frequently in private, and
twice in public. It is embarrassing for me to relate—but on
the occasion of the installation of my most distinguished successor, the King used as his mouthpiece the most illustrious
Duke, I mean the Duke of Norfolk, who is the Lord High
Treasurer of England, and he respectfully ordered the Duke
to proclaim publicly that he had unwillingly yielded to my
request for resignation; the King, however, was not satisfied
even with that extraordinary manifestation of good will toward me; at a much later date, he had the same pronounce-
ment repeated, in his presence, at a solemn session of the
Lords and Commons, this time using my successor as his
mouthpiece, on the formal occasion of his opening address
to that assembly which, as you know, we call Parliament.
Therefore, if you agree, there is no good reason for holding
back the publication of my letter. As to the statement in my
Epitaph that I was a source of trouble for heretics—I wrote
that just to be smart. I find that breed of men absolutely
loathsome, so much so that, unless they regain their senses,
I want to be as hateful to them as anyone can possibly be;
for my increasing experience with those men frightens me
with the thought of what the world will suffer at their hands.
I shall follow your advice and make no reply to the person
about whom you wrote, although I have held a lengthy letter
in readiness for some time now. My reason for holding back
is not that I have any regard for what he, or all of his co-
workers, may think or write about me, but because I do not
want to be burdened with the obligations of writing replies

to outsiders, when I feel the more immediate responsibility of answering our own associates. Best wishes, my dear Erasmus, and a long farewell; the best of luck always.

From my rural home at Chelsea.

INSCRIPTION ON THE TOMB OF THOMAS MORE [7]

Thomas More was born in London of respectable, though not distinguished, ancestry; he engaged to some extent in literary matters, and after spending several years of his youth as a pleader in the law courts and after having held the office of judge as an Under-Sheriff in his native city, he was admitted to the Court by the Unconquerable Henry the Eighth, who is the only King to have ever received the unique distinction of meriting the title "Defender of the Faith," a title earned by deeds of sword and pen; he was received at Court, chosen member of the King's Council, knighted, appointed Under-Treasurer and then Chancellor of Lancaster, and finally Chancellor of England by the special favor of his Sovereign. Meanwhile he was elected Speaker of the House of Commons; furthermore, he served as the King's ambassador at various times and in various places, last of all at Cambrai, as an associate and colleague of Cuthbert Tunstal, then Bishop of London and shortly after Bishop of Durham, a man whose equal in learning, wisdom, and virtue is seldom seen in the world today. In that place he witnessed, in the capacity of ambassador, to his great joy, the renewal of a peace treaty between the supreme monarchs of Christendom and the restoration of a long-desired peace to the world:

May heaven confirm this peace and make it a lasting one. He so conducted himself all through this series of high offices or honors that his Excellent Sovereign found no fault with his service, neither did he make himself odious to the nobles nor unpleasant to the populace, but he was a source of trouble to thieves, murderers, and heretics. His father, John More, was a knight and chosen by the King as member of the group of judges known as the King's Bench; he was an affable man, charming, irreproachable, gentle, sympathetic, honest, and

---

7. The monument was much damaged in the bombing of Chelsea Old Church, but has been most carefully restored.

upright; though venerable in age, he was vigorous for a man
of his years; after he had lived to see the day when his son was
Chancellor of England, he deemed his sojourn upon earth
complete and gladly departed for heaven. The son, all through
his father's lifetime, had been compared with him, and was
commonly known as the young More, and so he considered
himself to be; but now he felt the loss of his father, and as he
looked upon the four children he had reared and his eleven
grandchildren, he began, in his own mind, to grow old. This
feeling was increased by a serious chest ailment, that developed
soon after, as an indication of approaching old age. Now
sated with the passing things of this life, he resigned office
and, through the unparalleled graciousness of a most indulgent
Sovereign (may God smile favorably upon his enterprises),
he at length reached the goal which almost since boyhood
had been the object of his longing—to have the last years of
his life all to himself, so that he could gradually retire from
the affairs of this world and contemplate the eternity of the
life to come. Then he arranged for the construction of this
tomb for himself, to be a constant reminder of the unrelenting advance of death, and had the remains of his first wife
transferred to this place. That he may not have erected this
tomb in vain while still alive, and that he may not shudder
with fear at the thought of encroaching death, but may go
to meet it gladly, with longing for Christ, and that he may find
death not completely a death for himself but rather the gate-
way to a happier life, I beg you, kind reader, attend him with
your prayers while he still lives and also when he has done
with life.

EPITAPH THERETO ATTACHED

My beloved wife, Jane, lies here. I, Thomas More, intend
that this same tomb shall be Alice's and mine, too. One of
these ladies, my wife in the days of my youth, has made me
father of a son and three daughters; the other has been as
devoted to her stepchildren (a rare attainment in a step-
mother) as very few mothers are to their own children. The
one lived out her life with me, and the other still lives with
me on such terms that I cannot decide whether I did love the

one or do love the other more. O, how happily we could have
lived all three together if fate and morality permitted. Well,
I pray that the grave, that heaven, will bring us together. Thus
death will give what life could not.

End of the Epitaph

47

[192] To Elizabeth Barton.

Elizabeth Barton (1506?–1534) a maidservant in Aldington, Kent,
after a severe illness fell into trances and claimed to have visions
and make prophecies. At first she was considered "a good, simple
and saintly woman" and her revelations were said to have "marvelous holiness in rebuke of sin and vice." In 1527 she entered the
priory of St. Sepulchre, Canterbury, and from 1528 to 1532 she
worked against the King's divorce and prophesied his death. Eventually, she seems to have been used as a tool in the political situation. Several clergymen helped her in theology and legends of the
saints, and so were involved in her case.

In July 1533 Thomas Cromwell (see below, headnote to letter
49), at the King's command, sent to Archbishop Cranmer "touching
the demeanor of the hypocrite nun." Cranmer summoned the
Prioress to bring her nun before him and allowed the nun to talk;
she confessed that she had "never had a vision in her life, but
feigned them all." She and her counselors were arrested and required to do public penance before St. Paul's and again at Canterbury. On 20 April 1534 the Nun of Kent, two Friars Observant, two
monks, and a secular priest were drawn from the Tower to Tyburn
and there hanged and beheaded. These men, considered her "ac-
complices," had been the commission appointed by Archbishop
Warham to examine her in 1525, when they had pronounced in
her favor. Someone wrote to Cromwell c. November 1533, "The
phrase of Master More's letter I have utterly, as knoweth God,
forgotten, for I read it only superficially . . . Perceived no hurt
therein . . . Desired Gold and the woman to keep it safe for More's
discharge . . . conjectured that More, after he left Syon [*Correspondence,* Ep. 197, lines 120 f.], had heard something concerning
her being with the King and her revelation touching this laudable
marriage, which moved him to write that letter" (*L.P., 6,* 1467).

Chelsea
Tuesday ⟨1533?⟩

GOOD MADAM, AND MY RIGHT DEARLY BELOVED SISTER IN OUR
LORD GOD.

After my most hearty recommendation, I shall beseech you
to take my good mind in good worth, and pardon me that I
am so homely [1] as of myself unrequired,[2] and also without
necessity, to give counsel to you, of whom for the good in-
spirations, and great revelations that it liketh Almighty God
of his goodness to give and show, as many wise, well learned,
and very virtuous folk testify, I myself have need, for the
comfort of my soul, to require and ask advice, for surely, good
Madam, sith [3] it pleaseth God sometime to suffer such as are
far under and of little estimation, to give yet fruitful advertisement [4] to other as are in the light of the Spirit, so far above
them, that there were between them no comparison; as he
suffered his high prophet Moses to be in some things advised
and counseled by Jethro,[5] I cannot for the love that in our
Lord I bear you refrain to put you in remembrance of one
thing, which in my poor mind I think highly necessary to be
by your wisdom considered, referring the end and order
thereof, to God and his holy Spirit to direct you.

Good Madam, I doubt not, but that you remember that in
the beginning of my communication with you, I showed you
that I neither was, nor would be, curious of any knowledge
of other men's matters, and least of all any matter of princes
or of the realm, in case it so were that God had, as to many
good folks before time he hath, any things revealed unto you,
such things, I said unto your ladyship, that I was not only
not desirous to hear of, but also would not hear of. Now,
Madam, I consider well that many folk desire to speak with
you, which are not all peradventure [6] of my mind in this point,
but some hap to be curious and inquisitive of things that
little pertain unto their parts; and some might peradventure
happen to talk of such things as might peradventure after
turn to much harm, as I think you have heard how the late

1. familiar, rude.   2. unasked.   3. since.
4. admonition.   5. Exod. 18:12–27.   6. possibly.

Duke of Buckingham moved with the fame of one that was reported for an holy monk and had such talking with him as after was a great part of his destruction and disheriting [7] of his blood, and great slander and infamy of religion. It sufficeth me, good Madam, to put you in remembrance of such thing, as I nothing doubt your wisdom and the spirit of God shall keep you from talking with any persons, specially with lay persons, of any such manner things [8] as pertain to princes' affairs, or the state of the realm, but only to common [9] and talk with any person high and low, of such manner things as may to the soul be profitable for you to show and for them to know.

And thus my good Lady, and dearly beloved sister in our Lord, I make an end of this my needless advertisement unto you, whom the blessed Trinity preserve and increase in grace, and put in your mind to recommend me and mine unto him in your devout prayers. At Chelsea this Tuesday by the hand of

Your hearty loving Brother and Beadsman,[10]

THOMAS MORE, Kt.

48

[192*] To John Harris.

The following letter to John Harris (not in *Correspondence*) was called to my attention by Gary E. Haupt and R. S. Sylvester of Yale University. It is found on fols. 148–49 of MS Bodley 431, immediately after a transcript of More's *Treatise on the Blessed Body.* More is referring to his *Treatise on the Passion,* part of which must thus not have been written in the Tower, as is commonly supposed. He asks Harris to correct his earlier version of the passage and in the 1557 *Works* the changes were incorporated. The text forms a not unamusing (note the allusion to Burgensis) treatment of a scholarly problem by More.

John Harris was More's secretary and had been a tutor in the family. He married Dorothy Coly, Margaret Roper's maid. After More's death he was a schoolmaster, and was head of a school in Bristol at the beginning of Elizabeth's reign. He then went into exile in the Netherlands, settling at first in Louvain. He matriculated in the University 19 November 1565 and earned a living by

7. disinheriting.   8. any things of such kind.
9. commune, converse.   10. One who prays for another.

teaching Latin and Greek. The Clements and the Rastells had also found homes in Louvain.

Willesden, Sunday
⟨January–April 1534⟩

Neomenia,[1] the first day of the new moon next after the equinoctial in *Vere*,[2] that is to wit after the entering of the sun into *Aries*,[3] which is the eleventh or twelfth day of March, the day of next change of the moon after that, is the first day of the year with the Jews. And the fourteenth day after, which is *Quartadecima Luna*,[4] is the eating of their paschal lamb at night, and that day is not holy day till night. And on the morrow is their great feast day, that is to wit, the first day of the unleavened bread, but it beginneth in the evening before, and so do all their feasts, and their Sabbath days begin in the evening, and endure to the evening following, *A vespere ad vesperum seruabitis sabbata vestra:* [5] *Leuitici 23.* The year in which our Saviour was crucified, *Quartadecima Luna* [6] fell in *seria quinta*,[7] that is to wit upon the Thursday. And therefore in the evening that Thursday Christ made his Maundy, and so did all the Jews, for that was the very day appointed by the Scripture in Exodus.[8] And on the morrow (which was Good Friday, and which was *Quintadecima Luna*) [9] was the first day and the chief day of the unleavened bread, which feast began in the evening before, that is to wit, on Shere [10] Thursday, when the eating of the paschal lamb was, and therefore was eaten with unleavened bread. And so consequently Christ did consecrate in unleavened bread, for in that evening began *Primus dies Azimorum*,[11] as appeareth plainly by St. Matthew, St. Mark, and St. Luke. But the posterior Greeks say that Christ did not eat his paschal

1. new moon.   2. spring.   3. The ram, a sign of the zodiac.
4. fourteenth day (of the moon).
5. From evening to evening ye shall keep your sabbaths.
6. the fourteenth of the month.   7. Fifth series.
8. Exod. 12:43 f.   9. the fifteenth of the month.
10. Sheer ("Shere") was applied to Maundy Thursday, alluding to the purification of the soul by confession, and perhaps also to the practice of washing the altars on that day. The usual name Maundy Thursday comes from the Latin *mandatum*, a new commandment, from St. John 13:11–14.
11. first day of unleavened bread.

lamb in the day appointed by the law, that is to wit, *in vespere quartaedecimae Lunae*,[12] but they say he did prevent [13] the time by a day, and did eat it *in vespere decimae tertiae Lunae*.[14] But yet they said not that he ate it on the Wednesday, for in that I mistook them. But they say that the Thursday was *decimatertia Luna*,[15] and that *Quartadecima Luna* [16] (in which the paschal [17] should be eaten by the law) was on Good Friday, and that the Jews did eat it then, and that in that evening upon Good Friday (in which day Christ died) the Jews did eat the paschal lamb, and that on the morrow (which was the Sabbath day) was *Quintadecima Luna*,[18] and so therefore on that day was their great feast, that is to wit [19] the first day of the unleavened bread, which began they say on Good Friday in the evening at the rising of the moon. And for that cause they say that Christ did consecrate in leavened bread, because he consecrated on the Thursday, which was they say not *Quartadecima* [20] *Luna,* but *decima tertia*,[21] and that the unleavened bread came not in until the evening in *Quartadecima Luna*,[22] that was, they say, not till Good Friday in the evening, which they prove by the words of St. John cap. 13. *Ante diem festum paschae*,[23] and they say *festum paschae* was the feast of eating of the paschal lamb. And so our Lord, say they, made his Maundy before the feast of the eating of the paschal lamb, that is to wit, the day before *Quartadecima Luna*.[24] And so Shere Thursday they say was *decima tertia Luna*.[25] And therefore say they that the very day thereof (that is to wit, *Quartadecima Luna*) [26] was they say on Good Friday. And the Jews they say did eat that day after Christ's death, and that therefore they would not come in *pretorium, vt non contaminarentur, sed vt manducarent pascha*.[27] And that Christ (because he knew that he should

---

12. in the evening of the fourteenth of the month.
13. act in anticipation of.
14. in the evening of the thirteenth of the month.
15. the thirteenth.   16. the fourteenth of the month.
17. the paschal lamb.   18. the fifteenth of the month.
19. namely.   20. the fourteenth.   21. the thirteenth.
22. the fourteenth.   23. before the day of the feast of the Passover
24. the fourteenth.   25. the thirteenth.   26. the fourteenth.
27. St. John 18—"and they themselves entered not into the Praetorium, that they might not be defiled, but might eat the Passover."

that day be crucified) did prevent the day, and did eat it the day before, and therefore they had no one unleavened bread.

I put you in remembrance of this because I have mistaken it in the paper that you have, and have said that the Greeks held that Christ held his Maundy on Tenebrae Wednesday. I pray you, gentle John Harris, amend that fault of mine. *Ante diem festum Paschae*,[28] is meant by the first day of the feast of the unleavened loaves which was on Good Friday, that was *Quinta decima Luna*,[29] and the feast was called *festum Paschae*,[30] because it began in the evening on Shere Thursday, wherein the paschal lamb was eaten. *Quod abstinebant a pretorio (vt mundi manducarent Pascha)* [31] upon Good Friday, was for the unleavened bread which was also called by the name of Pascha, and continued seven days.

Burgensis [32] maketh another manner of reckoning, with which we shall not need to meddle; thus much is perplex enough.

From Willesden [33] this present Sunday, by

Your Lover THOMAS MORE Knight

28. before the feast of the Passover.   29. the fifteenth.
30. the feast of the Passover.
31. Because they kept away from the Praetorium so that they might eat the Passover undefiled.
32. Paul de Santa Maria, born in Burgos, c. 1351, distinguished for his scholarship and piety as a Jewish rabbi, was baptized in 1391, convinced by the writings of Thomas Aquinas. Two brothers, his daughter and three sons were baptized with him, but his wife remained loyal to Judaism until her death in 1420.
Burgensis studied in Paris and took his doctorate in Theology, was Bishop of Cartagena, and in 1415 Archbishop of Burgos, succeeded in his lifetime by his second son Alonso. He wrote *Additiones* to the postils of Nicholas de Lyra on the Bible. His Hebrew was superior, but many of his interpretations were rejected, particularly by Matthias Döring (Vulgate, Froben, Basel, 1506–08, p. 83, D).
33. A parish adjoining the county of London on the northwest. More may have gone there to visit the pilgrimage church of Our Lady of Willesden. His wife's son-in-law, Sir Giles Alington, had a country home in Willesden.

49

[194] To Thomas Cromwell.

Thomas Cromwell (1485?–1540) was a soldier for the French in Italy 1503, a merchant in the Netherlands until 1512, and then returned to London to practise as a solicitor. He entered Wolsey's service about 1520 and later superintended the building of the colleges the Cardinal founded in Ipswich and Oxford. After Wolsey's fall in 1529, Cromwell rose in the service of the King, became a member of Parliament and in 1530 a privy councilor. When it was clear that Pope Clement VII would not annul the marriage of Henry VIII and Catherine of Aragon, he considered that the divorce might be granted in England if the King were recognized as "Protector and Supreme Head of the English Church and Clergy." This was first included in the King's titles in a petition, 1531, from Convocation to the King, asking that the clergy be forgiven for breach of *Praemunire* in having supported the trial of the divorce by a legatine court held by Cardinals Campeggio and Wolsey. It was passed as a statute in the Act of Royal Supremacy 1534, and under it Fisher, Bishop of Rochester, and Sir Thomas More suffered.

The *Articles devised by the Whole Consent of the King's Council* were written as propaganda at the end of 1533; they called the Pope the "Bishop of Rome" and claimed the right to appeal from him to a General Council. More's *Answer to the Poisoned Book* (1533) is his reply to Tyndale's *The Supper of the Lord;* it is mainly an exposition of St. John 6.

Chelsea

1 February ⟨1533/4⟩

A letter written by Sir Thomas More to Master Thomas Cromwell (then one of the King's Privy Council) the first day of February in the year of our Lord God 1533, after the computation of the Church of England and in the twenty-fifth year of the reign of King Henry the VIII.

RIGHT WORSHIPFUL,[1] IN MY MOST HEARTY WISE I RECOMMEND ME UNTO YOU.

Sir, my cousin William Rastell hath informed me that your Mastership of your goodness showed him that it hath been reported that I have against the book of certain articles (which

1. distinguished, used in titles of address.

was late put forth in print by the King's honorable Council)
made an answer, and delivered it unto my said cousin to
print. And albeit that he for his part truly denied it, yet because he somewhat remained in doubt, whether your Mastership gave him therein full credence or not, he desired me for
his farther discharge [2] to declare you the very truth, sir, as
help me God neither my said cousin nor any man else, never
had any book of mine to print, one or other, since the said
book of the King's Council came forth. For of truth the last
book that he printed of mine was that book that I made
against an unknown heretic which hath sent over a work that
walketh in over many men's hands [3] named the *Supper of the
Lord,* against the blessed sacrament of the altar. My answer
whereunto, albeit that the printer (unaware to me) [4] dated
it Anno 1534, by which it seemeth to be printed since the
Feast of the Circumcision, yet was it of very truth both made
and printed and many of them gone before Christmas. And
myself never espied the printer's oversight in the date, in more
than three weeks after. And this was in good faith the last
book that my cousin [5] had of mine. Which being true as of
truth it shall be found, sufficeth [6] for his declaration in this
behalf.

As touching mine own self, I shall say thus much farther,
that on my faith I never made any such book nor ever thought
to do. I read the said book once over and never more. But
I am for once reading [7] very far off from many things, whereof
I would have meetly [8] sure knowledge, ere [9] ever I would make
an answer, though the matter and the book both, concerned
the poorest man in a town, and were of the simplest man's
making too. For of many things which in that book be touched,
in some I know not the law, and in some I know not the fact.
And therefore would I never be so childish nor so play the
proud arrogant fool, by whomsoever the book had been made,
and to whomsoever the matter had belonged, as to presume
to make an answer to the book, concerning the matter whereof

2. acquittal.   3. is in the hands of too many men.
4. without my knowledge.
5. Rastell was the son of John Rastell by his wife Elizabeth, More's
sister.
6. is adequate.   7. because I read the book only once.
8. suitably.   9. before.

I never were sufficiently learned in the laws, nor fully in-
structed in the facts. And then while the matter pertained
unto the King's Highness, and the book professeth openly that
it was made by his honorable Council, and by them put in
print with his Grace's license obtained thereunto I verily trust
in good faith that of your good mind toward me, though I
never wrote you word thereof, yourself will both think and
say so much for me, that it were a thing far unlikely, that
an answer should be made thereunto by me. I will by the
grace of Almighty God, as long as it shall please him to lend
me life in this world, in all such places (as I am of my duty
to God and the King's Grace bounden) truly say my mind,
and discharge [10] my conscience, as becometh a poor honest
true man, wheresoever I shall be by his Grace commanded.
Yet surely if it should happen any book to come abroad in the
name of his Grace or his honorable Council, if the book to
me seemed such as myself would not have given mine own
advice to the making, yet I know my bounden duty, to bear
more honor to my prince, and more reverence to his honorable
Council, than that it could become me for many causes, to
make an answer unto such a book, or to counsel and advise
any man else to do it. And therefore as it is a thing that I
never did nor intended, so I heartily beseech you if you shall
happen to perceive any man, either of evil will or of light-
ness,[11] any such thing report by [12] me, be so good master to
me, as help to bring us both together. And then never take
me for honest after, but if you find his honesty somewhat im-
paired in the matter.

Thus am I bold upon your goodness to encumber you with
my long rude [13] letter, in the contents whereof, I eftsones [14]
heartily beseech you to be in manner aforesaid good master
and friend unto me, whereby you shall bind me to be your
bedesman [15] while I live, as knoweth our Lord, whose especial
grace both bodily and ghostly [16] long preserve and keep you.

At Chelsea in the Vigil of the Purification of our Blessed
Lady by the hand of
Assuredly all your own,

THOMAS MORE, Knight

10. clear.   11. inconstancy.   12. of.
13. inelegant.   14. a second time.
15. to be one to pray for him.   16. spiritually.

50

[195] To Thomas Cromwell.

Chelsea

Saturday, ⟨February–March⟩ 1533/4

Another letter written by Sir Thomas More to Master Thomas Cromwell in February or in March in the year of our Lord God 1533, after the computation [1] of the Church of England, and in the twenty-fifth year of the reign of King Henry the Eighth.

RIGHT WORSHIPFUL.[2]

After right hearty recommendation, so it is that I am informed, that there is a bill [3] put in against me into the higher house before the Lords, concerning my communication with the Nun of Canterbury, and my writing unto her, whereof I not a little marvel, the truth of the matter being such as God and I know it is, and as I have plainly declared unto you by my former letters, wherein I found you then so good, that I am now bold eftsoons [4] upon your goodness to desire you to show me that favor, as that I might the rather by your good means, have a copy of the bill. Which seen, if I find any untrue surmise [5] therein as of likelihood there is, I may make mine humble suit unto the King's good Grace, and declare the truth, either to his Grace or by his Grace's commandment, wheresoever the matter shall require. I am so sure of my truth toward his Grace, that I cannot mistrust his gracious favor toward me, upon the truth known, nor the judgment of any honest man. Nor never shall there loss in this matter grieve me, being myself so innocent as God and I know me, whatsoever should happen me therein, by the grace of Almighty God, who both bodily and ghostly [6] preserve you. At Chelsea this present Saturday by the hand of

Heartily all your own,

THO. MORE, Knight

1. reckoning.   2. In titles of address: distinguished.
3. A Bill of Attainder, 21 February 1534, against the Nun of Kent and her colleagues, included More and Fisher, but for misprision not for treason.
4. again.   5. suspicion.   6. spiritually.

51

[197] To Thomas Cromwell.

In the reign of Queen Mary (1553–58), there was no question of the sincerity of the Nun of Kent, and much appreciation of her efforts in favor of Catherine of Aragon and her daughter. Therefore More's nephew, William Rastell, publishing the *Workes—in the Englysh Tonge* in 1557, omitted this letter.

Richard Resby (1490–1534) was educated at Winchester and New College, Oxford, B.A. 1510. He entered the Franciscan order in 1513 and was finally Warden of the Observants at Canterbury.

⟨March? 1534⟩

RIGHT WORSHIPFUL,[1]

After my most hearty recommendation, with like thanks for your goodness in the accepting of my rude [2] long letter, I perceive that of your further goodness and favor toward me, it liked your Mastership to break with [3] my son Roper of that, that I had had communication, not only with divers that were of acquaintance with the lewd [4] Nun of Canterbury, but also with herself; and had, over that, by my writing, declaring favor toward her, given her advice and counsel; of which my demeanor,[5] that it liketh you to be content to take the labor and the pain, to hear, by mine own writing, the truth, I very heartily thank you, and reckon myself therein right deeply beholden [6] to you.

It is, I suppose, about eight or nine years ago sith [7] I heard of that huswife [8] first; at which time the Bishop of Canterbury that then was, God assoil [9] his soul, sent unto the King's Grace a roll of paper in which were written certain words of hers, that she had, as report was then made, at sundry times spoken in her trances; whereupon it pleased the King's Grace to deliver me the roll, commanding me to look thereon and afterward show him what I thought therein. Whereunto, at another time, when his Highness asked me, I told him, that in good faith I found nothing in these words that I could anything

1. In titles of address: distinguished.   2. unskilled.
3. reveal to.   4. villainous or ignorant.   5. of which conduct.
6. obliged.   7. since.   8. worthless or pert woman.
9. absolve.

regard or esteem, for saving that some part fell in rhyme, and that, God wot,[10] full rude, else for any reason, God wot, that I saw therein, a right simple [11] woman might, in my mind, speak it of her own wit [12] well enough; howbeit, I said, that because it was constantly reported for a truth, that God wrought in her, and that a miracle was showed upon her, I durst not nor would not, be bold in judging the matter. And the King's Grace, as methought, esteemed the matter as light as it after proved lewd.[13]

From that time till about Christmas was twelvemonth,[14] albeit that continually, there was much talking of her, and of her holiness, yet never heard I any talk rehearsed,[15] either of revelation of hers, or miracle, saving that I had heard some times in my Lord Cardinal's days, that she had been both with his Lordship and with the King's Grace, but what she said either to the one or to the other, upon my faith, I had never heard any one word.

Now, as I was about to tell you, about Christmas was twelvemonth, Father Resby, Friar Observant, then of Canterbury, lodged one night at mine house; where after supper, a little before he went to his chamber, he fell in communication with me of the Nun, giving her high commendation of holiness, and that it was wonderful to see and understand the works that God wrought in her; which thing, I answered, that I was very glad to hear it, and thanked God thereof. Then he told me, that she had been with my Lord Legate in his life and with the King's Grace, too, and that she had told my Lord Legate a revelation of hers, of three swords that God hath put in my Lord Legate's hand, which if he ordered not well, God would lay it sore [16] to his charge, the first he said was the ordering of the spiritualty [17] under the Pope, as Legate, the second the rule that he bare in order of the temporalty [18] under the King, as his Chancellor. And the third, she said, was the meddling [19] he was put in trust with by the King, concerning the great matter of his marriage. And therewithal I said unto him that any revelation of the King's

10. God knows.   11. unlearned.   12. mind.
13. evil.   14. Christmas a year ago.   15. recounted.
16. grievously.   17. the clergy.   18. temporality.
19. action.

matters I would not hear of, I doubt not but the goodness of God should direct his highness with his grace and wisdom, that the thing should take such end, as God should be pleased with, to the King's honor and surety [20] of the realm. When he heard me say these words or the like, he said unto me, that God had specially commanded her to pray for the King; and forthwith he brake again [21] into her revelations, concerning the Cardinal that his soul was saved by her mediation; [22] and without any other communication went into his chamber. And he and I never talked any more of any such manner of matter, nor since his departing on the morrow, I never saw him after to my remembrance, till I saw him at Paul's cross.[23]

After this, about Shrovetide,[24] there came unto me, a little before supper, Father Rich,[25] Friar Observant of Richmond. And as we fell in talking, I asked him of Father Resby, how he did? and upon that occasion, he asked me whether Father Resby had anything showed me of the Holy Nun of Kent? and I said yea, and that I was very glad to hear of her virtue. I would not, quoth he, tell you again that you have heard of him already, but I have heard and known many great graces that God hath wrought in her, and in other folk, by her, which I would gladly tell you if I thought you had not heard them already. And therewith he asked me, whether Father Resby had told me anything of her being with my Lord Cardinal? and I said yea. Then he told you, quoth he, of the three swords; yea verily, quod I. Did he tell you, quoth he, of the revelations that she had concerning the King's Grace? Nay, forsooth, quoth I, nor if he would have done I would not have given him the hearing; nor verily no more I would in deed, for sith [26] she hath been with the King's Grace herself,

20. security.   21. began to speak again of.
22. intercession on behalf of. This the nun claimed in 1531.

23. The nun and the clergy who had helped her were forced to read their confessions in public penance before St. Paul's Cathedral, November 1533.

24. days of shriving just before Lent.

25. Hugh Rich was included in the Act of Attainder but was not executed at Tyburn. We do not know whether he had died or had been pardoned. He had been Warden at Canterbury, in which post Resby had succeeded him.

26. since.

and told him, methought it a thing needless to tell the matter
to me, or any man else. And when Father Rich perceived
that I would not hear her revelations concerning the King's
Grace he talked on a little of her virtue and let her revelations
alone; and therewith my supper was set upon the board [27]
where I required [28] him to sit with me, but he would in no
wise tarry but departed to London. After that night I talked
with him twice, once in mine own house, another time in his
own garden at the Friars, at every time a great space, but not
of any revelation touching the King's Grace, but only of other
mean folk,[29] I knew not whom, of which things some were
very strange and some were very childish. But albeit that he
said that he had seen her lie in her trance in great pains and
that he had at other times taken great spiritual comfort in
her communication, yet did he never tell me she had told him
those tales herself; for if he had I would, for the tale of Mary
Magdalene [30] which he told me, and for the tale of the host,
with which, as I heard, she said she was houseled,[31] at the
King's Mass at Calais; [32] if I had heard it of him as told unto
himself by her mouth for a revelation, I would have both
liked him and her the worse. But whether ever I heard that
same tale of Rich or of Resby or of neither of them both, but
of some other man since she was in hold,[33] in good faith I
cannot tell. But I wot [34] well when or where so ever I heard
it, methought it a tale too marvelous to be true, and very
likely that she had told some man her dream, which told it
out for a revelation. And in effect, I little doubted but that
some of these tales that were told of her were untrue; but yet
sith I never heard them reported, as spoken by her own mouth,
I thought nevertheless that many of them might be true, and

27. the table.   28. asked.   29. of low degree.

30. **Dr. Bocking**, a Benedictine monk at Canterbury, kept a book in
his own handwriting, of the nun's revelations. In 1534 the nun "confessed
that the letter purporting to have been written by Mary Magdalene in
Heaven, and sent to a widow in London, was written by a monk of St.
Augustine's in Canterbury, named Hawkeherst" (*L.P.*, 7, 72).

31. communicated.

32. "When the King was at Calais, she saw the host taken from the
priest with the blessed blood, and angels brought it to her to receive"
(*L.P.*, 6, 1466, p. 585).

33. in custody.   34. know.

she a very virtuous woman too; as some lies peradventure [35] written of some that be saints in heaven, and yet many miracles in deed done by them for all that.

After this I being upon a day at Syon talking with divers of the Fathers together at the grate, they showed me that she had been with them, and showed me divers things that some of them misliked in her and in this talking, they wished that I had spoken with her and said they would fain see how I should like her; whereupon, afterward, when I heard that she was there again, I came thither to see her and to speak with her myself. At which communication had, in a little chapel, there were none present but we two. In the beginning whereof I showed that my coming to her was not of any curious mind, anything to know of such things as folk talked, that it pleased God to reveal and show unto her, but for the great virtue that I had heard for so many years, every day more and more spoken and reported of her, I therefore had a great mind to see her, and be acquainted with her, that she might have somewhat the more occasion to remember me to God in her devotion and prayers; whereunto she gave me a very good virtuous answer that as God did of his goodness far better by her than such a poor wretch was worthy, so she feared that many folk yet beside that spake of their own favorable minds many things for her, far above the truth, and that of me she had many such things heard, that already she prayed for me and ever would, whereof I heartily thanked her.

I said unto her, "Madam, one Helen, a maiden dwelling about Totnam, of whose trances and revelations there hath been much talking, she hath been with me late [36] and showed me that she was with you, and that after the rehearsal of such visions as she had seen, you showed her that they were no revelations, but plain illusions of the devil and advised her to cast them out of her mind, and verily she gave therein good credence unto you and thereupon hath left [37] to lean [38] any longer unto such visions of her own, whereupon she saith, she findeth your words true, for ever since she hath been the less visited with such things as she was wont to be before." To this she answered me, "Forsooth, Sir, there is in this point

35. perhaps.   36. lately.   37. stopped.   38. leaning.

no praise unto me, but the goodness of God, as it appeareth, hath wrought much meekness in her soul, which hath taken my rude warning so well and not grudged to hear her spirit and her visions reproved." I liked her in good faith better for this answer than for many of those things that I heard reported by [39] her. Afterward she told me, upon that occasion how great need folk have, that are visited with such visions, to take heed and prove well of what spirit they come of, and in the communication she told me that of late the devil, in likeness of a bird, was fleeing [40] and flickering about her in a chamber, and suffered himself to be taken; and being in hands suddenly changed, in their sight that were present, into such a strange ugly fashioned bird, that they were all afraid, and threw him out at a window.

For conclusion, we talked no word of the King's Grace or any great personage else, nor in effect, of any man or woman, but of herself, and myself, but after no long communication had for or ever we met,[41] my time came to go home, I gave her a double ducat,[42] and prayed her to pray for me and mine, and so departed from her and never spake with her after. Howbeit, of truth I had a great good opinion of her, and had her in great estimation as you shall perceive by the letter that I wrote unto her. For afterward because I had often heard, that many right worshipful folks as well men as women used to have much communication with her, and many folk are of nature inquisitive and curious, whereby they fall sometime into such talking, as better were to forbear, of which thing I nothing thought while I talked with her of charity, therefore I wrote her a letter thereof, which sith it may be peradventure, that she brake [43] or lost, I shall insert the very copy thereof in this present letter.

Good Madam and my right dearly beloved Sister in our Lord God.—

[After quotation of letter to Elizabeth Barton:]

At the receipt of this letter she answered my servant that

---

39. of.   40. flying.
41. I.e. we did not talk for very long because I had to leave shortly after we met.
42. Venetian gold coin, worth nearly $5.   43. destroyed.

she heartily thanked me. Soon after this there came to mine house the proctor [44] of the Charterhouse at Sheen and one brother William with him, which nothing talked with me but of her and of the great joy that they took in her virtue, but of any of her revelations they had no communication. But at another time brother William came to me, and told me a long tale of her, being at the house of a Knight in Kent, that was sore troubled with temptation to destroy himself; and none other thing we talked of nor should have done of likelihood, though we had tarried together much longer. He took so great pleasure, good man, to tell that tale with all the circumstances at length. When I came again another time to Syon, on a day in which there was a profession, [45] some of the fathers asked me how I liked the Nun? And I answered that, in good faith, I liked her very well in her talking; "howbeit," quoth I, "she is never the nearer tried by that, for I assure you she were likely to be very bad, if she seemed good, ere I should think her other, till she happed to be proved naught"; and in good faith, that is my manner indeed, except I were set to search and examine the truth upon likelihood of some cloaked evil; for in that case, although I nothing suspected the person myself, yet no less than if I suspected him sore, [46] I would as far as my wit would serve me, search to find out the truth as yourself hath done very prudently in this matter; wherein you have done, in my mind, to your great laud and praise, a very meritorious deed in bringing forth to light such detestable hypocrisy, whereby every other wretch may take warning, and be feared [47] to set forth their own devilish dissimuled [48] falsehood, under the manner and color of the wonderful work of God; for verily, this woman so handled herself, with help of the evil spirit that inspired her, that after her own confession declared at Paul's cross, when I sent word by my servant unto the Proctor of the Charterhouse, that she was undoubtedly proved a false deceiving hypocrite; the good man had had so good opinion of her so long that he could at

44. Henry Man, professed and proctor at Sheen, which was renamed Richmond by Henry VII.
45. day of taking vows.   46. grievously.   47. afraid.
48. dissembled.

the first scantly [49] believe me therein. Howbeit it was   he
alone that thought her so very good, but many another
good man beside, as little marvel was upon so good report, th.
she was proved naught.

I remember me further, that in communication between
Father Rich and me, I counseled him, that in such strange
things as concerned such folk as had come unto her, to whom,
as she said, she had told the causes of their coming ere themselves spake thereof; and such good fruit as they said that
many men had received by her prayer he and such other as so
reported it, and thought that the knowledge thereof should
much pertain to the glory of God, should first cause the things
to be well and surely examined by the ordinaries,[50] and such
as had authority thereunto; so that it might be surely known
whether the things were true or not, and that there were no
lies intermingled among them or else the lies might after hap
to away [51] the credence of those things that were true. And
when he told me the tale of Mary Magdalene, I said unto
him, "Father Rich, that she is a good virtuous woman, in good
faith, I hear so many good folk so report her, that I verily
think it true; and think it well likely that God worketh some
good and great things by her. But yet are, you wot well, these
strange tales no part of our creed; and therefore before you
see them surely proved, you shall have my poor counsel not
to wed [52] yourself so far forth to the credence of them, as to
report them very surely for true, lest that if it should hap that
they were afterward proved false, it might minish [53] your
estimation in your preaching, whereof might grow great loss."
To this he thanked me for my counsel, but how he used it
after that, I cannot tell.

Thus have I, good Master Cromwell, fully declared you, as
far as myself can call to remembrance, all that ever I have
done or said in this matter wherein I am sure that never one
of them all shall tell you any farther thing of effect,[54] for if

49. hardly.
50. One who has immediate ecclesiastical jurisdiction—archbishop,
bishop or bishop's deputy.
51. to (take) away.
52. not to be obstinately attached to.   53. diminish.
54. of essential importance.

any of them, or any man else, report of me as I trust verily no
man will, and I wot well truly no man can, any word or deed
by me spoken or done, touching any breach of my loyal troth [55]
and duty toward my most redoubted [56] sovereign and natural
liege [57] lord, I will come to mine answer, and make it good in
such wise as becometh a poor true man to do; that whosoever
any such thing shall say, shall therein say untrue; for I neither
have in this matter done evil nor said evil, nor so much as any
evil thing thought, but only have been glad, and rejoiced of
them that were reported for good; which condition I shall
nevertheless keep toward all other good folk, for the false
cloaked hypocrisy of any of these, no more than I shall esteem [58] Judas the true apostle, for Judas the false traitor.

But so purpose I to bear myself in every man's company,
while I live, that neither good man nor bad, neither monk,
friar nor nun, nor other man or woman in this world shall
make me digress from my troth and faith, either toward God,
or toward my natural prince, by the grace of Almighty God;
and as you therein find me true, so I heartily therein pray you
to continue toward me your favor and good will, as you shall
be sure of my poor daily prayer, for other pleasure can I
none do you. And thus the blessed Trinity, both bodily and
ghostly,[59] long preserve and prosper you.

I pray you pardon me, that I write not unto you of mine
own hand, for verily I am compelled to forbear writing for a
while by reason of this disease of mine, whereof the chief
occasion is grown, as it is thought, by the stooping and leaning
on my breast, that I have used in writing. And this, eftsoons,[60]
I beseech our Lord long to preserve you.

55. loyalty.   56. feared.   57. entitled to feudal allegiance.
58. hold.   59. spiritually.   60. again.

52

[198] To Henry VIII.

Chelsea

5 March ⟨1534⟩

It may like your Highness [1] to call to your gracious remembrance, that at such time as of that great weighty room and office of your Chancellor (with which so far above my merits or qualities able and meet [2] therefor, your Highness had of your incomparable goodness honored and exalted me), ye were so good and gracious unto me, as at my poor humble suit to discharge and disburden me, giving me license with your gracious favor to bestow the residue of my life in mine age now to come, about the provision for my soul in the service of God, and to be your Grace's beadsman [3] and pray for you. It pleased your Highness further to say unto me, that for the service which I before had done you (which it then liked your goodness far above my deserving to commend) that in any suit that I should after have unto your Highness, which either should concern mine honor (that word it liked your Highness to use unto me) or that should pertain unto my profit, I should find your Highness good and gracious lord unto me. So is it now, gracious Sovereign, that worldly honor is the thing, whereof I have resigned both the possession and the desire, in the resignation of your most honorable office; and worldly profit, I trust experience proveth, and daily more and more shall prove, that I never was very greedy thereon.

But now is my most humble suit unto your excellent Highness, partly to beseech the same, somewhat to tender my poor honesty, but principally that of your accustomed goodness, no sinister [4] information move your noble Grace to have any more distrust of my truth and devotion toward you than I have, or shall during my life give the cause. For in this matter of the wicked woman of Canterbury [5] I have unto your trusty

1. Your Highness may like.   2. fit.
3. One who prays for another.   4. darkly suspicious.
5. Elizabeth Barton. See above, Letter 47, and introduction. Rastell changed "wicked woman of Canterbury" to "nun of Canterbury" when he printed this letter in the 1557 *Works*.

Counselor Master Thomas Cromwell, by my writing, as plainly declared the truth as I possibly can, which my declaration of his duty toward your Grace and his goodness toward me he hath, I understand, declared unto your Grace. In any part of all which my dealing, whether any other man may peradventure [6] put any doubt, or move any scruple of suspicion, that can I neither tell, nor lieth in mine hand to let,[7] but unto myself is it not possible any part of my said demeanor [8] to seem evil, the very clearness of mine own conscience knoweth in all the matter my mind and intent [9] so good.

Wherefore most gracious Sovereign, I neither will nor well it can become [10] me with your Highness to reason and argue the matter, but in my most humble manner prostrate at your gracious feet, I only beseech your Majesty with your own high prudence and your accustomed goodness consider and weigh the matter. And then if in your so doing, your own virtuous mind shall give you, that notwithstanding the manifold excellent goodness that your gracious Highness hath by so many manner ways used unto me, I be a wretch [11] of such monstrous ingratitude as could with any of them all, or with any other person living, digress from my bounden [12] duty of allegiance toward your good Grace, then desire I no further favor at your gracious hand, than the loss of all that ever I may lose in this world, goods, lands, and liberty and finally my life withal,[13] whereof the keeping of any part unto my self could never do me pennyworth of pleasure, but only should then my recomfort [14] be, that after my short life and your long, which with continual prosperity to God's pleasure [15] our Lord for his mercy send you I should once meet with your Grace again in heaven, and there be merry with you, where among mine other pleasures this should yet be one, that your Grace should surely see there then, that (howsoever you take me) I am your true beadman now and ever have been, and will be till I die, howsoever your pleasure be to do by me.[16]

Howbeit, if in the considering of my cause your high wisdom

6. possibly.   7. prevent.   8. conduct.
9. intention, purpose.   10. be fitting for.
11. despicable person.   12. moral.   13. besides.
14. comfort, consolation.   15. service.
16. it please you to do by me.

and gracious goodness perceive (as I verily trust in God you shall) that I none otherwise have demeaned [17] myself, than well may stand with my bounden duty of faithfulness toward your royal Majesty, then in my most humble wise I beseech your most noble Grace that the knowledge of your true gracious persuasion in that behalf may relieve the torment of my present heaviness,[18] conceived of the dread and fear (by that I hear such a grievous bill put by your learned Council into your high Court of Parliament [19] against me) lest your Grace might by some sinister information be moved anything to think the contrary, which if your Highness do not (as I trust in God and your great goodness the matter by your own high prudence examined and considered, you will not) then in my most humble manner I beseech your Highness further (albeit that in respect of my former request this other thing is very slight) yet sith [20] your Highness hath herebefore [21] of your mere [22] abundant goodness heaped and accumulated upon me (though I was thereto very far unworthy) from time to time both worship [23] and great honor, too, and sith I now have left off all such things and nothing seek or desire but the life to come and in the meanwhile pray for your Grace, it may like your Highness of your accustomed benignity [24] somewhat to tender [25] my poor honesty and never suffer by the mean [26] of such a bill put forth against me any man to take occasion hereafter against the truth to slander me; which thing should yet by the peril of their own souls do themself more hurt than me, which shall, I trust, settle mine heart, with your gracious favor, to depend upon the comfort of the truth and hope of heaven, and not upon the fallible opinion or soon spoken words of light [27] and soon changeable people.

And thus, most dread [28] and most dear sovereign Lord, I beseech the blessed Trinity preserve your most noble Grace, both in body and soul, and all that are your well willers,[29] and amend all the contrary, among whom if ever I be or ever have

17. conducted.   18. sadness, grief.
19. Parliament as a court of law or administration.   20. since.
21. in time past.   22. pure, unmixed.   23. distinction.
24. kindness of disposition.   25. esteem.   26. means.
27. irresponsible.   28. held in awe, revered.
29. well-wishers.

been one, then pray I God that he may with mine open shame and destruction declare it. At my poor [30] house in Chelsea, the fifth day of March, by the known rude hand of

Your most humble and most heavy [31] faithful subject and beadsman,

THO. MORE, Kg.

53

[199] To Thomas Cromwell.

Chelsea
5 March ⟨1534⟩

RIGHT WORSHIPFUL.[1]

After my most hearty recommendation,[2] it may please you to understand that I have perceived by the relation [3] of my son [4] Roper (for which I beseech almighty God reward you) your most charitable labor taken for me toward the King's gracious Highness, in the procuring at his most gracious hand, the relief and comfort of this woeful heaviness [5] in which mine heart standeth, neither for the loss of goods, lands, or liberty, nor for any respect either, of this kind of honesty [6] that standeth in the opinion of people and worldly reputation, all which manner things (I thank our Lord), I so little esteem for any affection [7] therein toward myself that I can well be content to jeopard,[8] lose, and forgo them all and my life therewith, without any further respite than even this same present day, either for the pleasure of God or of my prince.

But surely good Master Cromwell, as I by mouth declared unto you, some part (for all could I neither then say nor now write) it thoroughly pierceth my poor heart, that the King's Highness (whose gracious favor toward me far above all the things of this world I have evermore desired, and whereof both for the conscience of mine own true faithful heart and

30. of little worth.   31. sad, grieved.
1. In titles of address: distinguished.
2. A usual form for beginning a letter.   3. report.
4. The son-in-law who had married Margaret More.
5. sadness.   6. honorable position.   7. good disposition.
8. risk.

devotion toward him, and for the manifold benefits of his high
goodness continually bestowed upon me, I thought myself
always sure), should conceive any such mind or opinion of me,
as to think that in my communication either with the nun or
the friars, or in my letter written unto the nun, I had any
other manner mind,[9] than might well stand with the duty of
a tender loving subject toward his natural prince, or that his
Grace should reckon in me any manner of obstinate heart
against his pleasure in any thing that ever I said or did concerning his great matter of his marriage or concerning the
primacy of the Pope. Never would I wish other thing in this
world more lief,[10] than that his Highness in these things all
three, as perfectly knew my dealing, and as thoroughly saw
my mind, as I do myself, or as God himself, whose sight pierceth
deeper into my heart, than mine own.

For, Sir, as for the first matter, that is to wit [11] my letter or
communication with the nun (the whole discourse whereof in
my former letter I have as plainly declared unto you as I
possibly can), so pray I God to withdraw that scruple [12] and
doubt of my good mind, out of the King's noble breast and
none other wise, but as I not only thought none harm, but
also purposed good, and in that thing most, in which (as I
perceive) his Grace conceiveth most grief and suspicion, that
is to wit in my letter which I wrote unto her. And therefore
Sir, sith [13] I have by my writing declared the truth of my deed,
and am ready by mine oath to declare the truth of mine intent,[14] I can devise [15] no further thing by me to be done in
that matter, but only beseech almighty God to put into the
King's gracious mind, that as God knoweth the thing is indeed, so his noble Grace may take it. Now touching the second
point concerning his Grace's great matter of his marriage, to
the intent that you may see cause with the better conscience
to make suit unto his highness for me, I shall as plainly declare you my demeanor [16] in that matter as I have already
declared you in the other, for more plainly can I not.

Sir, upon a time at my coming from beyond the sea,[17] where

9. kind of intention.   10. dearly.   11. namely.
12. hesitation.   13. since.   14. intention.
15. contrive.   16. conduct.   17. From Calais, late September 1527.

I had been in the King's business, I repaired as my duty was
unto the King's Grace being at that time at Hampton Court.
At which time suddenly his Highness walking in the gallery,[18]
brake with me of [19] his great matter,[20] and showed me that it
was now perceived, that his marriage was not only against the
positive laws of the Church and the written law of God, but
also in such wise against the law of nature, that it could in no
wise by the Church be dispensable.[21] Now so was it that before my going over the sea, I had heard certain things moved
against the bull of the dispensation concerning the words of
the Law Levitical and the Law Deuteronomical to prove the
prohibition to be *de iure diuino,* but yet perceived I not at
that time but that the greater hope of the matter stood in certain faults that were founden in the bull, whereby the bull
should by the law not be sufficient. And such comfort was
there in that point as far as I perceived a good season,[22] that
the Council on the other part were fain [23] to bring forth a
brief,[24] by which they pretended those defaults [25] to be supplied, the truth of which brief was by the King's Council suspected, and much diligence was thereafter done for the trial of
that point, wherein what was finally founden either I never
knew or else I not remember.

But I rehearse [26] you this to the intent you shall know that
the first time that ever I heard that point moved, that it should
be in such high degree against the law of nature, was the time
in which as I began to tell you the King's Grace showed it me
himself, and laid the Bible open before me, and there read me
the words that moved his Highness and divers other erudite [27]
persons so to think, and asked me further what myself thought

18. Now called the Haunted Gallery.   19. disclosed to me.
20. The divorce was commonly spoken of as the "King's matter." There
was much controversy over two passages: Levit. 20:21 and Deut. 25:5.
Queen Catherine said that there was a papal brief in Spain granting
dispensation for the marriage with Henry, even if the marriage with
Arthur had been consummated. The latter point, in any case, Catherine
denied. Cf. below, Letter 59, note 42.
21. Subject to dispensation, the granting of a license by a pope, archbishop or bishop to do what is forbidden by ecclesiastical law.
22. for a good while.   23. glad.
24. short letter from the pope on matters of discipline.
25. defects.   26. repeat.   27. well-instructed, learned.

thereon. At which time not presuming to look [28] that his Highness should anything take that point for the more proved or
unproved for my poor mind in so great a matter, I showed
nevertheless as my duty was at his commandment what thing
I thought upon the words which I there read. Whereupon his
Highness accepting benignly [29] my sudden unadvised answer
commanded me to commune [30] further with Master Fox, now
his Grace's Almoner,[31] and to read a book [32] with him that
then was in making [33] for that matter. After which book read,
and my poor opinion eftsoons [34] declared unto his Highness
thereupon, his Highness like a prudent and a virtuous prince
assembled at another time at Hampton Court a good number
of very well learned men, at which time as far as ever I heard
there were (as was in so great a matter most likely to be) diverse opinions among them. Howbeit I never heard but that
they agreed at that time upon a certain form in which the book
should be made, which book was afterward at York Place in
my Lord Cardinal's chamber read in the presence of divers
bishops and many learned men. And they all thought that
there appeared in the book good and reasonable causes that
might well move the King's Highness, being so virtuous a
prince, to conceive in his mind a scruple against his marriage,
which, while he could not otherwise avoid, he did well and
virtuously for the acquieting [35] of his conscience to sue [36] and
procure [37] to have his doubt decided by judgment of the
Church.

After this the suit began, and the Legates sat upon the matter,[38] during all which time I never meddled therein, nor was
a man meet to do,[39] for the matter was in hand by an ordinary

28. expect.   29. graciously.   30. converse.
31. An official to a prince or a bishop, who distributes his alms.
32. *The Determinations of the most famous and most excellent universities of Italy and France, that it is unlawful for a man to marry his
brother's wife, that the pope hath no power to dispense therewith* (London, 1531), by Stokesley, Bishop of London, Edward Fox, the King's
Almoner, and Dr. Nicholas de Burgo, an Italian Augustinian friar.
33. in course of being written.   34. again.   35. quieting.
36. put in suit.   37. cause.
38. Cardinals Campeggio and Wolsey held a legatine court from 31
May to 23 July 1529.
39. nor was it fitting for a man to do so.

process of the spiritual law, whereof I could little skill. And
yet while the Legates were sitting upon the matter, it pleased
the King's Highness to send me in the company of my *Lord
of London* now of *Durham* [40] in embassiate [41] about the peace
that at our being there was concluded at Cambrai, between
his Highness and the Emperor and the French King. And after
my coming home his Highness of his only goodness (as far
unworthy as I was thereto) made me, as you well know, his
Chancellor of this realm, soon after which time his Grace
moved me again yet eftsoons, to look and consider his great
matter, and well and indifferently [42] to ponder such things as
I should find therein. And if it so were that thereupon it
should hap me to see such things as should persuade me to
that part, he would gladly use me among other of his councilors in that matter, and nevertheless he graciously declared
unto me that he would in no wise that I should other thing do
or say therein, than upon that that I should perceive mine
own conscience should serve me, and that I should first look
unto God and after God unto him, which most gracious words
was the first lesson also that ever his Grace gave me at my first
coming into his noble service. This motion was to me very
comfortable and much I longed beside anything that myself
either had seen, or by further search should hap to find for
the one part or the other, yet specially to have some conference
in the matter with some such of his Grace's learned Council
as most for his part had labored and most have found in the
matter.

Whereupon his Highness assigned unto me the now most
reverend fathers Archbishops of Canterbury and York with
Master Doctor Fox, now his Grace's Almoner and Master
Doctor Nicholas the Italian friar,[43] whereupon I not only
sought and read, and as farforth as my poor wit and learning
served me, well weighed and considered every such thing as I
could find myself, or read in any other man's labor that I
could get, which anything had written therein, but had also

---

40. Cuthbert Tunstal, at the head of the embassy to negotiate the
Treaty of Cambrai, 1529.

41. embassy.   42. without prejudice.

43. Thomas Cranmer, Edward Lee, Edward Fox, Nicholas de Burgo.

diligent conference with his Grace's councilors aforesaid, whose
honors and worships [44] I nothing mistrust in this point, but
that they both have and will report unto his Highness that
they never found obstinate manner or fashion in me, but a
mind as toward [45] and as conformable [46] as reason could in a
matter disputable require.

Whereupon the King's Highness being further advertised [47]
both by them and myself of my poor opinion in the matter
(wherein to have been able and meet to do him service I would
as I then showed his Highness have been more glad than of all
such worldly commodities [48] as I either then had or ever should
come to) his Highness graciously taking in gre [49] my good mind
in that behalf used of his blessed disposition in the prosecuting
of his great matter only those (of whom his Grace had good
number) whose conscience his Grace perceived well and fully
persuaded upon that part, and as well myself as any other to
whom his Highness thought the thing to seem otherwise, he
used in his other business, abiding (of his abundant goodness)
nevertheless gracious lord unto any man, nor never was willing
to put any man in ruffle [50] or trouble [51] of his conscience.

After this did I never nothing more therein, nor never any
word wrote I therein to the impairing [52] of his Grace's part
neither before nor after, nor any man else by my procure-
ment,[53] but settling my mind in quiet to serve his Grace in
other things, I would not so much as look nor wittingly [54] let
lie by me any book of the other part, albeit that I gladly read
afterward divers books that were made on his part yet, nor
never would I read the book that Master Abell [55] made on the
other side, nor other book which were as I heard say made in

44. formal titles for holders of certain offices.
45. favorable.   46. compliant.   47. informed.
48. profits, interests.   49. in good part.   50. confusion.
51. perplexity.   52. impairment.   53. instigation.
54. knowingly.
55. Thomas Abell, Queen Catherine's chaplain, was sent to Spain to
procure the papal brief, but secretly showed the Emperor that the Queen
most earnestly desired the original should not be sent, lest it be destroyed. Abell was imprisoned in the Tower as if he had been an accom-
plice of Elizabeth Barton and after six years' confinement was hanged as a
traitor July 1540. The book was his *Invicta Veritas*, 1532.

Latin beyond the sea, nor never give ear to the Pope's proceedings in the matter.

Moreover, whereas I had founden in my study a book that I had before borrowed of my Lord of Bath,[56] which book he had made of the matter at such time as the Legates sat here thereupon, which book had been by me merely gently cast aside, and that I showed him I would send him home his book again, he told me that in good faith he had long time before discharged his mind of that matter,[57] and having forgotten that copy to remain in my hands, had burned his own copy that he had thereof at home, and because he no more minded [58] to meddle anything in the matter, he desired me to burn the same book too. And upon my faith so did I.

Besides this, divers [59] other ways have I so used myself that if I rehearsed [60] them all, it should well appear that I never have had against his Grace's marriage any manner demeanor [61] whereby his Highness might have any manner cause or occasion of displeasure toward me, for likewise as I am not he which either can, or whom it could become,[62] to take upon him the determination or decision of such a weighty matter, nor boldly to affirm this thing or that therein, whereof divers points a great way pass my learning, so am I he that among other his Grace's faithful subjects, his Highness being in possession of his marriage [63] and this noble woman really [64] anointed Queen, neither murmur at it nor dispute upon it, nor never did nor will, but without any other manner meddling of the matter among his other faithful subjects faithfully pray to God for his Grace and hers both, long to live and well and their noble issue too, in such wise as may be to the pleasure of God, honor and surety to themselves, rest, peace, wealth, and profit unto this noble realm.

56. John Clerk, Bishop of Bath and Wells, 1523, became one of Catherine's counselors in 1528, but later joined in pronouncing the King's divorce.

57. dismissed that matter from his mind.

58. intended.   59. various.   60. repeated.

61. kind of conduct.   62. to whom it could be fitting.

63. Rastell omitted everything from here to the end of the paragraph.

64. Perhaps More wrote "rially," i.e. royally, to be ambiguous.

As touching the third point, the primacy of the Pope, I nothing meddle in the matter. Truth it is, that as I told you, when you desired me to show you what I thought therein, I was myself sometime not of the mind that the primacy of that see should be begun by the institution of God, until that I read in that matter those things that the King's Highness had written in his most famous book [65] against the heresies of Martin Luther, at the first reading whereof I moved the King's Highness either to leave out that point, or else to touch it more slenderly [66] for doubt of such things as after might hap to fall in question between his Highness and some pope as between princes and popes divers times have done. Whereunto his Highness answered me that he would in no wise anything minish [67] of that matter, of which thing his Highness showed me a secret cause [68] whereof I never had anything heard before. But surely after that I had read his Grace's book therein, and so many other things as I have seen in that point by this continuance of these ten year since and more have found in effect the substance of all the holy doctors from St. Ignatius,[69] disciple to St. John the Evangelist, unto our own days both Latins and Greeks so consonant and agreeing in that point, and the thing by such general councils so confirmed also, that in good faith I never neither read nor heard anything of such effect on the other side, that ever could lead me to think that my conscience were well discharged, but rather in right great peril if I should follow the other side and deny the primacy to be provided by God, which if we did, yet can I nothing (as I showed you) perceive any commodity that ever could come by that denial, for that primacy is at the leastwise instituted by the corps [70] of Christendom and for a great urgent cause in

65. *Assertio septem Sacramentorum 1521.*
66. less emphatically.   67. diminish.
68. Full papal power was necessary for the dispensation that had allowed his marriage. Perhaps the "secret cause" was that the King thought he had evidence that the marriage of Arthur and Catherine had been consummated. If it were a marriage only in name, dispensation would have been more readily granted. Cf. Reynolds, p. 161, note 2.
69. Ignatius, Bishop of Antioch, martyred in Rome c. A.D. 115.
70. body.

avoiding of schisms [71] and corroborate [72] by continual succession [73] more than the space of a thousand year at the least, for there are passed almost a thousand year sith [74] the time of holy St. Gregory.[75]

And therefore sith all Christendom is one corps, I cannot perceive how any member thereof may without the common assent of the body depart from the common head. And then if we may not lawfully leave it by ourself, I cannot perceive (but if the thing were a treating [76] in a general council) what the question could avail whether the primacy were instituted by God or ordained by the Church. As for the general councils assembled lawfully, I never could perceive but that in the declaration of the truths to be believed and to be standen to,[77] the authority thereof ought to be taken for undoubtable, or else were there in nothing no certainty, but through Christendom upon every man's affectionate reason, all thing might be brought from day to day to continual ruffle [78] and confusion, from which by the general councils, the spirit of God assisting, every such council well assembled keepeth and ever shall keep the corps of his Catholic Church.

And verily sith the King's Highness hath (as by the book of his honorable council appeareth) appealed to the general council from the Pope, in which council I beseech our Lord send his Grace comfortable speed, methinketh in my poor mind it could be no furtherance there unto his Grace's cause if his Highness should in his own realm before, either by laws making or books putting forth, seem to derogate and deny not only the primacy of the see apostolic,[79] but also the authority of the general councils too, which I verily trust his Highness intendeth not, for in the next general council it may well happen that this Pope may be deposed and another substituted in

71. breaches of the unity of the church not due, according to Augustine and other Fathers, to heretical belief.
72. corroborated, strengthened.
73. succeeding to the episcopate by authority in an unbroken line from St. Peter, the first pope.
74. since.   75. Gregory the Great, Pope 590–604.
76. to be discussed.   77. obeyed.   78. disorder.
79. Rome, the see of the Apostle St. Peter.

his room [80] with whom the King's Highness may be very well content; for albeit that I have for mine own part such opinion of the pope's primacy as I have showed you, yet never thought I the Pope above the general council nor never have in any book of mine put forth among the King's subjects in our vulgar tongue, advanced greatly the Pope's authority. For albeit that a man may peradventure [81] somewhat find therein that after the common manner of all Christian realms I speak of him as primate, yet never do I stick [82] thereon with reasoning and proving of that point. And in my book against the Masker,[83] I wrote not I wot [84] well five lines, and yet of no more but only St. Peter himself, from whose person many take not the primacy,[85] even of those that grant it none of his successors, and yet was that book made, printed, and put forth of very truth before that any of the books of the council was either printed or spoken of. But where as I had written thereof at length in my confutation [86] before, and for the proof thereof had compiled together all that I could find therefor, at such time as I little looked [87] that there should fall between the King's Highness and the Pope such a breach as is fallen since, when I after that saw the thing likely to draw toward such displeasure between them, I suppressed it utterly and never put word thereof into my book, but put out the remnant without it, which thing well declareth that I never intended anything to meddle in that matter against the King's gracious pleasure, whatsoever mine own opinion were therein.

And thus have I, good Master Cromwell, long troubled your Mastership with a long process [88] of these matters, with which I neither durst [89] nor it could become [90] me to encumber the King's noble Grace, but I beseech you for our Lord's love, that you be not so weary of my most cumbrous [91] suit but that it may like you [92] at such opportune time or times as your wisdom

80. place. Stapleton omitted "yet never thought I the Pope above the general council."
81. possibly.   82. dwell on the point.
83. *The Answer to a Poisoned Book*, 1533.   84. know.
85. not many take the primacy away from St. Peter.
86. More's *Confutation of Tyndale's Answer*, 1532–33.
87. expected.   88. discussion.   89. dared.
90. be fitting for me.   91. distressing.
92. it may please you.

may find to help that his Highness may by your goodness be
fully informed of my true faithful mind, and that in the matter of that wicked woman there never was on my part any
other mind [93] than good, nor yet in any other thing else never
was there nor never shall there be any further fault found in
me, than that I cannot in everything think the same way that
some other men of more wisdom and deeper learning do, nor
can find in mine heart otherwise to say than as mine own
conscience giveth [94] me, which condition hath never grown in
anything that ever might touch his gracious pleasure of any
obstinate mind or misaffectionate [95] appetite, but of a tim-
orous conscience rising happily [96] for lack of better perceiving,[97] and yet not without tender [98] respect unto my most
bounden [99] duty toward his noble Grace, whose only favor I
so much esteem that I nothing have of mine own in all this
world, except only my soul, but that I will with better will
forgo it than abide of his Highness, one heavy displeasant [100]
look. And thus I make an end of my long, troublous process,
beseeching the blessed Trinity for the great goodness ye show
me, and the great comfort ye do me, both bodily and ghostly [101]
to prosper [102] you, and in heaven to reward you. At Chelsea
the fifth day of March by

Your deeply bounden,[103]

                                        THO. MORE. Kg.

54

[200] To Margaret Roper.

For the first time in English history, an Act of Parliament was
passed to regulate the succession to the throne, to prevent inter-
ference as "in times past" by the pope. The Act of Succession states
that the marriage with Catherine is "adjudged to be against the
laws of Almighty God, and also accepted, reputed and taken of no
value nor effect." The marriage with Anne "we your said subjects—
do firmly accept, approve and ratify for good, and consonant to the
laws of Almighty God. . . . No man, of what estate, degree or condition soever he be, hath power to dispense with God's laws. . . .

93. intention.   94. prompts.   95. evil-disposed.
96. haply, by chance.   97. understanding.   98. careful.
99. binding.   100. displeased, angry.   101. spiritually.
102. to be propitious to.   103. indebted.

All the issue had and procreate, or hereafter to be had and procreate, between your Highness and your said most dear and entirely
beloved wife Queen Anne shall be your lawful children, and be
inheritable, and inherit according to the course of inheritance and
laws of this realm, the imperial crown of the same." No loyal
Catholic could conscientiously swear to these statements.

The traitor's death was to be the penalty for any who "maliciously
give occasion by writing, print, deed or act" to disturb the King
or the crown, or to derogate from the lawful matrimony between
the King and the said Queen Anne. Loss of goods and imprisonment for life were the penalties for misprision of treason, incurred
if any persons "by any words, without writing, or any exterior deed
or act, maliciously and obstinately shall publish, divulge or utter
any thing or things to the peril of your Highness, or to the slander
or prejudice of the said matrimony."

All persons "shall make a corporal oath . . . that they shall
truly, firmly and constantly, without fraud or guile, observe, fulfill,
maintain, defend and keep, to their cunning, wit, and uttermost of
their powers, the whole effects and contents of this present act."
Those who refuse the oath are guilty of misprision of treason.

The Act does not, however, contain the oath. Letters patent contained the form and appointed the commission. The commissioners
added to the oath a formula "abjuring any foreign potentate," and
the clergy thus had to renounce the pope. More was called upon
so to abjure, though "they sent for no more temporal men." We do
not know the form of the oath offered to More. In the following
November a second Act of Succession was passed and the oath offered to More and Fisher was "reputed the very oath intended by
the Act of Succession," and its form was included in the new act.

⟨Tower of London
c. 17 April 1534⟩

Sir Thomas More, upon warning [1] given him, came before the
King's Commissioners [2] at the Archbishop of Canterbury's
place [3] at Lambeth (the Monday the thirteenth day of April in
the year of our Lord 1534, and in the latter end of the twenty-
fifth year of the reign of King Henry the Eighth), where he refused the oath then offered unto him. And thereupon was he
delivered to the Abbot of Westminster [4] to be kept as a pris-

1. summons.

2. Archbishop Cranmer; Sir Thomas Audley, Chancellor; Thomas Duke
of Norfolk, Treasurer; and the Duke of Suffolk were commissioned to
receive the oath to the Act of Succession.

3. palace.

4. William Benson, born at Boston in Lincolnshire, B.D. Cambridge

oner, with whom he remained till Friday following, and then was sent prisoner to the Tower of London. And shortly after his coming thither he wrote a letter and sent unto his eldest daughter Mistress Margaret Roper, the copy whereof here followeth.

When I was before the Lords at Lambeth, I was the first that was called in, albeit Master Doctor the Vicar of Croydon [5] was come before me, and divers others. After the cause of my sending for, declared unto me (whereof I somewhat marveled in my mind, considering that they sent for no more temporal men [6] but me), I desired the sight of the oath, which they showed me under the great seal.[7] Then desired I the sight of the Act of the Succession, which was delivered me in a printed roll. After which read secretly by myself, and the oath considered with the act, I showed unto them that my purpose was not to put any fault either in the act or any man that made it, or in the oath or any man that sware it, nor to condemn the conscience of any other man. But as for myself in good faith my conscience so moved me in the matter that though I would not deny to swear to the succession, yet unto the oath that there was offered me I could not swear, without the iubarding [8] of my soul to perpetual damnation. And that if they doubted

---

1521, D.D. 1528, became Abbot of Westminster 1533. In 1540 he surrendered the Abbey to the King, and became the first Dean of the new Cathedral.

5. Rowland Phillips (c. 1468–?1538) M.A. Oxford, Warden of Merton College 1521–25, D.D. 1522, was collated to Croydon by Archbishop Morton in 1497, and held many other preferments. He was often in a difficult situation during the religious changes under Henry VIII. In 1531 he had confessed and been pardoned for "all offenses against the Crown and the Statute of Provisors." He was taken prisoner in the autumn of 1533, but was released and in March 1534 heard the sermons at Court, and in April was licensed to dispute with Hugh Latimer. More's letter shows that he took the Oath to the Succession, and in 1535 he labored "to bring the Carthusians into obedience to the King as head of this Church." In July 1537 he appeared before Cranmer but we have no information about his trial. In May 1538 he resigned the living of Croydon and received a pension "on account of his great age."

6. laymen.

7. The Act of Succession did not give the oath, but letters patent contained its form.

8. jeoparding, imperiling.

whether I did refuse the oath only for the grudge [9] of my conscience, or for any other fantasy,[10] I was ready therein to
satisfy them by mine oath. Which if they trusted not, what
should they be the better to give me any oath? And if they
trusted that I would therein swear true, then trusted I that of
their goodness they would not move [11] me to swear the oath
that they offered me, perceiving that for to swear it was against
my conscience.

Unto this my Lord Chancellor [12] said that they all were
sorry [13] to hear me say thus, and see me thus refuse the oath.
And they said all that on their faith I was the very first that
ever refused it; which would cause the King's Highness to conceive great suspicion of me and great indignation toward me.
And therewith they showed me the roll, and let me see the
names of the lords and the commons which had sworn, and
subscribed their names already.[14] Which notwithstanding when
they saw that I refused to swear the same myself, not blam-
ing [15] any other man that had sworn, I was in conclusion commanded to go down into the garden, and thereupon I tarried
in the old burned chamber,[16] that looketh into the garden and
would not go down because of the heat. In that time saw I
Master Doctor Latimer [17] come into the garden, and there
walked he with divers other doctors and chaplains of my Lord
of Canterbury, and very merry I saw him, for he laughed, and

9. uneasiness.   10. caprice.   11. urge, impel.
12. Sir Thomas Audley.   13. distressed.
14. signed as consenting parties.   15. censuring.
16. audience room.
17. Hugh Latimer (1492?–1555), Protestant martyr under Queen Mary,
B.A. Cambridge 1510, M.A. 1514, B.D. 1524, was ordained priest at
Lincoln 1515. He was suspected of Lutheran tendencies as early as 1525.
He was summoned before Convocation for heresy in 1532 because of his
views on pilgrimages, purgatory, invocations to saints, and power of the
keys, and was excommunicated. He recanted but was allowed to make
his submission on lesser charges, agreeing that "no man ought to preach
who has been forbidden by the bishops," and that "consecrations, sanc-
tifications and benedictions in the church are laudable and useful."
Stokesley, Bishop of London, pronounced absolution from heretical prav-
ity, "at the special request of our lord the King." By 1534, he was appointed to preach before the King on all the Wednesdays in Lent, but
was warned by Archbishop Cranmer to avoid controversy. He was made
royal chaplain and in August 1535 was chosen Bishop of Worcester, to
replace the Italian Ghinucci.

took one or twain about the neck so handsomely, that if they had been women, I would have went [18] he had been waxen [19] wanton. After that came Master Doctor Wilson [20] forth from the lords and was with two gentlemen brought by me, and gentlemanly [21] sent straight unto the Tower. What time my Lord of Rochester was called in before them, that cannot I tell. But at night I heard that he had been before them, but where he remained that night, and so forth till he was sent hither, I never heard. I heard also that Master Vicar of Croydon, and all the remnant [22] of the priests of London that were sent for, were sworn, and that they had such favor at the council's hand that they were not lingered [23] nor made to dance any long attendance to their travail [24] and cost, as suitors were sometimes wont to be, but were sped apace [25] to their great comfort so far forth that Master Vicar of Croydon, either for gladness or for dryness, or else that it might be seen (quod ille notus erat pontifici) [26] went to my Lord's buttery bar [27] and called for drink, and drank (valde familiariter).[28]

When they had played their pageant [29] and were gone out of the place, then was I called in again. And then was it declared unto me what a number had sworn, even since I went inside, gladly, without any sticking.[30] Wherein I laid no blame in no man, but for my own self answered as before. Now as

18. weened, supposed.   19. become.
20. Dr. Nicholas Wilson, B.A. Cambridge (Christ's College) 1508/9, D.D. 1533, was chaplain and confessor to the King, held church preferments, and in 1533 was Master of Michaelhouse, Cambridge. In Convocation he was in the minority which thought that the Pope could dispense for the marriage of Henry with his brother's widow. After two years' imprisonment in the Tower, he took the oath to the Succession and was released. He was preferred to the deanery of Wimborne in the diocese of Salisbury and held it until its dissolution in 1547. From June 1540 for some months he was again in the Tower "for having maintained the Pope's side." Released in 1541 he received further preferment, including a prebend at St. Paul's. He was appointed, with bishops and other doctors, to examine the New Testament in the English Bibles, as "many things needed reformation." He died in 1548.
21. as befits a gentleman.   22. remaining number.
23. caused to linger.   24. trouble.   25. expedited.
26. that he was known to the archbishop.
27. A board or ledge on the top of the buttery hatch, the half-door over which provisions are served.
28. very familiarly.   29. empty show.   30. hesitation.

well before as then, they somewhat laid unto me for obstinacy,
that where as before, sith [31] I refused to swear, I would not
declare any special part of that oath that grudged [32] my conscience, and open the cause wherefore. For thereunto I had
said to them, that I feared lest the King's Highness would as
they said take displeasure enough toward me for the only [33]
refusal of the oath. And that if I should open and disclose the
causes why, I should therewith but further exasperate his
Highness, which I would in no wise do, but rather would I
abide all the danger and harm that might come toward me,
than give his Highness any occasion of further displeasure than
the offering of the oath unto me of pure necessity constrained
me. Howbeit when they divers times imputed this to me for
stubbornness and obstinacy that I would neither swear the oath
nor yet declare the causes why, I declined [34] thus far toward
them that rather than I would be accounted for obstinate,[35] I
would upon the King's gracious license [36] or rather his such
commandment had [37] as might be my sufficient warrant [38] that
my declaration [39] should not offend his Highness, nor put me
in the danger of any of his statutes, I would be content to
declare the causes in writing; and over [40] that to give an oath
in the beginning, that if I might find those causes by any man
in such wise answered as I might think mine own conscience
satisfied, I would after that with all mine heart swear the
principal oath, too.

To this I was answered that though the King would give [41]
me license under his letters patent,[42] yet would it not serve
against the statute. Whereto I said that yet if I had them, I
would stand unto the trust of his honor at my peril for the
remnant. But yet it thinketh me,[43] lo, that if I may not declare
the causes without peril, then to leave them undeclared is no
obstinacy.

My Lord of Canterbury taking hold upon that that I said,[44]

31. since.   32. murmured against.
33. only for the refusal.   34. gave in.
35. be considered obstinate.   36. permission.
37. rather having such commandment.   38. safeguard.
39. exposition.   40. beyond.
41. that even if the King should give.
42. open letters to put an agreement on record.   43. I think.
44. what I had said.

that I condemned not the conscience of them that sware, said unto me that it appeared well that I did not take it for a very sure thing and a certain that I might not lawfully swear it, but rather as a thing uncertain and doubtful. But then (said my Lord) you know for a certainty and a thing without doubt that you be bounden to obey your sovereign lord your King. And therefore are ye bounden to leave off the doubt of your unsure conscience in refusing the oath, and take the sure way in obeying of your prince, and swear it. Now all was it so [45] that in mine own mind methought myself not concluded,[46] yet this argument seemed me [47] suddenly so subtle and namely with such authority coming out of so noble [48] a prelate's mouth, that I could again answer nothing thereto but only that I thought myself I might not well do so, because that in my conscience this was one of the cases in which I was bounden that I should not obey my prince, sith that whatsoever other folk thought in the matter (whose conscience and learning I would not condemn nor take upon me to judge), yet in my conscience the truth seemed on the other side. Wherein I had not informed my conscience neither suddenly nor slightly but by long leisure and diligent search for the matter. And of truth if that reason may conclude,[49] than have we a ready way to avoid all perplexities. For in whatsoever matters the doctors stand in great doubt, the King's commandment given upon whither side he list [50] soyleth [51] all the doubts.

Then said my Lord of Westminster to me that howsoever the matter seemed unto mine own mind, I had cause to fear that mine own mind was erroneous when I see the great council [52] of the realm determine of my mind the contrary,[53] and that therefore I ought to change my conscience. To that I answered that if there were no mo [54] but myself upon my side and the whole Parliament upon the other, I would be sore afraid to lean to mine own mind only against so many. But on the other side, if it so be that in some things for which

45. Even though I agreed to the extent.
46. that I thought myself (as a layman) not included.
47. to me.   48. notable.   49. truly if reason may conclude.
50. on whichever side is pleasing to him.   51. resolves.
52. Parliament.   53. determine contrary to my mind.
54. more.

I refuse the oath, I have (as I think I have) upon my part as
great a council and a greater too, I am not then bounden to
change my conscience, and confirm [55] it to the council of one
realm, against the general council of Christendom. Upon this
Master Secretary [56] (as he that tenderly favoreth me), said and
sware a great oath that he had lever [57] that his own only son [58]
(which is of truth a goodly young gentleman, and shall I trust
come to much worship) had lost his head than that I should
thus have refused the oath. For surely the King's Highness
would now conceive a great suspicion against me, and think
that the matter of the nun of Canterbury was all contrived [59]
by my drift.[60] To which I said that the contrary was true and
well known, and whatsoever should mishap [61] me, it lay not
in my power to help it without peril of my soul. Then did
my Lord Chancellor repeat before me my refusal unto Master
Secretary, as to him that was going unto the King's Grace.
And in the rehearsing, his Lordship repeated again that I
denied not but was content to swear to the succession. Whereunto I said that as for that point, I would be content, so that
I might see [62] my oath in that point so framed [63] in such a
manner as might stand with my conscience.

Then said my Lord: "Marry,[64] Master Secretary mark that
too, that he will not swear that neither but under some certain manner." "Verily no, my Lord," quoth I, "but that I will
see it made in such wise first, as I shall myself see, that I shall
neither be forsworn [65] nor swear against my conscience. Surely
as to swear to the succession I see no peril, but I thought and
think it reason that to mine own oath I look well myself, and
be of counsel also in the fashion,[66] and never intended to
swear for a pece,[67] and set my hand to the whole oath. Howbeit
(as help me God),[68] as touching the whole oath, I never with-
drew any man from it, nor never advised any to refuse it, nor

---

55. conform.   56. Thomas Cromwell.
57. liefer, rather.
58. Gregory Cromwell was just of age. He seems hardly to have deserved More's tribute.
59. devised.   60. controlling influence.
61. happen unfortunately to.   62. if I might see.
63. composed.   64. Interjection: Mary.   65. perjured.
66. and have counsel in the way.   67. piece, part.
68. so God help me.

never put, nor will, any scruple in any man's head, but leave
every man to his own conscience. And methinketh [69] in good
faith that so were it good reason [70] that every man should
leave me to mine."

55

[201] To Margaret Roper.

Tower of London
⟨April–May? 1534⟩

A letter written with a coal [1] by Sir Thomas More to his daughter Mistress Margaret Roper, within a while after he was
prisoner in the Tower.

MINE OWN GOOD DAUGHTER.

Our Lord be thanked, I am in good health of body, and in
good quiet of mind; and of worldly things I no more desire
than I have. I beseech him make you all merry in the hope
of heaven. And such things as I somewhat longed to talk with
you all, concerning the world to come, our Lord put them
into your minds, as I trust he doth, and better, too, by his
Holy Spirit, who bless you and preserve you all. Written with
a coal by your tender loving father, who in his poor prayers
forgetteth none of you all, nor your babes, nor your nurses,
nor your good husbands, nor your good husbands' shrewd [2]
wives, nor your father's shrewd wife neither, nor our other
friends. And thus fare you heartily well for lack of paper.

THOMAS MORE, Knight

Our Lord keep me continually true, faithful and plain,[3] to
the contrary whereof I beseech him heartily never to suffer me
to live. For as for long life (as I have often told thee, Meg) I
neither look for, nor long for, but am well content to go, if
God call me hence tomorrow. And I thank our Lord I know
no person living that I would had one philip [4] for my sake, of
which mind [5] I am more glad than of all the world beside.

69. I think.   70. it would be good reason.
1. charcoal used for writing.   2. clever.
3. straightforward.
4. A smart stroke with the nail joint of the finger.
5. state of mind.

Recommend me to [6] your shrewd Will and mine other sons,[7] and to John Harris [8] my friend, and yourself knoweth to whom else, and to my shrewd wife above all, and God preserve you all, and make and keep you his servants all.

56

[202] To Margaret Roper.

Tower of London
⟨May? 1534⟩

Within a while after Sir Thomas More was in prison in the Tower, his daughter Mistress Margaret Roper wrote and sent unto him a letter,[1] wherein she seemed somewhat to labor to persuade him to take the oath (though she nothing so thought) to win thereby credence [2] with Master Thomas Cromwell, that she might the rather get liberty to have free resort [3] unto her father (which she only [4] had for the most time of his imprisonment) unto which letter her father wrote an answer, the copy whereof here followeth.

OUR LORD BLESS YOU ALL.

If I had not been, my dearly beloved daughter, at a firm and fast [5] point (I trust in God's great mercy), this good great while before, your lamentable [6] letter had not a little abashed me,[7] surely far above all other things, of which I hear divers times not a few terrible toward me. But surely they all touched me never so near, nor were so grievous [8] unto me, as to see you, my well-beloved child, in such vehement [9] piteous manner labor to persuade unto me that thing wherein I have of pure necessity for respect unto mine own soul so often given you so precise answer before. Wherein as touching the points of your letter, I can make none answer, for I doubt not but you well remember that the matters which move my conscience

6. commend me to the favor of.
7. William Roper, William Daunce, Giles Heron, John More.
8. For John Harris see above, Letter 48.
1. Margaret Roper's letter is not extant.   2. confidence, trust.
3. access.   4. she alone.   5. steadfast.
6. distressing.   7. destroyed my self-confidence
8. intense, severe.   9. passionate.

(without declaration whereof I can nothing touch the points) I have sundry times showed you that I will disclose them to no man. And therefore daughter Margaret, I can in this thing no further, but like as you labor [10] me again to follow your mind, to desire and pray you both again to leave off such labor, and with my former answers to hold yourself content.

A deadly grief unto me, and much more deadly than to hear of mine own death (for the fear thereof, I thank our Lord, the fear of hell, the hope of heaven and the passion of Christ daily more and more assuage) is that I perceive my good son your husband, and you my good daughter, and my good wife, and mine other good children and innocent friends, in great displeasure and danger of great harm thereby. The let [11] whereof, while it lieth not in my hand, I can no further but commit all unto God. (Nam in manu Dei) saith the scripture (cor regis est, et sicut diuisiones aquarum quocunque voluerit, impellit illud),[12] whose high goodness I most humbly beseech to incline the noble heart of the King's Highness to the tender [13] favor of you all, and to favor me no better than God and myself know that my faithful heart toward him and my daily prayer for him, do deserve. For surely if his Highness might inwardly see my true mind such as God knoweth it is, I would (I trust) soon assuage [14] his high displeasure. Which while I can in this world never in such wise show but that his Grace may be persuaded to believe the contrary of me, I can no further go, but put all in the hands of him, for fear of whose displeasure for the safeguard of my soul stirred by mine own conscience (without insectation [15] or reproach laying to any other man's) I suffer and endure this trouble. Out of which I beseech him to bring me, when his will shall be, into his endless bliss of heaven, and in the meanwhile, give me grace and you both in all our agonies and troubles, devoutly to resort prostrate unto the remembrance of that bitter agony, which our Saviour suffered before his passion at the Mount.[16] And if we diligently so do, I verily trust we shall find therein great comfort and consolation. And thus my dear

10. urge.   11. hindrance, stoppage.   12. Prov. 21:1.
13. gentle.   14. soften, appease.
15. pursuing with words, railing.   16. St. Matt. 26:36–46.

daughter the blessed spirit of Christ for his tender mercy govern and guide you all, to his pleasure and your weal [17] and comforts both body and soul.

Your tender loving father,

THOMAS MORE, Knight [18]

57

[204] To All His Friends.

Roper tells us that Margaret's visit was permitted when More "had remained in the Tower a little more than a month." Their conversation began "after the seven psalms and litany said."

In August, Alice Alington, More's step-daughter, wrote Margaret Roper that the Chancellor had "come to take a course at a buck in our park," and gave her the opportunity to speak for her father. Sir Thomas Audley reminded her that he had helped in the affair of the Nun, but now "marveled that my father is so obstinate in his own conceit, as that everybody went forth withal save only the blind Bishop and he." He callously refused help, putting Lady Alington off with the telling of two of Aesop's fables. Margaret shared the letter with her father when she next visited him. The reply to her step-sister is a repetition of the dialogue with her father. It is so characteristic of More that when it was printed, after More's and Margaret's deaths, the remaining members of the family circle could not tell whether the writer was More himself, or Margaret.

Tower of London

⟨1534⟩

Within a while after Sir Thomas More had been in prison in the Tower, his daughter Mistress Margaret Roper obtained license of the King, that she might resort unto her father in the Tower, which she did. And thereupon he wrote with a coal [1] a letter to all his friends, whereof the copy followeth.

17. well-being.
18. Margaret answered this letter, telling her father that the family found comfort in "the experience we have had of your life past and godly conversation." She desired "above all worldly things to be in John Wood's stead to do you some service." John à Wood was More's servant, who attended him in the Tower. He saved More's works written during his imprisonment.
1. charcoal used for writing.

TO ALL MY LOVING FRIENDS.

For as much as being in prison I cannot tell what need I may have, or what necessity I may hap to stand in, I heartily beseech you all, that if my well beloved daughter Margaret Roper (which only of all my friends hath by the King's gracious favor license to resort to me) do anything desire of any of you, of such things as I shall hap to need, that it may like you no less to regard and tender [2] it, than if I moved it unto you and required it of you personally present myself. And I beseech you all to pray for me, and I shall pray for you.

Your faithful lover and poor bedeman,[3]

THOMAS MORE, Knight, prisoner

58

[207] To Dr. Nicholas Wilson.

Tower of London

1534

A letter written and sent by Sir T. More to Master Doctor Nicholas Wilson [1] (then both prisoners in the Tower of London) in the year of our Lord God 1534, and in the twenty-sixth year of the reign of King Henry the Eighth.

Our Lord be your comfort and whereas I perceive by sundry means that you have promised to swear the oath, I beseech our Lord give you thereof good luck. I never gave any man counsel to the contrary in my days nor never used any ways to put any scruple in other folks' conscience concerning the matter. And whereas I perceive that you would gladly know what I intend to do, you wot [2] well that I told you when we were both abroad that I would therein neither know your mind nor no man's else, nor you nor no man else should therein know mine, for I would be no part taker [3] with no man nor of truth never I will, but leaving every other man to their own conscience myself will with good grace follow mine.

2. attend to.   3. One who prays for another.
1. For Dr. Wilson see above, Letter 54, intro.   2. know.
3. partisan.

For against mine own to swear were peril of my damnation
and what mine own shall be tomorrow myself cannot be sure
and whether I shall have finally the grace to do according
to mine own conscience or not hangeth in God's goodness and
not in mine, to whom I beseech you heartily remember me
in your devout prayers and I shall and daily do remember
you in mine, such as they be, and as long as my poor short life
shall last, any thing that I have, your part shall be therein.

59

[208] To Dr. Nicholas Wilson.

Tower of London

1534

Another letter written and sent by Sir Thomas More to Master
Doctor Wilson (then both prisoners in the Tower) in the year
of our Lord 1534, and in the twenty-sixth year of the reign of
King Henry the Eighth.

MASTER WILSON IN MY RIGHT HEARTY WISE I RECOMMEND [1] ME
TO YOU.

And very sorry am I to see you, beside the trouble that you
be in by this imprisonment with loss of liberty, goods, revenues
of your livelihood and comfort of your friends' company,
fallen also into such agony and vexation of mind through
doubts falling in your mind that diversely [2] to and fro toss
and trouble your conscience to your great heaviness of heart
as I (to no little grief of mine own mind for your sake) perceive. And so much am I for you, good Master Doctor, the
more sorry for that it lieth not in me to give you such kind
of comfort as meseemeth [3] you somewhat desire and look for
at mine hand.

For whereas you would somewhat hear of my mind in your
doubts, I am a man at this day very little meet [4] therefor. For
this you know well, good Master Doctor, that at such time as
the matter came in such manner in question as mine opinion
was asked therein amongst other and yet you made privy

1. commend.   2. in diverse ways.   3. it seems to me.
4. suitable.

thereunto before me, you remember well that at that time you and I many things talked together thereof. And by all the time after by which I did at the King's gracious commandment both seek out and read and commen [5] with all such as I knew made privy to the matter to perceive what I might therein upon both sides and by indifferent [6] weighing of everything as near as my poor wit and learning would serve to see to which side my conscience could incline, and as my own mind should give me so to make his Highness report which way myself should hap to think therein. For other commandment had I never of his Grace in good faith, saving that this knot [7] his Highness added thereto that I should therein look first unto God and after God unto him, which word was also the first lesson that his Grace gave me what time I came first into his noble service and neither a more indifferent commandment nor a more gracious lesson could there in my mind never King give his counselor or any his other [8] servant.

But as I began to tell you by all this long time,[9] I cannot now tell how many years, of all those that I talked with of the matter and with whom I most conferred [10] those places of Scripture and of the old holy Doctors that touched either the one side or the other, with the councils and laws on either side, that speak thereof also, the most, as I trow [11] you wot [12] well, was yourself. For with no man communed I so much and so often thereof as with you, both for your substantial learning and for your mature judgment, and for that [13] I well perceived ever in you that no man had or lightly could have a more faithful respect unto the King's honor and surety [14] both of body and soul than I ever saw that you had.

And yet among many other things which I well liked in you, one specially was that I well perceived in the thing that the King's Grace did put you in trust with,[15] your substantial [16] secret manner. For where I had heard (I wot not now of whom) that you had written his Highness a book of that matter from

5. confer, discuss.   6. impartial.   7. bond, obligation.
8. any other servant of his.   9. in all this long time.
10. compared.   11. think.   12. know.   13. because.
14. security.   15. in which the King's Grace trusted you.
16. essentially.

Paris before, yet in all those years of our long acquaintance
and often talking and reasoning upon the thing, I never heard
you so much as make once any mention of that book. But else
(except there were any other things in that book that you
peradventure [17] thought not on) I suppose that all that ever
came to your mind, that might in the matter make for the
one side or the other comprised [18] either in the Scripture or
in the old ancient Doctors, I verily think in my mind that
you did communicate with [19] me and I likewise with you and
at the least wise I remember well that of those points which
you call now newly to your remembrance there was none at
that time forgotten.

I remember well also by your often [20] conference [21] in the
matter that by all the time in which I studied about it, you
and I were in every point both twain [22] of one opinion and
remember well that the laws and councils and the words of
Saint Augustine *De ciuitate Dei* and the epistle of Saint Ambrose *Ad paternum* and the epistle of Saint Basil translated
out of Greek and the writing of Saint Gregory [23] you and I
read together and over that the places of the Scripture self [24]
both in Leviticus [25] and in the Deuteronomy and in the Gospel [26] and in Saint Paul's epistles [27] and over [28] this in that
other place of Saint Augustine that you remember now and
beside that other places of his, wherein he properly toucheth [29]
the matter expressly with the words of Saint Jerome and of
Saint Chrysostom too, and I cannot now remember of how
many more. But I verily think that on your part, and I am
very sure that on my part, albeit that it had been peradventure
over long to show and read with you every man's book that
I read by myself, whereto the parties peradventure that trusted
me therewith gave me no leave to show their books further
as you peradventure used the like manner with me; yet in
good faith as it was of reason my part in that case to do, you

17. possibly.   18. comprehended.   19. impart to.
20. frequent.   21. action of taking counsel.   22. two.
23. For references on the opinions of the Fathers, consult the *Catholic
Encyclopaedia*, "Divorce."
24. itself.   25. Levit. 20:21.
26. Deut. 25:5; St. Mark 10; St. Matt. 19.
27. 1 Cor. 7; 1 Tim. 5:14.   28. besides.   29. considers.

and I having both one commandment indifferently [30] to consider the matter, everything of Scripture and of the Doctors I faithfully communed with you and as I suppose verily so did you with me too, so that of me, good Master Doctor, though I had all the points as ripe in mind now as I had then and had still all the books about me that I then had, and were as willing to meddle [31] in the matter as any man could be, yet could you now no new thing hear of me, more than you have, I wyn,[32] heard often before, nor I wyn I of you neither.

But now standeth it with me in far other case. For afterward when I had signified unto the King's Highness mine own poor opinion in the matter which his Highness very graciously took in good part and that I saw further progress in the matter wherein to do his Grace service to his pleasure I could not, and anything meddle [33] against his pleasure I would not, I determined utterly with myself to discharge [34] my mind of any farther studying or musing [35] of the matter and thereupon I sent home again such books as I had saving that some I burned by the consent of the owner that was minded [36] as myself was no more to meddle of [37] the matter, and therefore now good Master Doctor I could not be sufficient and able to reason those points again though I were minded thereto sith [38] many things are out of my mind which I never purpose to look for again nor though I would were never like to find again while I live. Besides this, all that ever I looked for was, you wot well, concerning two or three questions to be pondered and weighed by the study of scripture and the interpreters of the same, save for somewhat that hath been touched in the same by the canon [39] laws of the Church.

But then were there at that time in the matter other things more, divers faults found in the bull [40] of the dispensation,[41] by which the King's Council learned in the spiritual law reckoned the bull vicious, partly for untrue suggestion, partly

30. impartially.   31. concern myself.   32. ween, suppose.
33. contend.   34. disburden.   35. pondering.
36. disposed.   37. engage in.   38. since.
39. Church laws from councils and decrees of the popes.
40. Pope's edict, with leaden *bulla* or seal.
41. Ecclesiastical license to do what is otherwise forbidden by canon law.

by reason of unsufficient suggestion.[42] Now concerning those points I never meddled. For I neither understand the doctors of the law nor well can turn their books. And many things have there since in this great matter grown in question wherein I neither am sufficiently learned in the law nor full informed of the fact and therefore I am not he that either murmur or grudge, make assertions, hold opinions or keep dispicions [43] in the matter, but like the King's true, poor, humble subject daily pray for the preservation of his Grace, and the Queen's Grace and their noble issue and of all the realm, without harm doing or intending, I thank our Lord, unto any man living.

Finally as touching the oath, the causes for which I refused it, no man wotteth [44] what they be for they be secret in mine own conscience, some other peradventure, than those that other men would ween,[45] and such as I never disclosed unto any man yet nor never intend to do while I live. Finally as I said unto you, before the oath offered unto us when we met in London at adventure [46] I would be no part taker [47] in the matter but for mine own self follow mine own conscience, for which myself must make answer unto God, and shall leave every other man to his own, so say to you still and I dare say further that no more never intended you neither.[48] Many things every man learned [49] wotteth well there are, in which every man is at liberty without peril of damnation to think which way him list [50] till the one part be determined for necessary to be believed by a general council [51] and I am not he that take upon me to define or determine of what kind or nature everything is that the oath containeth, nor am so bold or presumptuous to blame or dispraise the conscience of other men, their truth nor their learning neither, nor I meddle with no man but of

42. Henry took the position that the dispensation could not allow the marriage with a brother's widow, if that first marriage had really been consummated. But before the trial Catherine showed Cardinal Campeggio the copy of a brief of Pope Julius II which dispensed for the marriage, though considering that the marriage with Arthur had been consummated. This, in any case, Catherine denied.

43. disputations.   44. knows.   45. suppose.
46. by chance.   47. partisan.
48. neither did you intend more.   49. learned man.
50. he is inclined.
51. Determined by a general council as necessary belief.

myself, nor of no man's conscience else will I meddle but of mine own. And in mine own conscience I cry God mercy, I find of mine own life, matters enough to think on.

I have lived, methinks,[52] a long life and now neither I look nor I long to live much longer. I have since I came in the Tower looked once or twice to have given up my ghost [53] ere [54] this and in good faith mine heart waxed [55] the lighter with hope thereof. Yet forget I not that I have a long reckoning and a great to give account of,[56] but I put my trust in God and in the merits of his bitter passion, and I beseech him give me and keep me the mind to long to be out of this world and to be with him. For I can never but trust that who so long to be with him shall be welcome to him and on the other side my mind giveth me verily that any that ever shall come to him shall full heartily wish to be with him or [57] ever he shall come at [58] him. And I beseech him heartily to set your heart at such rest and quiet as may be to his pleasure and eternal weal [59] of your soul and so I verily trust that he shortly shall and shall also if it be his pleasure incline the King's noble heart to be gracious and favorable to you and me both, sith we be both twain of true faithful mind unto him, whether we be in this matter of one mind both,[60] or of diverse. *Sicut diuisiones aquarum, ita cor regis in manu Domini, quocunque voluerit, inclinabit illud.*[61] And if the pleasure of God be on any of us both otherwise to dispose,[62] I need to give you no counsel nor advice.

But for myself I most humbly beseech him to give me the grace in such wise patiently to conform my mind unto his high pleasure therein, that after the troublous storm of this my tempestuous time his great mercy may conduct me into the sure haven of the joyful bliss of heaven, and after at his further pleasure (if I have any) [63] all mine enemies too, for there shall we love together well enough and I thank our Lord for my part so do I here too. Be not angry now though I pray not like for you; you be sure enough I would my friends fare no worse

52. it seems to me.   53. to have died.   54. before.
55. grew.   56. I.e., to God.   57. before.   58. to.
59. happiness.   60. both of one mind.   61. Proverbs 21:1.
62. To dispose otherwise for either of us.
63. This clause should follow *enemies.*

than they, nor yet they, so help me God, no worse than myself.

For our Lord's sake, good Master Wilson, pray for me for I pray for you daily and sometime when I would be sorry but if I thought you were asleep. Comfort yourself, good Master Doctor, with remembering God's great mercy and the King's accustomed goodness, and by my troth I think that all his Grace's Council favoreth you in their hearts. I cannot judge in my mind any one of them so evil as to be of the mind that you should do otherwise than well. And for conclusion in God is all. *Spes non confundit.*[64] I pray you pardon my scribbling for I cannot always so well endure to write as I might sometime. And I pray you when ye see time convenient at your pleasure, send me this rude bill again. *Quia quanquam nihil inest mali, tamen propter ministrum nolim rescire.*[65]

60

[210] To Margaret Roper.

Margaret wrote sympathetically of More's being "shut up again" more closely in the Tower. He had been allowed to hear Mass in one of the chapels and to be in the garden with Dame Alice More and Margaret.

Tower of London

1534

A letter written and sent by Sir Thomas More to his daughter Mistress Roper answering her letter here next before.

THE HOLY SPIRIT OF GOD BE WITH YOU.

If I would with my writing (mine own good daughter) declare how much pleasure and comfort your daughterly loving letters were unto me, a peck of coals would not suffice to make me the pens. And other pens have I (good Margaret) none

64. Rom. 5:5.
65. "Because, although there is nothing evil (disloyal or treasonous) in it, yet on account of the servant I would not wish them to discover it." George Golde, the Lieutenant's servant, carried letters for prisoners. More wished to keep letters to prove their harmlessness, but Golde said there was no better keeper than the fire and burned them.

here: and therefore can I write you no long process,[1] nor dare adventure,[2] good daughter, to write often.

The cause of my close keeping [3] again did of likelihood grow of my negligent [4] and very plain true word which you remember. And verily where as my mind gave me (as I told you in the garden) that some such thing were likely to happen, so doth my mind alway give me that some folk yet ween [5] that I was not so poor as it appeared in the search, and that it may therefore happen that yet eftsoon [6] ofter than once, some new sudden searches may hap to be made in every house of ours as narrowly as is possible. Which thing if ever it so should hap can make but game [7] to us that know the truth of my poverty but if they find out my wife's gay girdle and her golden beads. Howbeit I verily believe in good faith that the King's Grace of his benign pity will take nothing from her.

I thought and yet think that it may be that I was shut up again upon some new causeless suspicion, grown peradventure [8] upon some secret sinister information, whereby some folk haply [9] thought that there should be found out against me some other greater things. But I thank our Lord whensoever this conjecture hath fallen in my mind, the clearness of my conscience hath made my heart hop for joy. For one thing am I very sure of hitherto, and trust in God's mercy to be while I live, that as often I have said unto you, I shall for anything toward my prince never take great harm, but if I take great wrong, in the sight of God, I say, howsoever it shall seem in the sight of men. For to the world, wrong may seem right sometime by false conjecturing, sometimes by false witnesses, as that good Lord said unto you, which is I dare say my very good lord in his mind, and said it of very good will. Before the world also, my refusing of this oath is accounted an heinous [10] offense, and my religious fear [11] toward God is called obstinacy toward my Prince. But my Lords of the Council before whom I refused it might well perceive by the heaviness of my heart appearing well more ways than

· 1. narrative.   2. try.   3. strict confinement.
4. careless.   5. think.   6. again.   7. sport.
8. perhaps.   9. by chance
10. criminal.   11. mingled feeling of dread and reverence.

one unto them that all sturdy stubbornness whereof obstinacy
groweth was very far from my mind. For the clearer proof
whereof, sith [12] they seemed to take for one argument of obstinacy in me that refusing of the oath, I would not declare
the causes why, I offered with a full heart, that albeit I rather
would endure all the pain and peril of the statute than by
declaring of the causes, give any occasion of exasperation unto
my most dread Sovereign Lord and Prince, yet rather than
his Highness should for not disclosing the causes account me
for stubborn and obstinate, I would upon such his gracious
license and commandment as should discharge me of his displeasure and peril of any statute declare those points that
letted [13] my poor conscience to receive that oath; and would
over that be sworn before, that if I should after the causes
disclosed and declared find them so answered as my conscience
should think itself satisfied, I would thereupon swear the oath
that I there refused. To this, Master Secretary answered me
that though the King's Grace gave me such a license, yet it
could not discharge me against [14] the statutes in saying anything that were by them upon heinous [15] pains prohibited. In
this good warning he showed himself my special tender friend.

And now you see well, Margaret, that it is no obstinacy to
leave the causes undeclared, while I could not declare them
without peril. But now is it accounted great obstinacy that
I refuse the oath, whatsoever my causes be, considering that
of so many wiser and better men none sticked [16] thereat. And
Master Secretary of a great zeal that he bare unto me sware
there before them a great oath that for the displeasure that
he thought the King's Highness would bear me, and the suspicion that his Grace would conceive of me, which would
now think in his mind that all the Nun's business was wrought
and devised by me, he had liefer [17] than I should have refused
the oath that his own only son (which is a goodly young
gentleman of whom our Lord send him much joy) had had
his head stricken off. This word Margaret, as it was a marvelous
declaration of Master Secretary's great good mind and favor
toward me, so was it an heavy hearing to me that the King's

12. since.   13. prevented.   14. exempt me from.
15. severe.   16. scrupled.   17. rather.

Grace, my most dread Sovereign Lord, were likely to conceive such high suspicion of me and bear such grievous indignation toward me, for the thing which without the danger and peril of my poor soul lay not in my hand to help, nor doth.

Now have I heard since that some say that this obstinate manner of mine in still refusing the oath shall peradventure force and drive the King's Grace to make a further law for me. I cannot let [18] such a law to be made. But I am very sure that if I died by such a law, I should die for that point innocent afore [19] God. And albeit (good daughter) that I think our Lord that hath the hearts of Kings in his hand would never suffer of his high goodness, so gracious a Prince, and so many honorable men, and so many good men as be in the Parliament to make such an unlawful law, as that should be if it so mishapped,[20] yet lest I note that point unthought upon, but many times more than one revolved and cast in my mind before my coming hither, both that peril and all other that might put my body in peril of death by the refusing of this oath. In devising whereupon, albeit (mine own good daughter) that I found myself (I cry God mercy) very sensual [21] and my flesh much more shrinking from pain and from death than methought it the part of a faithful Christian man, in such a case as my conscience gave me, that in the saving of my body should stand the loss of my soul, yet I thank our Lord, that in that conflict the Spirit had in conclusion the mastery, and reason with help of faith finally concluded that for to be put to death wrongfully for doing well (as I am very sure I do, in refusing to swear against mine own conscience, being such as I am not upon peril of my soul bounden [22] to change whether my death should come without law, or by color [23] of a law) it is a case in which a man may leese [24] his head and yet have none harm, but instead of harm inestimable good at the hand of God.

And I thank our Lord (Megge) since I am come hither I set by [25] death every day less than other. For though a man

18. prevent. 19. before. 20. unfortunately happened.
21. depending on the senses only and not on the intellect or spirit.
22. bound. 23. under the pretext. 24. lose.
25. esteem.

leese of his years in this world, it is more than manifold
recompensed by coming the sooner to heaven. And though it
be a pain to die while a man is in health, yet see I very few
that in sickness die with ease. And finally, very sure am I that
whensoever the time shall come that may hap to come, God
wot [26] how soon, in which I should lie sick in my death bed
by nature, I shall then think that God had done much for me,
if he had suffered me to die before by the color of such a law.
And therefore my reason showeth me (Margaret) that it were
great folly for me to be sorry to come to that death, which I
would after wish that I had died. Beside that, that a man may
hap with less thank of God and more adventure [27] of his
soul to die as violently and as painfully by many other chances
as by enemies or thieves. And therefore mine own good
daughter I assure you (thanks be to God) the thinking of any
such albeit it hath grieved [28] me ere [29] this, yet at this day
grieveth me nothing. And yet I know well for all this mine
own frailty, and that Saint Peter which feared it much less
than I, fell in such fear soon after that at the word of a
simple girl he forsook and forsware [30] our Saviour.[31] And
therefore am I not (Megge) so mad [32] as to warrant [33] myself
to stand. But I shall pray, and I pray thee mine own good
daughter to pray with me, that it may please God that hath
given me this mind, to give me the grace to keep it.

And thus have I mine own good daughter disclosed unto
you the very secret bottom of my mind, referring the order
thereof only to the goodness of God, and that so fully that
I assure you Margaret on my faith I never have prayed God to
bring me hence nor deliver me from death, but referring all
thing whole unto his only pleasure, as to him that seeth better
what is best for me than myself doth. Nor never longed I
since I came hither to set my foot in mine own house, for
any desire of or pleasure of my house, but gladly would I
sometime somewhat talk with my friends, and specially my
wife and you that pertain to my charge. But sith that God
otherwise disposeth,[34] I commit all wholly to his goodness

---

26. knows.   27. peril.   28. troubled.   29. before.
30. denied on oath.   31. Matt. 26:69–75.   32. unwise.
33. pledge.   34. ordains.

and take daily great comfort in that I perceive that you live together so charitably and so quietly; I beseech our Lord continue it. And thus, mine own good daughter, putting you finally in remembrance that albeit if the necessity so should require, I thank our Lord in this quiet and comfort is mine heart at this day, and I trust in God's goodness so shall have grace to continue, yet (as I said before) I verily trust that God shall so inspire and govern the King's heart that he shall not suffer his noble heart and courage to requite my true faithful heart and service with such extreme unlawful and uncharitable dealing, only for the displeasure that I cannot think so as other do. But his true subject will I live and die, and truly pray for him will I, both here and in the other world too.

And thus mine own good daughter have me recommended to my good bedfellow and all my children, men, women and all, with all your babes and your nurses and all the maids and all the servants, and all our kin, and all our other friends abroad. And I beseech our Lord to save them all and keep them. And I pray you all pray for me, and I shall pray for you all. And take no thought for me whatsoever you shall hap to hear, but be merry in God.

61

[211] To Margaret Roper.

Tower of London
1534

Another letter written and sent by Sir Thomas More (in the year of our Lord, 1534 and in the twenty-sixth year of King Henry the Eighth) to his daughter Mistress Roper, answering a letter [1] which she wrote and sent unto him.

THE HOLY SPIRIT OF GOD BE WITH YOU.

Your daughterly loving letter, my dearly beloved child, was and is, I faithfully assure you, much more inward comfort unto me than my pen can well express you, for divers things that I marked therein but of all things most especially, for that God of his high goodness giveth you the grace to consider

1. Margaret's letter is lost.

the incomparable difference between the wretched estate of
this present life and the wealthy state of the life to come, for
them that die in God, and to pray God in such a good
Christian fashion that it may please him (it doth me good
here to rehearse your own words) "of his tender pity so firmly
to rest our love in him, with little regard of this world, and so
to flee sin and embrace virtue, that we may say with Saint
Paul, *Mihi viuere Christus est et mori luchrum.* And this,
Cupio dissolui et esse cum Christo." [2] I beseech our Lord, my
dearly beloved daughter, that wholesome prayer that he hath
put in your mind, it may like him to give your father the
grace daily to remember and pray, and yourself as you have
written it even so daily devoutly to kneel and pray it. For
surely if God give us that, he giveth us and will give us therewith all that ever we can well wish. And therefore good Marget,
when you pray it, pray it for us both, and I shall on my part
the like, in such manner as it shall like our Lord to give me,
poor wretch,[3] the grace, that likewise as in this wretched world
I have been very glad of your company and you of mine,
and yet would if it might be (as natural charity bindeth the
father and the child) so we may rejoice and enjoy each other's
company, with our other kinsfolk, allies,[4] and friends ever-
lastingly in the glorious bliss of heaven, and in the meantime
with good counsel and prayer each help other thitherward.

   And where you write these words of yourself, "But good
father, I wretch am far, far, farthest of all other from such
point of perfection, our Lord send me the grace to amend my
life, and continually to have an eye to mine end, without
grudge [5] of death, which to them that die in God, is the gate
of a wealthy life to which God of his infinite mercy bring us
all. Amen. Good Father strenght [6] my frailty with your devout
prayers." The father of heaven mote [7] strenght thy frailty, my
good daughter and the frailty of thy frail father too. And let
us not doubt but he so will, if we will not be slack [8] in calling
upon him therefor. Of my poor prayers, such as they be, ye
may be bold to reckon. For Christian charity and natural love

2. Phil. 1:21, 23.   3. one sunk in deep distress.
4. relatives by marriage.   5. fear.   6. strengthen.
7. must.   8. remiss.

and your very daughterly dealing (*funiculo triplici,* as saith the Scripture, *difficile rumpitur*) [9] both bind me and strain me thereto. And of yours I put as little doubt.

That you fear your own frailty Marget, nothing misliketh me.[10] God give us both twain [11] the grace to despair of our own self, and whole [12] to depend and hang upon the hope and strength of God. The blessed apostle Saint Paul found such lack of strength in himself that in his own temptation he was fain thrice to call and cry out unto God, to take that temptation from him. And yet sped he not of his prayer,[13] in the manner that he required. For God of his high wisdom, seeing that it was (as himself saith) necessary for him to keep him from pride that else he might peradventure [14] have fallen in, would not at his thrice praying, by and by [15] take it from him, but suffered him to be panged [16] in the pain and fear thereof, giving him yet at the last this comfort against his fear of falling (*Sufficit tibi gratia mea*).[17] By which words it well seemeth that the temptation was so strong (whatsoever kind of temptation it was) that he was very feared [18] of falling, through the feebleness of resisting that he began to feel in himself. Wherefore for his comfort God answered (*Sufficit tibi gratia mea*) putting him in surety, that were he of himself never so feeble and faint, nor never so likely to fall, yet the grace of God was sufficient to keep him up and make him stand. And our Lord said further (*Virtus in infirmitate proficitur*). [19] The more weak that man is, the more is the strength of God in his safeguard declared. And so Saint Paul saith (*Omnia possum in eo qui me confortat*). [20]

Surely Megge a fainter heart than thy frail father hath, canst you not have. And yet I verily trust in the great mercy of God, that he shall of his goodness so stay [21] me with his holy hand that he shall not finally suffer me to fall wretchedly from his favor. And the like trust (dear daughter) in his high goodness I verily conceive of you. And so much the more, in

9. Eccles. 4:12.   10. I do not disapprove.   11. two.
12. wholly.   13. attained he not his prayer.   14. possibly.
15. straightway.   16. affected.   17. 2 Cor. 12:7–10.
18. afraid.   19. 2 Cor. 12:9.   20. Phil. 4:13.
21. support.

that there is neither of us both, but that if we call his benefits
to mind and give him oft thanks for them, we may find
tokens [22] many, to give us good hope for all our manifold
offenses toward him, that his great mercy, when we will
heartily call therefor, shall not be withdrawn from us. And
verily, my dear daughter, in this is my great comfort, that
albeit I am of nature so shrinking from pain that I am almost
afeard of a fillip,[23] yet in all the agonies that I have had,
whereof before my coming hither (as I have showed you ere [24]
this) I have had neither small nor few, with heavy fearful
heart, forecasting [25] all such perils and painful deaths, as by
any manner of possibility might after fall unto me, and in
such thought lain long restless and waking, while my wife
had weened [26] I had slept, yet in any such fear and heavy
pensiveness [27] (I thank the mighty mercy of God) I never in
my mind intended to consent that I would for the enduring
of the uttermost do any such thing as I should in mine own
conscience (for with other men's I am not a man meet [28]
to take upon me to meddle) think to be to myself, such as
should damnably cast me in the displeasure of God. And this
is the least point that any man may with his salvation come
to, as far as I can see, and is bounden if he see peril to examine
his conscience surely by learning and by good counsel and be
sure that his conscience be such as it may stand with his
salvation, or else reform it. And if the matter be such as both
the parties may stand with salvation, then on whither [29] side
his conscience fall, he is safe enough before God. But that
mine own may stand with my own salvation, thereof I thank
our Lord I am very sure. I beseech our Lord bring all parts [30]
to his bliss.

It is now, my good daughter, late. And therefore thus I
commend you to the holy Trinity, to guide you, comfort you
and direct you with his Holy Spirit, and all yours and my wife
with all my children and all our other friends.

                                      THOMAS MORE, Knight

22. signs of divine power.
23. afraid of a small tap with the finger.   24. before.
25. imagining beforehand.   26. thought.   27. melancholy.
28. fit.   29. whichever.   30. sides in the contention.

62

[213] To Master Leder.

Tower of London
Saturday
16 January 1534/5

A letter written by Sir Thomas More to one Master Leder,[1] a virtuous priest, the sixteenth day of January in the year of our Lord 1534 after the computation[2] of the Church of England, and in the twenty-sixth year of the reign of King Henry the Eighth.

The tale that is reported, albeit I cannot but thank you though you would it were true, yet I thank God it is a very vanity. I trust in the great goodness of God, that he shall never suffer it to be true. If my mind had been obstinate indeed I would not let[3] for any rebuke or worldly shame plainly to confess the truth. For I purpose not to depend upon the fame of the world. But I thank our Lord that the thing that I do is not for obstinacy but for the salvation of my soul, because I cannot induce mine own mind otherwise to think than I do concerning the oath.

As for other men's consciences, I will be no judge of, nor I never advised any man neither to swear nor to refuse, but as for mine own self if ever I should mishap[4] to receive the oath (which I trust our Lord shall never suffer me), ye may reckon sure that it were expressed and extorted by duresse[5] and hard handling.[6] For as for all the goods of this world, I thank our Lord I set not much more by than I do by dust.[7] And I trust both that they will use no violent forcible ways, and also that if they would, God would of his grace and the rather a great deal through good folks' prayers give me strength to stand. *Fidelis Deus* (saith Saint Paul) *qui non patitur vos tentari supra id quod potestis ferre, sed dat cum*

1. Master Leder seems not otherwise known.   2. reckoning.
3. refrain.   4. have the misfortune.   5. compulsion.
6. More feared that he would be put to the torture.
7. esteem them as worth no more than I do esteem dust.

tentatione prouentum vt possitis sustinere.[8] For this I am very sure, that if ever I should swear it, I should swear deadly against mine own conscience. For I am very sure in my mind that I shall never be able to change mine own conscience to the contrary; as for other men's, I will not meddle of.

It hath been showed me that I am reckoned willful and obstinate because that since my coming hither I have not written unto the King's Highness and by mine own writing made some suit unto his Grace. But in good faith I do not forbear it of any obstinacy, but rather of a lowly mind and a reverent, because that I see nothing that I could write but that I fear me sore [9] that his Grace were likely rather to take displeasure with me for it than otherwise, while his Grace believeth me not that my conscience is the cause but rather obstinate willfulness. But surely that my let [10] is but my conscience, that knoweth God to whose order I commit the whole matter. *In cuius manu corda regum sunt.*[11] I beseech our Lord that all may prove as true faithful subjects to the King that have sworn as I am in my mind very sure that they be, which have refused to swear.

In haste, the Saturday the sixteenth day of January by the hand of your beadsman,[12]

THOMAS MORE, Knight and prisoner

63

[214] To Margaret Roper.

More wrote, "fearing lest she, being (as he thought) with child, should take some harm."

On April 20 John Houghton; Augustine Webster; Robert Lawrence; the priors of the Charterhouses of London, Beauvale and Axholme; and Dr. Richard Reynolds of the Bridgettine monastery of Syon were arrested and were brought to trial on the 28th for denying that the King was Supreme Head of the English Church. They urged that the obedience to the Pope was "to the salvation of man of necessity, and that this superiority of the Pope was a sure truth and manifest of the law of God, and instituted by Christ as

8. 1 Cor. 10:13.   9. I am greatly afraid.   10. hindrance.
11. Prov. 21:1.   12. One who prays for another.

necessary to the conservation of the spiritual unity of the mystical body of Christ" (*L.P., 8,* no. 801; Hughes, *1,* 280).

Tower of London

2 or 3 May 1535

A letter written and sent by Sir Thomas More to his daughter Mistress Roper, written the second or third day of May, in the year of our Lord 1535 and in the twenty-seventh year of the reign of King Henry the Eighth.

OUR LORD BLESS YOU.

MY DEARLY BELOVED DAUGHTER.

I doubt not but by the reason of the Councilors resorting hither, in this time (in which our Lord be their comfort) these fathers of the Charterhouse and Master Reynolds of Syon that be now judged to death for treason (whose matters and causes I know not) may hap to put you in trouble and fear of mind concerning me being here prisoner, specially for that it is not unlikely but that you have heard that I was brought also before the Council here myself. I have thought it necessary to advertise [1] you of the very truth, to the end that you neither conceive more hope than the matter giveth, lest upon other turn [2] it might aggrieve your heaviness, nor more grief and fear than the matter giveth of, on the other side. Wherefore shortly ye shall understand that on Friday the last day of April in the afternoon, Master Lieutenant [3] came in here unto me and showed me that Master Secretary [4] would speak with me. Whereupon I shifted my gown and went out with Master Lieutenant into the gallery to him. Where I met many, some known and some unknown, in the way. And in conclusion coming into the chamber where his Mastership sat with Master Attorney,[5] Master Solicitor,[6] Master Bedill,[7] and

1. inform.   2. change.

3. Sir Edmund Walsingham, an old friend, who felt himself "bounden . . . to make him good cheer," but could not "without the King's indignation."

4. Cromwell.

5. Sir Christopher Hales, Attorney General since 1525.

6. Richard Rich was newly appointed as Solicitor General. He was an able lawyer, but treacherous and cruel. Roper (pp. 84–91) shows how More proved Rich's perjury in evidence against himself.

7. Thomas Bedill (d. 1537), Clerk of the Privy Council, had been en-

Master Doctor Tregonnell,[8] I was offered to sit with them, which in no wise I would.

Whereupon Master Secretary showed unto me that he doubted not but that I had by such friends as hither had resorted to me seen the new statutes made at the last sitting of the Parliament. Whereunto I answered: "Yea verily. Howbeit for as much as being here, I have no conversation with any people, I thought it little need for me to bestow much time upon them, and therefore I redelivered the book shortly and the effect of the statutes I never marked nor studied to put in remembrance." Then he asked me whether I had not read the first statute of them, of the King being Head of the Church. Whereunto I answered, "Yes." Then his Mastership declared unto me that sith [9] it was now by act of Parliament ordained that his Highness and his heirs be, and ever right have been, and perpetually should be Supreme Head in yerth [10] of the Church of England under Christ, the King's pleasure was that those of his Council there assembled should demand mine opinion, and what my mind was therein. Whereunto I answered that in good faith I had well trusted that the King's Highness would never have commanded any such question to be demanded of me, considering that I ever from the beginning well and truly from time to time declared my mind unto his Highness, and since that time I had (I said) unto your Mastership Master Secretary also, both by mouth and by writing. And now I have in good faith discharged my mind of all such matters, and neither will dispute King's titles nor Pope's, but the King's true faithful subject I am and will be, and daily I pray for him and for all his, and for you all that are of his honorable Council, and for all the realm, and otherwise than thus I never intend to meddle.

Whereunto Master Secretary answered that he thought this manner [11] answer should not satisfy nor content the King's Highness, but that his Grace would exact a more full answer. And his Mastership added thereunto that the King's Highness

gaged in affairs connected with the divorce case. He was now obtaining oaths to the Royal Supremacy.

8. Sir John Tregonwell (d. 1565), now principal judge of the Court of Admiralty, had been proctor for the King in the divorce case.

9. since.   10. on earth.   11. kind of.

was a prince not of rigor but of mercy and pity, and though that he had found obstinacy at some time in any of his subjects, yet when he should find them at another time confyrmable [12] and submit themself, his Grace would show mercy. And that concerning myself, his Highness would be glad to see me take such confyrmable ways, as I might be abroad in the world again among other men as I have been before.

Whereunto I shortly (after the inward affection [13] of my mind) answered for a very truth that I would never meddle in the world again, to have the world given me. And to the remnant [14] of the matter I answered in effect as before, showing that I had fully determined with myself neither to study nor meddle with any matter of this world, but that my whole study should be upon the passion of Christ and mine own passage out of this world.

Upon this I was commanded to go forth for a while, and after called in again. At which time Master Secretary said unto me that though I was prisoner and condemned to perpetual prison, yet I was not thereby discharged of mine obedience and allegiance unto the King's Highness. And thereupon demanded me whether that I thought that the King's Grace might exact of me such things as are contained in the statutes and upon like pains [15] as he might of other men. Whereto I answered that I would not say the contrary. Whereto he said that likewise as the King's Highness would be gracious to them that he found conformable, so his Grace would follow the course of his laws toward such as he shall find obstinate. And his Mastership said further that my demeanor [16] in that matter was of a thing that of likelihood made now other men so stiff [17] therein as they be.

Whereto I answered, that I give no man occasion to hold any point one or other, nor never gave any man advice or counsel therein one way or other. And for conclusion I could no further go, whatsoever pain should come thereof. I am, quoth I, the King's true faithful subject and daily bedesman [18] and pray for his Highness and all his and all the realm. I do nobody harm, I say none harm, I think none harm, but wish

12. conformable.　　13. feeling.　　14. remainder.
15. punishment.　　16. conduct.　　17. obstinate.
18. one who prays for another.

everybody good. And if this be not enough to keep a man alive in good faith I long not to live. And I am dying already, and have since I came here, been divers times in the case [19] that I thought to die within one hour, and I thank our Lord I was never sorry for it, but rather sorry when I saw the pang [20] past. And therefore my poor body is at the King's pleasure— would God my death might do him good.

After this Master Secretary said, "Well ye find no fault in that statute, find you any in any of the other statutes after?" Whereto I answered, "Sir, whatsoever thing should seem to me other than good, in any of the statutes or in that statute either, I would not declare what fault I found, nor speak thereof." Whereunto finally his mastership said full gently that of anything that I had spoken, there should none advantage be taken, and whether he said further that there be none to be taken, I am not well remembered.[21] But he said that report should be made unto the King's Highness, and his gracious pleasure known.

Whereupon I was delivered [22] again to Master Lieutenant, which was then called in, and so was I by Master Lieutenant brought again into my chamber, and here am I yet in such case as I was, neither better nor worse. That that shall follow lieth in the hand of God, whom I beseech to put in the King's Grace's mind that thing that may be to his high pleasure, and in mine, to mind only the weal [23] of my soul, with little regard of my body.

And you with all yours, and my wife and all my children and all our other friends both bodily and ghostly [24] heartily well to fare. And I pray you and all them pray for me, and take no thought whatsoever shall happen me. For I verily trust in the goodness of God, seem it never so evil to this world, it shall indeed in another world be for the best.

Your loving father,

THOMAS MORE Knight [25]

19. condition.   20. brief, keen spasm of pain.
21. do not remember.   22. handed over.   23. good.
24. spiritually.
25. On 4 May, Margaret was allowed to visit her father again, and together they saw the monks start on their martyrs' journey to Tyburn, to be hanged as traitors. The authorities had probably thought Margaret

64

[216] To Margaret Roper.

The Commission of the King's Council were now Archbishop Cranmer; Sir Thomas Audley; Charles Brandon, Duke of Suffolk; Thomas Boleyn, Earl of Wiltshire and Ormonde, the Lord Privy Seal; and Thomas Cromwell, the King's principal Secretary.

⟨Tower of London
3 June 1535⟩

Another letter written and sent by Sir Thomas More to his daughter Mistress Roper, written in the year of our Lord 1535, and in the twenty-seventh year of the reign of King Henry the Eighth.

OUR LORD BLESS YOU AND ALL YOURS.

Forasmuch, dearly beloved daughter, as it is likely that you either have heard or shortly shall hear that the Council was here this day, and that I was before them, I have thought it necessary to send you word how the matter standeth. And verily to be short I perceive little difference between this time and the last, for as far as I can see the whole purpose is either to drive me to say precisely the one way, or else precisely the other.

Here sat my Lord of Canterbury, my Lord Chancellor, my Lord of Suffolk, my Lord of Wiltshire, and Master Secretary. And after my coming, Master Secretary made rehearsal [1] in what wise he had reported unto the King's Highness, what had been said by his Grace's Council to me, and what had been answered by me to them at mine other being before them last. Which thing his Mastership rehearsed in good faith very well, as I knowledged [2] and confessed and heartily thanked him therefor. Whereupon he added thereunto that the King's Highness was nothing content nor satisfied with mine answer, but thought that by my demeanor [3] I had been occasion [4] of

---

would move her father by her distress at this sight. More said, "Lo, dost thou not see, Meg, that these blessed fathers be now as cheerfully going to their deaths as bridegrooms to their marriage?"

1. related.   2. acknowledged.   3. conduct.   4. cause.

much grudge [5] and harm in the realm, and that I had an
obstinate mind and an evil toward him and that my duty was,
being his subject, and so he had sent them now in his name
upon my allegiance to command me, to make a plain and
terminate [6] answer whether I thought the statute lawful or
not and that I should either knowledge and confess it lawful
that his Highness should be Supreme Head of the Church
of England or else to utter plainly my malignity.[7]

Whereto I answered that I had no malignity and therefore
I could none utter. And as to the matter I could none other
answer make than I had before made, which answer his
Mastership had there rehearsed. Very heavy [8] I was that the
King's Highness should have any such opinion of me. Howbeit
if there were one that had informed his Highness many evil
things of me that were untrue, to which his Highness for
the time gave credence,[9] I would be very sorry that he should
have that opinion of me the space of one day. Howbeit if I
were sure that other should come on the morrow by whom his
Grace should know the truth of mine innocency, I should in
the meanwhile comfort myself with consideration of that. And
in like wise now though it be great heaviness [10] to me that
his Highness have such opinion of me for the while, yet have
I no remedy to help it, but only to comfort myself with this
consideration that I know very well that the time shall come,
when God shall declare my truth toward his Grace before him
and all the world. And whereas it might haply [11] seem to be
but small cause of comfort because I might take harm here
first in the meanwhile, I thanked God that my case was such
in this matter through the clearness of mine own conscience
that though I might have pain I could not have harm, for a
man may in such case leese [12] his head and have no harm.
For I was very sure that I had no corrupt [13] affection, but that
I had always from the beginning truly used myself to looking
first upon God and next upon the King according to the lesson
that his Highness taught me at my first coming to his noble
service, the most virtuous lesson that ever prince taught his

5. injurious influence.   6. final.   7. deep-rooted ill will.
8. weighed down with sorrow.   9. accepted as true.
10. sorrow.   11. perhaps.   12. lose.   13. evil.

servant; whose Highness to have of me such opinion is my great heaviness, but I have no mean [14] as I said to help it, but only comfort myself in the meantime with the hope of that joyful day in which my truth towards him shall well be known. And in this matter further I could not go nor other answer thereto I could not make.

To this it was said by my Lord Chancellor and Master Secretary both that the King might by his laws compel me to make a plain answer thereto, either the one way or the other.

Whereunto I answered I would not dispute [15] the King's authority, what his Highness might do in such case, but I said that verily under correction it seemed to me somewhat hard. For if it so were that my conscience gave me against the statutes (wherein how my mind giveth me I make no declaration), then I nothing doing nor nothing saying against the statute, it were a very hard thing to compel me to say either precisely with it against my conscience to the loss of my soul, or precisely against it to the destruction of my body.

To this Master Secretary said that I had ere this when I was Chancellor examined heretics and thieves and other malefactors and gave me a great praise above my deserving in that behalf. And he said that I then, as he thought and at the leastwise Bishops did use to examine heretics, whether they believed the Pope to be head of the Church and used to compel them to make a precise answer thereto. And why should not then the King, sith [16] it is a law made here that his Grace is Head of the Church, here compel men to answer precisely to the law here as they did then concerning the Pope.

I answered and said that I protested that I intended not to defend any part or stand in contention, [17] but I said there was a difference between those two cases because that at that time as well here as elsewhere through the corps [18] of Christendom the Pope's power was recognized for an undoubted thing which seemeth not like a thing agreed in this realm and the contrary taken for truth in other realms, whereunto Master Secretary answered that they were as well burned for the denying of that as they be beheaded for denying of this, and therefore as good

14. means, opportunity.   15. contest.   16. since.
17. strife, dispute.   18. body.

reason to compel them to make precise answer to the one as to the other.

Whereto I answered that sith in this case a man is not by a law of one realm so bound in his conscience, where there is a law of the whole corps of Christendom to the contrary in matter touching belief, as he is by a law of the whole corps though there hap to be made in some place a law local [19] to the contrary, the reasonableness or the unreasonableness in binding a man to precise answer standeth not in the respect or difference between heading [20] or burning, but because of the difference in charge of conscience, the difference standeth between heading and hell.

Much was there answered unto this both by Master Secretary and my Lord Chancellor over [21] long to rehearse. And in conclusion they offered me an oath by which I should be sworn to make true answer to such things as should be asked me on the King's behalf, concerning the King's own person.

Whereto I answered that verily I never purposed to swear any book oath [22] more while I lived. Then they said that was very obstinate if I would refuse that, for every man doth it in the Star Chamber [23] and everywhere. I said that was true but I had not so little foresight but that I might well conjecture what should be part of my interrogatory [24] and as good it was to refuse it at the first, as afterward.

Whereto my Lord Chancellor answered that he thought I guessed truth, for I should see them and so they were showed me and they were but twain.[25] The first whether I had seen the statute. The other whether I believed that it were a lawful made interrogatory [26] or not. Whereupon I refused the oath and said further by mouth that the first I had before confessed, and to the second I would make none answer.

Which was the end of the communication and I was thereupon sent away. In the communication before it was

19. local law.   20. beheading.   21. too.
22. oath of special solemnity, on a book (the Bible).
23. judicial sittings of the King's Council, meeting in the Star Chamber at Westminster, usually for criminal jurisdiction.
24. questioning, interrogation.   25. two.
26. question formally put to an accused person; the 1557 *Works* print "statute."

said that it was marveled that I stack [27] so much in my conscience while at the uttermost I was not sure therein. Whereto
I said that I was very sure that mine own conscience so informed as it is by such diligence as I have so long taken
therein may stand with mine own salvation. I meddle not
with the conscience of them that think otherwise, every man
suo domino stat et cadit.[28] I am no man's judge. It was also
said unto me that if I had as lief [29] be out of the world as in
it, as I had there said, why did I not speak even out plain
against the statute. It appeared well I was not content to die
though I said so. Whereto I answered as the truth is, that I
have not been a man of such holy living as I might be bold to
offer myself to death, lest God for my presumption might
suffer me to fall, and therefore I put not myself forward, but
draw back. Howbeit if God draw me to it himself, then trust
I in his great mercy, that he shall not fail to give me grace
and strength.

In conclusion Master Secretary said that he liked me this
day much worse than he did the last time, for then he said
he pitied me much and now he thought that I meant not
well, but God and I know both that I mean well and so I
pray God do by me.[30]

I pray you be you and mine other friends of good cheer
whatsoever fall of me,[31] and take no thought for me but pray
for me as I do and shall do for you and all them.

Your tender loving father,

THOMAS MORE, Kg.

65

[217] To Antonio Bonvisi.

Bonvisi had sent More a warm camlet gown (of the hair of the
Angora goat) and gifts of wine and meat.

Bonvisi himself suffered later as a loyal Catholic. He fled from
England in 1544. His house (and also Clement's) was seized in 1550,
and he was specially excepted from the pardon of the Parliament of
1553. He recovered his property under Queen Mary and when he
died in 1558 left it to his nephew. He was buried in Louvain.

27. persisted.   28. Rom. 14:4.   29. if I were as willing to.
30. deal with me.   31. fall to my lot.

Tower of London
1535

Sir Thomas More a little before he was arraigned and condemned (in the year of our Lord 1535, and in the twenty-
seventh year of the reign of King Henry the Eighth), being
shut up so close in prison in the Tower that he had no pen
nor ink, wrote with a coal[1] a pistle[2] in Latin to Master
Anthony Bonvisi (merchant of Luke[3] and then dwelling in
London), his old and dear friend, and sent it unto him, the
copy whereof here followeth. [Latin text follows in *1557*.]

The translation into English of the Latin pistle next before.

GOOD MASTER BONVISI OF ALL FRIENDS MOST FRIENDLIEST, AND TO
ME WORTHILY DEARLIEST BELOVED, I HEARTILY GREET YOU.

Sith[4] my mind doth give me (and yet may chance falsely but
yet so it doth) that I shall not have long liberty to write unto
you, I determined therefore while I may to declare unto you
by this little epistle of mine how much I am comforted with
the sweetness of your friendship, in this decay of my fortune.

For afore[5] (right Worshipful[6] Sir) although I always delighted marvelously in this your love towards me, yet when
I consider in my mind that I have been now almost this forty
years not a guest, but a continual nursling[7] in Master Bonvisi's house, and in the mean season[8] have not showed myself
in requiting you again, a friend, but a barren lover only, my
shamefastness[9] verily made that that sincere sweetness, which
otherwise I received of the revolving[10] of your friendship,
somewhat waxed[11] sourish, by reason of a certain rustical[12]
shame as neglecting of my duty toward you. But now I comfort myself with this, that I never had the occasion[13] to do
you pleasure. For such was always your great wealth that there
was nothing left in which I might be unto you beneficial. I
therefore (knowing that I have not been unthankful to you
by omitting my duty toward you but for lack of occasion and

1. charcoal pencil.   2. an epistle.
3. Lucca, in northern Italy.   4. since.   5. before.
6. distinguished.   7. object of a nurse's care.
8. meanwhile.   9. ashamedness.   10. turning.
11. became.   12. unmannerly.   13. opportunity.

opportunity, and seeing moreover all hope of recompense taken away, you so to persevere in love toward me, binding me more and more to you, yea rather so to run forward still, and as it were with a certain indefatigable course to go forth, that few men so fawn upon their fortunate friends, as you favor, love, foster and honor me, now overthrown, abjected,[14] afflicted, and condemned to prison) cleanse myself both from this bitterness (such as it is) of mine old shamefastness and also repose myself in the sweetness of this marvelous friendship of yours.

And this faithful prosperity of this amity and friendship of yours towards me (I wot [15] not how) seemeth in a manner to counterpoise [16] this unfortunate shipwreck of mine, and saving the indignation of my Prince, of me no less loved than feared, else as concerning all other things, doth almost more than counterpoise. For all those are to be accounted amongst the mischances of fortune. But if I should reckon the possession of so constant friendship (which no storms of adversity hath taken away, but rather hath fortified and strengthed [17]) amongst the brittle [18] gifts of fortune, then were I mad.[19] For the felicity of so faithful and constant friendship in the storms of fortune (which is seldom seen) is doubtless a high and a noble gift proceeding of a certain singular [20] benignity of God. And indeed as concerning myself, I cannot otherwise take it nor reckon it, but that it was ordained by the great mercy of God, that you, good Master Bonvisi, amongst my poor friends, such a man as you are and so great a friend, should be long afore provided that should by your consolation assuage [21] and relieve a great part of these troubles and griefs of mine, which the hugeness [22] of fortune hath hastily brought upon me. I therefore my dear friend and of all mortal men to me most dearest do (which now only [23] I am able to do) earnestly pray to Almighty God, which hath provided you for me, that sith he hath given you such a debtor as shall never be able to pay you, that it may please him of his benignity

14. cast down.   15. know.   16. balance, compensate for.
17. strengthened.   18. fragile.   19. unwise.
20. unique.   21. soften.   22. heavy weight.
23. is the only thing that.

to requite this bountifulness of yours, which you every day thus plenteously [24] pour upon me. And that for his mercy sake he will bring us from this wretched [25] and stormy world into his rest, where shall need no letters, where no wall shall dissever [26] us, where no porter shall keep us from talking together, but that we may have the fruition [27] of the eternal joy with God the Father, and with his only begotten Son our Redeemer Jesu Christ, with the holy spirit of them both, the Holy Ghost proceeding from them both. And in the mean season, Almighty God grant both you and me, good Master Bonvisi, and all mortal men everywhere, to set at naught all the riches of this world, with all the glory of it, and the pleasure of this life also, for the love and desire of that joy. Thus of all friends most trusty, and to me most dearly beloved, and as I was wont to call you the apple of mine eye, right heartily fare ye well. And Jesus Christ keep safe and sound and in good health, all your family, which be of like affection toward me as their master is.

Thomas More: I should in vain put to it, yours, for thereof can you not be ignorant, since you have bought it with so many benefits. Nor now I am not such a one that it forceth [28] whose I am.

66

[218] To Margaret Roper.

Tower of London
5 July 1535

Sir Thomas More was beheaded at the Tower hill in London on Tuesday the sixth day of July in the year of our Lord 1535, and in the twenty-seventh year of the reign of King Henry the Eighth. And on the day next before, being Monday and the fifth day of July, he wrote with a coal [1] a letter to his daughter Mistress Roper, and sent it to her (which was the last thing that ever he wrote). The copy whereof here followeth.

24. abundantly.   25. miserable.   26. separate.
27. possession.   28. matters.   1. charcoal pencil.

Our Lord bless you good daughter and your good husband and your little boy and all yours and all my children and all my godchildren and all our friends. Recommend [2] me when you may to my good daughter Cecilye,[3] whom I beseech our Lord to comfort, and I send her my blessing and to all her children and pray her to pray for me. I send her an handekercher [4] and God comfort my good son her husband. My good daughter Daunce hath the picture in parchment that you delivered me from my Lady Coniers; her name is on the back side. Show her that I heartily pray her that you may send it in my name again for a token from me to pray for me.

I like special [5] well Dorothy Coly,[6] I pray you be good unto her. I would wit [7] whether this be she that you wrote me of. If not I pray you be good to the other as you may in her affliction and to my good daughter Joan Aleyn [8] to give her I pray you some kind answer, for she sued [9] hither to me this day to pray you be good to her.

I cumber [10] you good Margaret much, but I would be sorry, if it should be any longer than tomorrow, for it is Saint Thomas even, and the utas of Saint Peter [11] and therefore tomorrow long I to go to God, it were a day very meet [12] and convenient for me. I never liked your manner toward me better than when [13] you kissed me last for I love when daughterly love and dear charity hath no leisure to look to worldly courtesy.

2. commend.

3. for the names mentioned in this paragraph see above, Letter 17 and Introduction.

4. handkerchief.   5. specially.

6. Margaret Roper's maid. Margaret sent her to the Tower every day during More's imprisonment, often with gifts. She married John Harris, More's secretary. Together they preserved many of More's letters and took them to the Low Countries in their exile.

7. know.

8. Another of Margaret Roper's maids. She had been educated in More's "School" and so is called "daughter."

9. appealed.   10. trouble.

11. The eve of the translation of the relics of St. Thomas of Canterbury (Becket), kept in England on 7 July. Octave of the feast of St. Peter, 29 June.

12. fitting.

13. When she embraced her father on Tower Wharf, on his return from Westminster Hall after conviction and sentence.

Fare well my dear child and pray for me, and I shall for you and all your friends that we may merrily meet in heaven. I thank you for your great cost.[14]

I send now unto my good daughter Clement [15] her algorism stone [16] and I send her and my good son and all hers God's blessing and mine.

I pray you at time convenient recommend me to my good son John More. I liked well his natural fashion.[17] Our Lord bless him and his good wife my loving daughter,[18] to whom I pray him be good, as he hath great cause, and that if the land of mine come to his hand, he break not my will concerning his sister Daunce. And our Lord bless Thomas and Austen [19] and all that they shall have.

14. expenditure of labor.
15. Margaret Gyge, now wife of John Clement.
16. Probably a slate.
    17. John More had knelt on Tower Wharf and asked his father's blessing.
18. Anne Cresacre, once More's ward.
19. The children of John More and Anne Cresacre.

INDEX